# Children's Authors and Illustrators
# Too Good to Miss

# RECENT TITLES IN THE POPULAR AUTHOR SERIES

# Children's Authors and Illustrators Too Good to Miss

## Biographical Sketches and Bibliographies

### Sharron L. McElmeel

**Popular Authors Series**

**LIBRARIES UNLIMITED**

*A Member of the Greenwood Publishing Group*

Westport, Connecticut • London

**Library of Congress Cataloging-in-Publication Data**

McElmeel, Sharron L.
    Children's authors and illustrators too good to miss : biographical sketches and
bibliographies / Sharron L. McElmeel.
       p. cm.
    Includes bibliographical references and index.
    ISBN 1–59158–027–7
    1. Children's literature, American—Bio-bibliography. 2. Illustration of
books—United States—Bio-bibliography. 3. Authors, American—21st
century—Biography. 4. Authors, American—20th century—Biography.
5. Illustrators—United States—Biography. I. Title. II. Series.
PS490.M398 2004
  810.9′9282′09051—dc22      2004044202

British Library Cataloguing in Publication Data is available.

Library of Congress Catalog Card Number: 2004044202
ISBN: 1–59158–027–7

First published in 2004

Libraries Unlimited, 88 Post Road West, Westport, CT 06881
A Member of the Greenwood Publishing Group, Inc.
www.lu.com

Printed in the United States of America

The paper used in this book complies with the
Permanent Paper Standard issued by the National
Information Standards Organization (Z39.48–1984).

10  9  8  7  6  5  4  3  2  1

*For E.J.M, forty plus years—and Michael, Deborah, Thomas, Steven, Matthew, Suzanne, Michael, Jade, Aubrey, E.J., and Kylie.*

# Contents

# Preface

One of my fondest memories is of lazy summer days long ago, when I would ride horses with my sister to a far corner of the family farm, hitch our horses to a tree, and sit in an abandoned stone cabin to read through the sunny afternoon. I grew up on a dairy and grain farm in the heartland of the United States—Iowa. There were few books in my family's home and no public libraries nearby (and few schools had any sort of library). But those books that were available to us were well read. By the time I was a teen, the family copies of Grimm's fairy tales and the tales of Hans Christian Andersen were well worn and tattered from use.

My abiding love of story deepened when my husband Jack and I read countless bedtime stories aloud to our six children. Now it is my grandchildren who help me enjoy even more stories and books.

It is in the spirit of encouraging curiosity and interest in books and reading that I offer these profiles of authors and illustrators with whom others might make literacy connections. I hope these profiles and comments engender curiosity, learning, and an appreciation of literature and contribute to the emergence of a community of literacy everywhere this book is read.

# Introduction: Connecting with Books and Their Creators

Almost 50 years ago, Mauree Applegate inspired educators with her book, *Easy in English, An Imaginative Approach to the Teaching of the Language Arts* (Harper & Row, 1960). In that book she said, "School is no longer merely a place where a child learns to read but where attitudes toward reading are as important as the reading itself."[1]

Applegate's comments ring as true today as they did in 1960. We must not only teach young people to communicate through reading and writing but we must also teach them to want to communicate through the written word—to want to read and write. Young learners must be encouraged to read and to practice their skills with real reading. They must be given the opportunity to read, to interact with others, to speak and listen, and they must have the opportunity to read and write in relation to their own experiences and in relation to shared experiences.

Educators today, as in decades past, are concerned with comprehension but research has made clear that comprehension takes place when readers have connections to the literature they are reading. Prior knowledge is very important for making those connections and so are direct connections with the literature itself.

Some of those direct connections can be formed through activities inspired by topics and themes in a book and through learning about a book and its creator. Study guides, literature activity guides, and basal reading manuals all help educators extend reading experiences with young readers. Packaging these books together—with connections and experiences—helps establish reading connections and encourages even more reading. Thematic approaches, connecting books and readers with a topic based on the curriculum or individual interest, creates a reading list that will stimulate exploration through reading.

## Author and Illustrator Focus Units, a Starting Point

Focusing the readers' attention on an author or illustrator provides a structure for the sharing of literature and for building better readers and writers. This focus fosters respect for the body of work of a writer or illustrator. The links between the author's or illustrator's many works become apparent as those works are read and savored. As the reader searches for more of an author's work or for books with similar themes, they begin to view the library as a wonderful source for reading material. Young readers feel a growing sense of achievement as they begin to recognize connections between the works of different writers and as they identify universal themes and topics. Once a connection is found, the mind is challenged to think in new terms and the more a reader learns about literature, the more ways the reader will find to bring books into his or her "work place." Literature enriches the curriculum and fits easily into every subject area.

## Why Study Authors?

When young readers meet authors, in person or through author guides and Web sites, they develop a loyalty to these authors and their books and they come back to that author and their books again and again. These connections inspire young people and foster not only a love of books but also a love of reading and writing.

Learning about authors and illustrators helps students view book creators as real people. The ability to identify favorite authors diminishes the readers feelings of intimidation related to the task of selecting appropriate or interesting books to read. Studying about an author also creates a relaxed setting, another factor that enhances the opportunities for comprehension and motivates even more reading.

According to Kathy Short in *Literature as a Way of Knowing* author studies expand choices and give students the opportunity to learn about strategies that they can use in their reading, writing, and illustrating.[2]

## Selecting Authors and Illustrators

What authors should you select for your author or illustrator study? The most popular authors' names show up time and time again. For example, virtually any educator who has read in the field of children's literature will recognize the names Dr. Seuss, Tomie dePaola, Beatrix Potter, Steven Kellogg, Beverly Cleary, and Eric Carle. Ask for recommendations for books to read aloud and invariably you will hear such titles as *The Very Hungry Caterpillar* (Eric Carle) or *Ramona* (Beverly Cleary).

These and dozens of other noteworthy book creators and their works have enjoyed a high level of popularity for several decades. Those mainstays are featured in two published volumes, *100 Most Popular Children's Authors: Biographical Sketches and Bibliographies* and *100 Most Popular Picture Book Authors and Illustrators: Biographical Sketches and Bibliographies*.[3] The selection on the authors and illustrators featured in those two books was largely determined by a nation-wide survey, which intended to identify the 100 most recognizable authors and illustrators in the field of children's literature. The results of that survey were also reported in *Library Talk*.[4] Readers who picked up those previous volumes of profiles and browsed the table of contents invariably recognized many of the subjects.[5] Many educators were already sharing books by the authors and illustrators included in those volumes and those stellar authors and illustrators are shared again and again, as they should be, all the way through elementary school. Certainly they are mainstays in the library and, dare I say, in most classrooms in the nation.

It was early in the year during my first year in a particular elementary library media center when a parent stopped into the library and asked if I would recommend some good read alouds for her second-grade student. In the course of the conversation, she expressed concern that it seemed as if each of her daughter's three teachers thus far had attended the same workshop where they were introduced to the same books and literature activities. She wondered aloud how many times one child could enjoy hearing *Stone Soup* and then making "stone soup."

But what prompted her visit on this particular day was not that the kindergarten teacher, the first grade teacher, and now her daughter's second-grade teacher had put that exact activity in their lesson plan but now the second grade teacher was beginning to read aloud *Charlotte's Web*. This mother had attended the same grade school as her daughter and had the same second grade teacher who also read aloud *Charlotte's Web* to this mother's class. Now, the mother was not questioning whether *Charlotte's Web* was an appropriate read aloud, because she personally had loved the story, but she wondered if there had been any new books published—books worthy of being read aloud. She was comfortable reading these fondly remembered titles in her home to her child but was looking to the school for *new* titles that would stimulate and interest her child in a more contemporary manner.

In her own way, this mother was expressing something that my all-time favorite storyteller (and now children's book author) Carol Otis Hurst once said at a reading conference at which she was a keynote speaker. In talking about stories to share with young readers and listeners, she expressed admiration for the writer E. B. White and for *Charlotte's Web* but then added that it was time to "give it a rest."[6] Hurst's point was that we need to continue our exploration of literature and discover some of the wonderful new authors and books that have recently been published.

Hurst's comments at that conference prompted me to look at the authors and illustrators I was focusing on in my library. My list seemed dominated by the books I had loved reading to my own children. The authors they loved—I now loved. I had virtually no books in my own childhood, so I clung to those that I had shared with my six children. I have no doubt that part of my love for certain authors and illustrators came from the personal connections that I made to those books. But similar to Hurst, I came to understand that there are many new authors and illustrators writing new books that are relevant for today's readers. It was my job to introduce those books and authors to the readers with whom I worked so I began searching for new authors to showcase in my own literature sessions with young children.

I started by taking a closer look at those book creators who were mentioned on best-book lists, those who were award winners, and names that for one reason or another had not appeared on the earlier lists and thus were not profiled in *100 Most Popular Children's Authors* and *100 Most Popular Picture Book Authors and Illustrators*. The authors I wanted to find were the authors and illustrators who for one reason or another were just emerging into the field of children's literature.

I gained some satisfaction in knowing that years earlier I had invited Leo and Diane Dillon to speak at a large book conference before they had been named the recipients of their second Caldecott Award. And I organized a five-school artist's residency for David Wisniewski when he was struggling to find his place in the world of children's books—later he was awarded the Caldecott award for *The Golem*. I delighted in realizing that "I knew them when . . . "

It is those up-and-coming authors and illustrators—the authors and illustrators that are too good to miss—that I seek to identify here. My purpose is to call attention to 45 of today's best and tomorrow's most popular authors and illustrators who have garnered awards or honors or who will probably be in that category in the near future. (Yes, in some cases I am attempting to predict the future.) These authors and illustrators are not necessarily well known now, and you may or may not have read their books, but they are the most promising, most likely to succeed, and most apt to become tomorrow's classics.

In some cases, the author or illustrator has been around for a long time but has not, until recently, received recognition in the field of children's literature. For example, Simms Taback has been illustrating children's books for a couple of decades but it was only after he created his second version of *Joseph Had a Little Overcoat* (Viking, 1999) that he was given the Caldecott Award for 2000, thus becoming much better known than he had ever been before. In 2004, Simms Taback turned 72—certainly not a young new author but new to many readers—and hopefully he will have several more books to offer readers in the future. His recent successes also encourage readers to look back to his previous offerings and locate earlier books that he illustrated.

Carol Otis Hurst is another such discovery. For years she has been a highly sought-after storyteller. However, it was not until a few years ago that she turned to writing those stories down. In 2001, two of her stories were published and one became a Boston Globe-Horn Book winner. Several more of her books have been published in recent years with more yet to come. Even though she will be 71 in 2004, she is a new author.

Other authors and illustrators in this book are of a younger generation. There is Laurie Halse Anderson, who first caught my attention as the author of *Turkey Pox* (Whitman, 1996). After I featured her book on a Web site along with another title, *Arthur's Chicken Pox* by Marc Brown (Little, Brown, 1994), she wrote me a note saying how pleased she was to find her name alongside that of Marc Brown's. Brown, of course, is one of those revered authors who is well known and read widely in homes, libraries, and classrooms—an author whom my children loved, one whom I loved, and one whom few primary teachers miss sharing in their classrooms. That Web site mention came shortly after *Turkey Pox* was published and now, less than 10 years later, Anderson has made a definite mark in the area of literature for young readers with her young adult novel *Speak* (Farrar Straus Giroux, 1999), her recent titles for the Wild at Heart series for Pleasant Company, and *Thank You, Sarah! The Woman Who Saved Thanksgiving* (Simon & Schuster, 2002). In spite of her recent celebrity, Anderson is a new author to many. Although her recognition has come mostly for her young adult titles, this recognition has also spurred renewed interest in her picture books and series titles for a slightly younger reading audience. Today, many authors would love to have their name listed alongside hers! (Alas, her popularity has kept her so busy that she does not seem to answer communications directed to her. In such instances books such as this become even more important by helping young readers make connections to the author or illustrator.)

## Organization and Format

The chapters in this book are organized alphabetically by author name. Similar to my previous author guides, this book is designed to introduce users to children's authors and illustrators and their works. To that end, each chapter contains a brief biographical profile with a photo, along with a selected bibliography of the individual's publications and resources for learning more about the author or illustrator.

However, there are some noteworthy differences in content and format between this volume and the previously published volumes already mentioned. These authors, because of the types of books or the nature of the biographical information, demanded a slightly different treatment. The content of each author's or illustrator's "Book Connection" varies according to the type of books that the particular author or illustrator created and what information is available about that particular book creator. The goal of each section, however, is to provide an extra note or two that will help readers make one more connection to the author's or illustrator's work.

The book lists for each of the authors or illustrators also vary in terms of categories of books listed. The book lists are intended to be selective rather than comprehensive. References within the narrative stand alone in context of the author or illustrator's life. Generally, the book lists focus on the author's or illustrator's most recent works, those that have been the author's or illustrator's most popular titles, and titles representative of the individual's current work. (Those who wish to have a comprehensive book list of the books created by a particular person might consult the main authority of such lists, the Library of Congress. Holdings can be checked online at <http://catalog.loc.gov>. Often the Library of Congress will also provide information about books that are forthcoming.)

Likewise, suggestions for further reading differ in length according to what resources are available. I have, in each case attempted to provide information that will entice readers into the books mentioned in conjunction with each author or illustrator. Selected genre and titles are included at the beginning of each entry to give the reader an idea of the types of books the author or illustrator helps to create and books they are most know for.

Also, each entry states the author or illustrator's birthplace and birth date with as much specificity as could be obtained. Some authors decline to offer this information and research yields conflicting information. For example, biographical information offered by Scholastic about David Diaz says (in a first person account) that he was born in Fort Lauderdale, Florida. However, a reliable source that shared interview information with me says he was born in New York and shortly after moved to Ft. Lauderdale where he grew up. I chose to use the New York version as I was familiar with the first-hand account but because he also declines to offer his birth date, verification of either story is difficult. Some authors prefer to keep some information confidential for personal security but when that information is available, it becomes a piece of information that may help the reader make one more connection to the author or illustrator and his or her work.

There will be, in many people's minds, some obvious oversights in this book. For example, J. K. Rowling is certainly a new author since the publication of the first two volumes of *100 Most Popular. . . .* Rowling's Harry Potter series has put a focus on children's books like no other title ever has. But despite the near absence of her name on *The Official Harry Potter Website* at <http://www.harrypotter.warnerbros.com>, there are literally thousands of articles and Web sites that provide information about Rowling and the origin of Harry Potter. Given that one can only profile so many authors and illustrators in a volume of this type and the fact that the overriding goal of this book is to showcase authors and illustrators that might be, at this point in time, relatively unknown to the many readers and thus overlooked by teachers in many classrooms, we decided it was not necessary to profile J. K. Rowling. She is probably known to anyone who has any interest whatsoever in children's books.

In contrast, such authors as Toni Buzzeo and Deborah Wiles, who are just now arriving on the scene but certainly authors to watch as future award winners, are new and relatively unknown to many. Information about them is scarce in print form. Both authors have Web sites—<http://www.tonibuzzeo.com> and <http://www.deborahwiles.com> —but as with many entries in this book, if an author is a relative unknown, readers would not know to search for information about that author. Being able to browse through a book such as this one should serve to introduce new authors to readers.

Inevitably, many readers will think certain authors and illustrators have been overlooked. It is not our intent to create a comprehensive resource that includes every single author or illustrator of note. In fact, some of my personal favorites such as illustrator Jeni Reeves, author Sharelle Byers Moranville, and author Barbara Santucci are missing from this volume and from the earlier ones. In time, these three as well as many others, are sure to emerge as award winners. They are authors and illustrators to watch and perhaps you will find their names in my next book.

But for now, turn to a page in this book, browse the table of contents, introduce yourself to Cynthia Leitich Smith, Jane Kurtz, Robert Florczak, Linda Sue Park, and dozens of others, read a profile, find a book or two, and begin to enjoy some great new books by some of this century's authors and illustrators that are indeed too good to miss. Make your own list of authors and illustrators that you would add to this list and investigate their books and background. Write to their publisher and request biographical brochures. Check the Internet for official Web pages. Use periodical indexes to locate articles and interviews with the author or illustrator. A starting point might be the author links on the Internet at <http://www.mcelmeel.com/curriculum/authorlinks>.

Whether used as a reference title or a resource for author study units, this book is meant to enhance the experience of reading and deepen the appreciation of books. It contains information about 45 authors or illustrators—none of whom have been profiled in the two previous volumes. I hope the information I have provided will introduce you and your students to some authors you were not previously well-acquainted with and help you find that the biographical information that provides meaningful connections for young readers—connections to a particular author or illustrator and to her or his books.

Read, share, and enjoy.

*Sharron L. McElmeel*
*Cedar Rapids, Iowa*

## Notes

1. Maure Applegate, *Easy in English: An Imaginative Approach to the Teaching of the Language Arts* (New York: Harper & Row, 1960), p. 15.

2. Kathy Short, *Literature As a Way of Knowing* (Portland, ME: Stenhouse Publishers, 1997), p. 51.

3. Sharron McElmeel, *100 Most Popular Children's Authors: Biographical Sketches and Bibliographies* (Westport, CT: Libraries Unlimited, 1999); and Sharron McElmeel, *100 Most Popular Picture Book Authors and Illustrators: Biographical Sketches and Bibliographies* (Westport, CT: Libraries Unlimited, 2000).

4. Sharron McElmeel and Lin Buswell, "Reader's Choices," *Library Talk* 11 (Jan/Feb, 1998): 12–13.

5. Table of contents available online at <http://www.mcelmeel.com/writing/page_pix.html> and <http://www.mcelmeel.com/writing/page_chi.html>.

6. Carol Hurst, *Celebrate Reading: A Conference,* Cedar Rapids, Iowa, July 1995.

# Laurie Halse Anderson

◆ Family stories ◆ Historical fiction ◆ Holidays

**Potsdam, New York**
October 23, 1961

📖 *Turkey Pox*

📖 *Thank You, Sarah! The Woman Who Saved Thanksgiving*

## About the Author

Laurie Halse Anderson, the daughter of Frank Halse Jr. and Joyce Halse, grew up in central New York State. During her childhood in the Syracuse area, Laurie wrote newspaper columns, letters, and stories using her father's typewriter. Her father was a United Methodist minister who was, among many other things, a poet. Laurie and her younger sister Lisa could often be found in their father's office where Laurie would sit on the floor and watch her father write poetry or read the comics to her.

Animals played an important part throughout Laurie's childhood even though she had allergies to some of them—cats especially. Her own first poem was about her kitten, Soot. Anderson rescued Soot when the tiny kitten was abandoned in front of their home. She hid the kitten in her bedroom for three days before her parents discovered it. Despite her misgivings about another pet (Smokey was already a resident cat), Laurie's mother allowed her to keep the kitten. When Smokey and Soot died, Laurie and Lisa adopted two more cats and then the family got a black Lab.

Laurie's grandfather was a forest ranger whose family had lived in the Adirondack Mountains for generations. He often took his granddaughters on hikes among the trees in the mountains, which helped instill in Laurie a love of nature. This love, along with an interest in many different animals later would influence her writing.

When Laurie was in the second grade, her teacher taught the students the Haiku form of poetry and Laurie's love of words continued to grow. She tried to read every book in the library and became known as an insatiable reader; she always seemed to have a book in her hand. Among her favorite books were the Little House series by Laura Ingalls Wilder, *Heidi* by Johanna Spyr, *Little Women* by Louisa May Alcott, various titles by Judy Blume, *The Borrowers* by Mary Norton, and especially *Charlotte's Web* by E. B. White.

1

Although Laurie loved reading and writing and often wrote poetry and drew comic strips in elementary and middle school, she did not plan to become a writer. Her future plans were to become a doctor, she even had a professional stethoscope when she was 11. However, during her high school years she began to write short stories.

By the time Laurie reached high school age, she found herself at a new school, Fayetteville-Manlius High School, just outside of Syracuse. The school was filled with exclusive groups and Laurie was definitely part of the group she later referred to as "dirt bags." Her clothes were unfashionable and her family was relatively poor. By the time Laurie was in the tenth and eleventh grades, she had moved into the "jock/Eurotrash" group because of her participation on the swim team and on the track team as a shot putter. Even though she was one of the tallest girls in school, she never garnered any attention from the group that played basketball.

In general, high school was a place to endure rather than enjoy. Laurie survived because of a couple of friends and a boyfriend from a nearby school. During her senior year she left home to be a foreign exchange student in Denmark where she lived on a pig farm. She burned off crops, picked up rocks from the fields, learned to butcher pigs and ducks, and shoveled a lot of manure. Laurie even took care of new baby piglets one night when a sow went into labor while she was babysitting at a neighbor's farm. She spent 13 months in Denmark, learned to speak Danish, and had a very good time.

When she returned to the states Laurie took some time off before entering Onondaga Community College in Syracuse. She took a part-time job on a dairy farm, rising at 3:30 A.M. to milk cows. After a year at the community college, Laurie went on to earn an undergraduate degree in languages and linguistics at Georgetown University in Washington, D.C.

It was at Georgetown where she met and married her husband, Greg Anderson. One of their first acquisitions was a cat whose large ears earned him the name Yoda. Two more cats and two daughters, Stephanie and Meredith, soon followed and later, the family adopted a German Shepard, Canute, from an animal shelter. Canute was very gentle with the children and often accompanied Laurie on her daily runs. When her daughters were young, Laurie Anderson worked as a reporter for the *Philadelphia Inquirer* and later as a freelance writer and editor. Canute lay on her feet as she wrote and Mittens, their cat, was always nearby.

When her younger daughter went off to first grade in 1992, Anderson resolved to focus on a book-writing career. She sat down to write and set her goal to get a book published in five years. It did not take her long to realize, however, that she did not know the first thing about writing a book. After struggling for a time she found an advertisement for a one-day conference of the Eastern Pennsylvania chapter of the Society of Children's Book Writers and Illustrators (SCBWI). Anderson attended the conference and loved the support and encouragement she received. On returning to her home, Laurie was energized and began to write. However, after receiving rejection after rejection from publishers, she realized that she still had a lot to learn. The next year Anderson attended the SCBWI chapter's conference in the Pocono Mountains. These SCBWI conferences provided her with the opportunity to meet editors and other authors and soon her writing began to sell. It had taken Anderson just four years to get a book into publication.

Although Anderson has gained her most fame in the young adult market, her first two books were picture books. The first, *Nedito Runs* (Henry Holt, 1996), tells the story of a young Kenyan girl who runs to school each day. *Turkey Pox* (A. Whitman, 1996) is about a girl who comes down with chicken pox. The girl and her family almost miss her grandma's Thanksgiving dinner until grandmother saves the day and the turkey.

Anderson's third picture book, *No Time for Mother's Day* (A. Whitman, 1999), was published the same year as her first novel, *Speak* (Farrar Straus Giroux, 1999). This novel catapulted Anderson into the center of writers for young readers. *Speak* was nominated for the 1999 National Book Award for Young People's Literature and was named an honor book on the Prinz Award list for that year.

Anderson's love of animals had grown throughout her childhood and into her life as an adult and now animals were filling the nooks and crannies in her writing. Within a few short years Laurie had 19 titles published several of which were titles in the Wild at Heart series for the Pleasant Company. In this series, five sixth-graders volunteer at the Wild at Heart Veterinary Clinic that Maggie's grandmother, Dr. J. J. MacKenzie (Dr. Mac) runs. The youngsters are very adept and resourceful in dealing with the animals and dilemmas associated with the clinic. The eleventh title in the series, *Masks,* features a cat character named Mittens in a tale involving a research lab and the ethics of caring for animals used for research. The clinic volunteers have helped save Manatee Rescue operations, shut down puppy mills, and investigated the origin of a flock of parrots that mysteriously appear in the town. Anderson's genuine love of animals and her dedication to accuracy and to her writing have contributed to the credibility and popularity of this series.

Various incidents in her life have influenced Anderson's novels for older readers. One night, Anderson was awakened from her sleep when in a dream she heard a child sobbing. That child became the main character, Melinda, in her award winning *Speak.* In that book, Melinda was plagued with many of the problems that Anderson dealt with while growing up. In one of the episodes, Melinda uses a tree as the subject of an art project. As Anderson wrote about that, she realized she had selected a tree as the subject for a ninth-grade art project of her own. Once that subconscious connection was recognized, she tweaked the final draft of the manuscript to make the thread run throughout the book.

Her next book, *Fever, 1793* (Simon & Schuster, 2000), is the result of a newspaper article Anderson read while the family was stuck in a traffic jam in August 1993. The article was about the epidemic of Yellow Fever that swept through Philadelphia in 1793. Anderson immediately recognized that the story had wonderful elements of conflict and fear and she began to write a book about it. As the story of Matilda "Mattie" Cook emerged, so did the picture of eighteenth-century Philadelphia. At first, Anderson envisioned Mattie as a 10-year-old orphan but as the writing developed she decided she could better tell the story if Mattie was an adolescent. Anderson had to do a lot of research to create an accurate setting for this book. As she became more comfortable with the characters, the story moved from being told in the third-person point of view to a first-person perspective. Although some historic figures have cameo appearances in a few episodes, Anderson deliberately kept historical and fictional characters from interacting with one another in an effort to keep readers from being confused.

A third novel, *Catalyst* (Viking, 2002), resulted from Anderson's desire to write about a "kid who looks like she has it all together."[1] Chemistry was not Anderson's favorite subject in high school but for this book she spent considerable time learning about chemistry and used her knowledge to create a thread throughout the book.

Today, Anderson continues to write for several age levels. A recent picture book, *Thank You, Sarah! The Woman Who Saved Thanksgiving* (Simon & Schuster, 2002), tells of Sarah Hale's 38-year campaign to get Thanksgiving declared a national holiday. At the same time she was working on books to fulfill a two-book deal with Viking Publishers.

Laurie Halse Anderson is a full-time writer who enjoys the part of her job that allows her to live in her imagination, work in her pajamas, stay close to the refrigerator, and be available when her children need her. Her normal workday begins at 6:30 A.M and her writing starts shortly after she gets her daughters off to school. Most of her writing is accomplished in the morning and the business contacts, returning telephone calls, writing letters, and other details are taken care of in the afternoon. When her daughters, Meredith and Stephanie, come home from school, Anderson calls a halt to her work for the day, although she does find time for more reading before bedtime.[2] Anderson and her family live in a suburb of Philadelphia.

## Book Connections

Many particulars in the books that Laurie Halse Anderson writes include references or similarities to details of her life. In her novels *Speak* and *Catalyst,* the high school setting is based on Anderson's own high school in Syracuse, New York. Similar to Kate Malone, a character from *Catalyst,* Anderson is the daughter of a minister. Kate used running as a way to escape, and while Anderson did not run during her high school days, she did take up running to get herself back in shape after her daughters were born.

Charity is the main character in both *Turkey Pox* and a later picture book, *No Time for Mother's Day.* Trees were an important part of Anderson's youth and the tree theme flows through *Speak,* as the character Melinda attempts to deal with the peer pressure that influences her experiences.

Research is a pinnacle of Anderson's books. Historic titles are well based in the facts and even her contemporary fiction benefits from her research in malls and in places where young people are present. From those informal encounters Anderson picks up ideas for dialogue that is appropriate for the situations that she wants to write about.

## Books Written by Laurie Halse Anderson

### Fiction

*Catalyst* (Viking, 2002). Young adult.

*Fever, 1793* (Simon & Schuster, 2000). Young adult.

*Masks:* Wild at Heart #11 (Pleasant Company, 2003).

*Race to the Finish:* Wild at Heart #12 (Pleasant Company, 2003).

*Speak* (Farrar Straus Giroux, 1999). Young adult.

### Picture Books

*Nedito Runs.* Illustrated by Anita Van Der Merwe. (Henry Holt & Co., 1996).

*No Time for Mother's Day.* Illustrated by Dorothy Donohue. (A. Whitman, 1999).

*Thank You, Sarah! The Woman Who Saved Thanksgiving.* Illustrated by Matt Faulkner. (Simon & Schuster, 2002).

*Turkey Pox.* Illustrated by Dorothy Donohue. (A. Whitman, 1996).

# For More Information

## Articles

Anderson, Laurie Halse. "The Writing of *Fever 1793.*" *School Library Journal* 47.5 (May 2001): 44.

Florence, Debbi Michiko. "An Interview with Children's Author Laurie Halse Anderson." In Debbi Michiko Florence's Library—Children's Fiction (2003). March 2004. <http://debbimichikoflorence.com/index.2ts?page=lauriehalse anderson>.

Schwartz, Dana. "Author Profile: Laurie Halse Anderson." March 2004. <http://www.teenreads.com/authors/au-anderson-laurie.asp>.

## Web Sites

Anderson, Laurie Halse. *Laurie's Bookshelf—Laurie Halse Anderson.* Nov. 2003. <http://www.writerlady.com>.

# Notes

1. Debbi Michiko Florence, "An Interview with Children's Author Laurie Halse Anderson," 2003 in Debbi Michiko Florence's Library, <http://debbimichikoflorence.com/index.2ts?page= lauriehalseanderson>.

2. Ibid.

# Tedd Arnold

◆  Family stories  ◆   Humor

**Elmira, New York**
January 20, 1949

📖 *No Jumping on the Bed!*

📖 *No More Water in the Tub*

**Huggly Series**

📖 *Huggly Goes to School*

📖 *Huggly's Snow Day*

## About the Author/Illustrator

Tedd Arnold was born in Elmira, New York on January 20, 1949. After living in Philadel-phia, his family moved back to Elmira and when his father, a machinist, lost his job they moved to Gainesville, Florida. Arnold finished his school years in Florida where he took his first art lessons in a studio above the Happy Hour Pool Hall. Arnold always enjoyed drawing and since his grade school years he wanted to be an artist.

After earning his undergraduate degree at the University of Florida, Arnold entered the working world as a commercial illustrator and design executive. While working in the commercial art field he also tried to write. Arnold had read many of the books his wife was using in her primary school classroom and he thought, "the books had just a few words on a page; what could be so hard?"[1]

Arnold spent six years submitting his work to children's publishers but all of his ideas were rejected. After six years, he met a man who was an agent for children's book authors. Arnold gave him some ideas for books that he wanted to sell and in three months, Arnold had a contract to write and illustrate a book. In 1985, his first books were published and he also began illustrating books for other writers. His first mark in the world of children's books was made with the publication of *No More Jumping on the Bed!* (Dial, 1987). It was the first book he both wrote and illustrated.

At the time Arnold wrote the story, he, his wife, Carol, and their son, Walter, were living in an apartment in Yonkers, New York. Walter was a notorious bed jumper. The apartment was in an old building and one day the ceiling collapsed. Walter began jump-ing on his bed and *No More Jumping on the Bed!* resulted.[2] Walter was just four when that book was published and Tedd and Carol's second son, William, had just been born. It took eight more years until William got a book of his own. Arnold's *No More Water in the*

*Tub* (Dial, 1995) features a young boy snorkeling in his bathtub and the text is composed of rhyming prose.

Between those two books, Arnold wrote and illustrated *The Signmaker's Assistant* (Dial, 1992). Arnold noticed the similarity in style of the signs in the neighborhood that he passed through on his way from Yonkers to New York City and he began to think about the difference the sign maker was actually making in the community. He imagined humorous ways one could make an impact as a sign maker and those thoughts were the beginnings of *The Signmaker's Assistant.*

Arnold's rhyming prose was most likely influenced by the Dr. Seuss books that he read in his childhood but when asked what children's books he enjoyed most as a child he replied, "Mother Goose."[3] Arnold's love of Mother Goose has resulted in two collections of Mother Goose rhymes. One collection became a set of four board books and the second set was a collection of the rhymes illustrated with cross-stitched samplers that Arnold designed.

In 1997, Tedd Arnold created a book series featuring the character Huggly. Huggly is a monster that wants to try people things and when he does he realizes that there's more involved to being a human than he knew. One of the most humorous titles is *Huggly Takes a Bath* (Scholastic, 1998). The little green monster slides out of his home under the little boy's bed only to discover a small room attached to the room with the bed in it. This small room will immediately be recognized by readers as a bathroom but Huggly only knows that there are things that spray water, a slippery cube that gets all sudsy, and bottles of pretty-smelling stuff that are perfect for making a monster slime pit. Each of the books about Huggly deals with one human activity such as getting pizza, dressing, and going to human school. Much of what went on around Arnold during his childhood and now as a dad contributes to what goes into his books.

One day, one of Arnold's sons was found clutching a Bible, pale as a ghost, and refusing to talk. He was losing a tooth and did not realize that this was something that was normal; he thought he was falling apart. A note about that incident went into Arnold's notebook of possible ideas and 10 years later the idea was expanded to create the story for *Parts* (Dial, 1987).[4] In *Parts,* the boy's skin was flaking off, lint was coming out of his belly button, and his teeth were falling out. *Parts* ended up winning numerous awards and spawning a sequel, *More Parts* (Dial, 2001). In *More Parts,* the chief protagonist mentally pictures the literal interpretations of some body-related figurative phrases such as, "I'll bet that broke your heart," "give him a hand," "Hold your tongue," and "jumps out of his skin." Arnold's humorous illustrations bring this book to a very funny level.

Many of the books Arnold illustrates are books he has written himself but he also illustrates books written by other authors. In 2002, Arnold illustrated *Giant Children* (Dial), a book of very humorous poems by Brod Bagert. Earlier he illustrated *Axel Annie* (Dial, 1999) a book written by friend Robin Pulver. Pulver and Arnold are both members of a writing group that meets in their western New York community. They meet with other writers to react to one another's works in progress. Arnold actually says he spends little time writing as most of his time is spent at the drawing table.[5] The members of the group share and discuss any illustrations in progress as well as their writing.

When Arnold is not working on writing or illustrating a book he might be found in the countryside making sketches of some of the buildings in the surrounding area. Several sketches of buildings in the country near his home are located on his Web site, <http://www.teddarnold.com>. He enjoys traveling, reading, and collecting books, particularly editions of Mother Goose verses. One of the verses he enjoys is "Sing a Song of

Sixpence" and when he found out that it was written in 1744 he tried to find a sixpence that was at least that old. He ended up finding one with a 1575 date and consequently began his coin collection.[6]

As the Arnold's sons were growing up the family often read together, especially in the evening. During those times one of their cats, a big white one named Cody, would hear them reading and come to where they were and plop right in the middle of the family—on the book if he could. The white cat showed up in *The Signmaker's Assistant*[7] and in many other books. Friskie is also a feline resident of the Arnold household.

Tedd and Carol Arnold and their two sons live in a large two-and-a-half story home nestled in a stand of tall trees in Elmira, New York. A round turret graces one corner of the house and a covered front porch extends a warm welcome. In the winter, the snow-covered land surrounding the house is the perfect place for winter adventures just like the adventures Huggly has in *Huggly's Snow Day* (Scholastic, 2002).

## Book Connections

Tedd Arnold is an artist. During his college days he often drew pictures and then wrote a line or two as a caption for the pictures. Now his humorous and colored-filled illustrations, created with watercolors and color pencils, are drawn to accompany his stories. How does Arnold create his illustrations? After drawing a sketch on tracing paper with a plain graphite pencil just the way he wants it, Arnold turns the picture over and covers the back with graphite. Once he turns it back over he can retrace the lines of his drawing and the outline of the drawing is transferred in a faint gray line onto more expensive illustrative paper. Once that is done Arnold retraces the faint gray lines with a brown pencil and begins to watercolor. First the underlying shadows are painted in with browns or dark blue paints. Using several layers of watercolor application Arnold then layers on the bright colors. Sometimes he uses an airbrush to create special effects and often paints a bottom layer of color to make the top layer appear brighter and more vibrant. Once the colors are applied, Arnold uses colored pencils to draw on top of the watercolors and scribble in the solid areas of the illustration to create texture and more interest. The final step is to outline everything in black and apply the finishing touches. Each drawing is completed in one to two days.[8] These illustrations provide each of Arnold's books with an added layer of humor and frivolity.

## Books Written and Illustrated by Tedd Arnold

*Five Ugly Monsters* (Scholastic, 1995).

*Green Wilma* (Dial, 1993).

Huggly Series

*Huggly and the Toy Monster* (Scholastic, 1998).

*Huggly Gets Dressed* (Scholastic, 1997).

*Huggly Goes to School* (Scholastic, 2000).

*Huggly Takes a Bath* (Scholastic, 1998).

*Huggly's Christmas* (Scholastic, 2002).

*Huggly's Pizza* (Scholastic, 2000).

*Huggly's Snow Day* (Scholastic, 2002).

*Mother Goose's Words of Wit and Wisdom* (Dial, 1990).

*No Jumping on the Bed!* (Dial, 1987).

*No More Water in the Tub* (Dial, 1995).

*Parts* (Dial, 1997).

*The Signmaker's Assistant* (Dial, 1992).

## Books Illustrated by Tedd Arnold

*Axel Annie.* Written by Robin Pulver. (Dial, 1999).

*Giant Children.* Written by Brod Bagert. (Dial, 2002).

*Lasso Lou and Cowboy McCoy.* Written by Barbara Larmon Failing. (Dial, 2003).

## For More Information

### Web Sites

Arnold, Tedd. *Tedd Arnold.* March 2004. <http://www.teddarnold.com>.

## Notes

1. Tedd Arnold, "Books, Kids, and a Cat," presentation at Iowa Reading Association Convention Author Luncheon, Des Moines, Iowa, 8 Apr. 1995.
2. Ibid.
3. Ibid.
4. Tedd Arnold, "There's an Author Loose in School," presentation at the Tennessee Association School Librarians conference, Paris Landing State Park, Tennessee, 19 Oct. 2001.
5. Arnold, "Books, Kids, and a Cat."
6. Tedd Arnold, conversation with author, Paris Landing State Park, Tennessee, 19 Oct. 2001.
7. Arnold, "Books, Kids, and a Cat."
8. Ibid.

# Mary Azarian

**Washington, D.C.**
December 8, 1940

📖 *The Gardener's Alphabet*

📖 *Snowflake Bentley*

📖 *A Symphony for Sheep*

## About the Author/Illustrator

For more than 30 years Mary Azarian has been creating beautiful art with woodcuts. In 1999, she was awarded the coveted Caldecott Medal for the illustrations she created for Jacqueline Briggs Martin's text in the book *Snowflake Bentley* (Houghton Mifflin, 1998).

Mary Azarian was born December 8, 1940 in Washington, D.C. An only child, she grew up in what was then a rural area of Virginia on her grandparents' small farm. Her grandfather raised chickens and sold eggs and her grandmother, Annie, gardened. Her uncle Winnie was also a gardener and had a large vegetable garden and farm stand. In fact, both sides of her family had many gardeners.[1]

Describing her childhood, Mary says "it was a wonderful childhood. I had a pony and spent hours exploring the countryside and woods."[2] Azarian's home was just 15 miles from the center of Washington, D.C. The area, says Azarian, "is now covered with asphalt. When I lived there the road was dirt and the nearest neighbor was 1/4 mile away."[3]

Mary Azarian enrolled in Smith College where she studied painting and printmaking with Leonard Baskin. After graduating in 1963, Mary and her husband, Tom, moved to Cabot, a small community in Vermont where they gardened and cared for chickens, cows, sheep, horses, and oxen on their small hill farm. At the time, Vermont had more cows than people.[4] It was on this small farm that the couple raised their three sons and sought to be as self-sufficient as possible. Later, Mary Azarian established her own print shop where she began making and selling woodcut prints and paintings. Even now, as a very successful children's book illustrator, the bulk of her time is spent on the actual production of prints. She usually illustrates only one book a year.[5]

One of Mary's first books, *A Farmer's Alphabet* (David R. Godine, 1981), began during those early days when, seeking to supplement the family income, she took a job

**11**

teaching in a rural one-room schoolhouse. She painted a set of alphabet posters that used images from the rural Vermont setting to use in the classroom. Before the birth of her second son, Azarian quit teaching and in 1969 she established Farmhouse Press. In the late 1970s, a Vermont arts organization offered grants for a body of work based on a Vermont theme. Azarian designed wood blocks for a set of alphabet posters that were subsequently funded by the arts organization and the state of Vermont printed a set for every primary classroom in the state.

Azarian then attempted to interest book publishers in her artwork but the response was less than favorable. A year later, however, David R. Godine called to say that he had heard about the woodcut alphabet and would like to take a look at the prints. In 1981, his publishing house released the cards in book form, as *A Farmer's Alphabet*.[6]

Mary's book illustration projects during the next few years were few. But in the early 1990s she acquired an agent, actually two, who worked together and they soon obtained projects for her. By the time she was awarded the Caldecott Medal, she had illustrated almost 40 children's books.

After creating a wood block any number of prints can be made from the block and many who create woodcuts rely on others to make the actual prints. Azarian, however, creates the prints herself. At first she printed by hand but later she began to use a nineteenth-century Vandecock proof hand press. In the early 2000s she returned to hand printing some of her prints because hand printing produces unique results from the hand rubbing that cannot be duplicated with the use of a press. Azarian's early prints were black and white and adding color would normally require a separate color block. Azarian developed a technique to hand color the prints with water-based paints. The hand painting creates a unique print as the colors vary from print to print.

Mary's prints sold at small craft fairs and local shops. Thousands of her prints sold and many homes in Vermont and across the country display prints that she has created. She is also interested in political issues and often contributes "biting political posters . . . to scores of organizations promoting social and economic justice."[7]

In her printmaking work Mary does it all: carving, printing, painting, pacing, shipping, and bookkeeping.[8] Although the prints pulled from any wood block will have very subtle variations, in general the prints are nearly identical so the printing process is not as challenging as the actual carving of the blocks. Azarian has carved "well over a thousand blocks" and has printed multiple prints from each block. Because much of her work time is devoted to production, she often welcomes the opportunity to create the blocks for a book. It is a one-time effort that "fills me with joy."[9]

Azarian also describes herself as a "fanatic gardener."[10] She keeps a large flower and vegetable garden that is home to lilies, salvias, blue veronica, lilacs, peonies, hydrangeas, monkshood, bee balm, sedum, and daffodils.[11] Her art of printmaking and her love of gardening came together when she created *A Gardener's Alphabet* (Houghton Mifflin, 2000). If Mary is not working on illustrating she is gardening (or playing tournament bridge).

Azarian usually works seven days a week but she says, "I have to gear myself up every day, especially when I'm working on new projects. Despite 30 plus years as a woodcut printmaker I almost never approach new design challenges with confidence. I am always fearful that I won't get it right."[12]

Her studio is on the second floor of the old farmhouse that she moved to in the early 1990s. A Macintosh computer sits side-by-side with the nineteenth-century press that she still uses. As Azarian carves and prints, she can view the outside through the many windows that line her studio. It is here that Azarian creates her book illustrations as well as the many prints, note cards, and calendars she creates each year.

In 1998 three books with her illustrations were released. One of the books she illustrated was *Barn Cat* by Carol P. Saul (Little, Brown, 1998). Azarian used her own cat, Big Kitty, as a model for that rhyming verse that followed a charming cat throughout a day. A second book featured a connection to Wilson "Snowflake" Bentley. As a long-time Vermont resident, Mary Azarian knew of the work of Wilson A. Bentley. Throughout his lifetime Bentley studied and photographed snowflakes and his interest in the snowflake was more important than making money. Bentley lived on a small farm in the Vermont countryside near Jericho, and was interested in his community. He was a financial contributor to the Fresh-Air Fund and Jericho was one of the areas where families often hosted New York tenement children who were sent by the fund to experience country life. In *Faraway Summer* (HarperCollins, 1998), Johanna Hurwitz tells the story of a poor Jewish orphan who leaves her crowded New York tenement for a country vacation where she meets and becomes friends with Bentley. It was while Azarian was working on the small black and white woodcuts for Hurwitz's novel that she received the manuscript for *Snowflake Bentley.* The fact that both books included Bentley as a character is, according to Azarian, "absolutely coincidental" and "both strange and wonderful."[13]

During the summer, Mary spends a lot of the time in her garden but in the winter, snow surrounds her house and her windowed studio looks out on snow-covered fields. It was on one of those snow-covered days in 1999 that she and a friend spent an evening at another friend's "house concert" and then enjoyed a moonlight ski. The skiing conditions were so good "it was like skiing on velvet."[14] By the next morning the temperature had dropped and it was several degrees below zero. Azarian's friend left for town and Azarian was soon settled into a favorite chair by the fireside with a book to read. It wasn't long before her friend returned; his car was stuck in the snow. They pushed the car out of the snow but discovered a tire was flat. On their return to the house, Azarian heard the phone ringing. Azarian thought to herself that "some idiot was calling at such an insensitive time; it was before 8:00 A.M."[15] But she answered the phone; it was the Caldecott committee, informing her of the award. By that time, Mary could only think "such a joke was in poor taste."[16] In fact, when she was convinced that the call was legitimate she called her oldest son who said that she should not get "too excited as they will probably call back and tell you they miscounted."[17]

Mary Azarian was very pleased with her award and now is invited to share her art with many school children. She also receives many letters from readers. One letter was a congratulatory letter from an 88-year-old man. Wilson Bentley, the subject of *Snowflake Bentley* had died in 1931 but this man had met him. At the time of their meeting Bentley had been wearing three overcoats while collecting snowflakes. Azarian has said that she thought it was a wonderful letter.

Mary Azarian continues to work on her woodcuts, now often printing them by hand and on fine rice paper. Her gardens have been photographed for magazines and appear on her Web site, <http://www.maryazarian.com>. Her woodcuts and the projects she has been involved in over the past 35 years give clues to her own favorites: cooking from scratch, the color blue, playing bridge, gardening, the art of Chris Van Allsburg, and medieval and Renaissance choral music. Each morning she enjoys an hour of reading before her morning walk and the beginning of her workday in her studio, which she begins as early as possible. On a good day she is done by 2:00 P.M. and seldom works

Dear Young Book Lovers,

        Reading was one of my
greatest pleasures as a child.
A trip to the library was always
a treat for me — a world of endless
possibilities

        I urge you to make reading
a life-long activity. It can
fuel your imagination, teach you
new things, inspire you and entertain
you for your whole life. So...
turn off the TV and pick up a
book and LIVE!

                    Mary Azarian

beyond 4:00 P.M. But because she creates her own schedule, she can take a day off now and then to work the entire day in her garden. She says she creates art pieces that are intended to please only her and she enjoys working with fabric design, mainly painting on silk.

Mary Azarian has three grown sons—Ethan, Jesse, and Tim—all musicians or artists. As a full-time printmaker, she has been selling woodcut prints and paintings since 1969 and many of her works are available on her Web site. With her beagle, Hilda, and three cats, Phoebe, Trey, and Big Kitty, she continues to make her home in Vermont and create art in her Farmhouse Press studio.

## Book Connections

Mary Azarian's woodcuts are beautiful pieces of art whether they are in the form of a print or within a children's book. According to a description of her printing process given by Terry J. Allen, a friend of twenty years, Azarian begins by sitting "on a stool facing the outside view"[18] as she carves the wood block. The wood she favors for the blocks include fine-grained wood from Japan, basswood, or pine. She sketches a detailed drawing directly on the block and then carves away the parts of the block that she does not want to be printed onto her paper. Many of her prints are printed on a very thin Japanese paper made from vegetable fiber. She uses a brayer, a soft rubber cylinder on a handle, to roll the ink or paint across the surface of the carved block. When she prints using her cast-iron printer she puts the carved block, ink side up, under the press and lays a sheet of paper directly over the block. She then rolls the press's large wheel over the block and the inked portions of the block print black while the carved out portions remain white. The process is repeated, sometimes for hours, producing just one print at a time. After the black ink dries, Azarian adds color with acrylic paints that she waters down to produce a translucent effect. She applies the same color to each print and then she moves on to another color. All the blue wheelbarrows would be painted blue, then all the orange pumpkins, and so forth. With the color being added by hand, there are subtle changes in each print, however, when Azarian produces wood blocks for a book, she creates one master print of the illustration that will appear in the book and adds the color to that print. The publisher uses the finished pieces of art to make the master plates for the book's illustrations.

## Books Illustrated by Mary Azarian

*Barn Cat.* Written by Carol P. Saul. (Little, Brown, 1998).

*A Farmer's Alphabet.* Written by Mary Azarian. (David R. Godine, 1981).

*A Gardener's Alphabet.* Written by Mary Azarian. (Houghton Mifflin, 2000).

*The Man Who Lived Alone.* Written by Donald Hall. (David R. Godine, 1984).

*Miss Bridie Chose a Shovel.* Written by Leslie Connor. (Houghton Mifflin, 2004).

*Snowflake Bentley.* Written by Jacqueline Briggs Martin. (Houghton Mifflin, 1998).

*A Symphony for the Sheep.* Written by C. M. Millen. (Houghton Mifflin, 1996).

*When the Moon Is Full: A Lunar Year.* Written by Penny Pollock. (Little, Brown, 2001).

## For More Information

### Articles

Allen, Terry J. "Mary Azarian." *Horn Book Magazine* 75.4 (July/August 1999): 430–434.

Azarian, Mary. "Caldecott Medal Acceptance." *Horn Book Magazine* 75.4 (July/August 1999): 423–430.

Martin, Tovah. "Carving Country Memories." *Victoria* 10.4 (April 1996): 80+.

McElmeel, Sharron. "Author Profile: Mary Azarian—Woodcut Artist." *Library Talk* 13.1 (January/February 2000): 18–19.

## Books

Hart, Lilias MacBean. *The Four Seasons of Mary Azarian.* Illustrated by Mary Azarian. Boston: David R. Godine, 2000.

## Web Sites

Azarian, Mary. *Mary Azarian, Vermont Woodcut Artist and Book Illustrator.* March 2004. <http://www.maryazarian.com>.

# Notes

1. Mary Azarian, letter to the author, 12 July 1999.
2. Ibid.
3. Ibid.
4. Mary Azarian, "Caldecott Award Acceptance Speech," Caldecott—Newbery Banquet, New Orleans, Louisiana, 17 June 1999.
5. Azarian, letter.
6. Azarian, "Caldecott Award Acceptance Speech."
7. Terry J. Allen, "Mary Azarian," *Horn Book Magazine* 75.4 (July/August 1999): 430.
8. Azarian, "Caldecott Award Acceptance Speech."
9. Ibid.
10. Ibid.
11. Tovah Martin, "Carving Country Memories," *Victoria* 10.4 (April, 1996): 80.
12. Azarian, letter.
13. Ibid.
14. Azarian, "Caldecott Award Acceptance Speech."
15. Ibid.
16. Ibid.
17. Ibid.
18. Allen, "Mary Azarian."

# Haemi Balgassi

◆ Historical fiction ◆ School fiction

**Seoul, South Korea**
July 2, 1967

📖 *Peacebound Trains*
📖 *Tae's Sonata*

## About the Author

Haemi Balgassi spent her early childhood in South Korea. She recalls, "my first years are tinged golden with memories of living in Seoul with my maternal grandmother, my mother, and a young aunt (my mother's younger sister). My father was away in Tokyo, Japan, much of that time on business."[1] Haemi also fondly remembers her all time favorite pet, a doting hound named Spotty.

By the time she was four, her father's company transferred him back to an office in Seoul and the family was then able to move into a home of their own. Soon after, Haemi's younger sister, Sumi, was born. After Haemi finished first grade, her family moved to the northeastern region of the United States. Her interest in writing was sparked in elementary school when she received recognition in a statewide creative writing contest. By the time she was in high school, writing had become a passion. She was poetry editor for the school's literary magazine and earned the school's highest honor for writing poetry during her junior and senior years. She interviewed her mother about her experiences during the Korean War and wrote an essay, "War Child." That essay later formed the basis for her award-winning story *Peacebound Trains* (Clarion, 1996).

Shortly after graduating from high school, Haemi enlisted in the U.S. Army, partly so she could qualify for the G.I. Bill. However, Haemi's army time did not last long due to an injury that forced her release from duty. Later, she entered college and focused on business and computer science—something practical as compared to creative writing. It wasn't until her first daughter, Adria, was born that she began to seriously consider writing.

At first Haemi Balgassi wrote and published short stories and poetry for adults. She was actively writing in that field when Adria was born. At that time, she began to explore children's literature with her daughter. Balgassi fell in love with children's literature and

**17**

she began to write in that field. Her first book, *Peacebound Trains*, was drawn directly from her family heritage and the grandmother she had lived with in Seoul became the inspiration for the story. The main character for that book was given the name Sumi—in honor of Balgassi's younger sister.

Balgassi's second book, *Tae's Sonata* (Clarion, 1997), is a reflection on her own struggle to balance her Korean and American identities and to sort out the balance between her home and her school lives. *Tae's Sonata,* a middle-grade novel, tells the story of a Korean-American eighth grader who is assigned to a class project with one of the most popular boys in the class. The fact that Tae is paired with Josh earns her the spite of a popular clique of girls. When Tae's best friend begins to hang out with the clique, Tae feels lonely but begins to view others around her in a different light. She realizes that Philip—the only other Korean American in school—is not as stuck up as she thought and Josh, despite being very popular, is also a very nice person. Along with universal teenage problems Haemi also deals with the racial and ethnic dynamics in Tae's life.

Haemi, her husband, Joseph, and their two daughters, Adria and Louisa, currently live in Massachusetts. Balgassi's favorite foods include eggs, mushrooms, her mother's fried shrimp, and thin string pastas with light non-tomato sauce. But her favorite dish is her mother's Lobster Cantonese—a dish that her mother made for her every year on her birthday. Her favorite color, at one time, was forest green but now she is more likely to say that twilight blue is her favorite. After spending some time off from writing while her daughters were young she is now working on several new projects—a middle-grade novel and several picture books.

## Book Connections

Both of Haemi's books feature Korean-American protagonists and explore intergenerational relationships. In both stories the mother-daughter relationship is important. The story of *Peacebound Trains* was originally told to Balgassi by her grandmother, who died when Balgassi was 11 years old. It describes a dangerous rooftop train ride in 1950 during the first harsh winter of the Korean War. Balgassi's grandmother took that ride along with her daughters—Balgassi's own mother, who was just five years old, and two of Balgassi's aunts, one nine years old and the youngest not quite ten months old. During her high school days, Balgassi asked her mother about the trip and her mother added more details and a different dimension to the stories. Balgassi wrote an essay about the story but she knew that someday she would write that story for a wider audience. Ten years later, the story found its way to a publisher as *Peacebound Trains.*

Chris K. Soentpiet's illustrations for this book won him the Society of Illustrators Gold Medal. *Peacebound Trains* is featured on the U.S. Government's official Korean War 50th Anniversary Web site. It is the only children's book to receive this honor.

## Books Written by Haemi Balgassi

*Peacebound Trains.* Illustrated by Chris Soentpiet. (Clarion, 1996).

*Tae's Sonata* (Clarion, 1997).

Dear Readers,

   I can't imagine what my childhood would have been like without the books that filled it. I think back on some of their characters and remember and cherish them as I do the best of friends.

   Fill your lives with good books, just as I hope you do good friends. You will be the richer for it.

                    Haemi Balgassi

## For More Information

### Web Sites

Balgassi, Haemi. *Children's Author: Haemi Balgassi.* March 2004. <http://www.haemibalgassi.com>.

## Note

1. Haemi Balgassi, letter to the author, 25 Oct. 2002.

# Fred Bowen

♦  Sports fiction

---
**Marblehead, Massachusetts**
August 3, 1953

---

**AllStar SportStory Series**

📖  *Final Cut*

📖  *Off the Rim*

## About the Author

From the time he was able to say "Go, Red Sox," Fred Bowen was a sports fan. Born on August 3, 1953 in Marblehead, Massachusetts, Fred was the sixth child in an Irish Catholic family of seven children; he has two sisters and four brothers. Fred recalls that his entire family was "sports crazy."[1] In fact, when Fred's older brother, Rich, was born on October 7, 1948, his father and his mother's physician were attending the World Series game between the Cleveland Indians and the Boston Red Sox. According to Bowen, his mother seemed to understand, after all, "they had tickets to the World Series."[2]

At the age of six Fred was a batboy for his big brother Rich's Little League team. When he reached fifth grade, during the 1960s, he was playing Little League baseball and Midget football. Fred also liked to read about sports. Under the covers at night by the light of a flashlight, he read the Chip Hilton series. The series, popular in the 1950s and written by Clair Bee, is best described as a Hardy Boys type series but with sports. In the classroom during lessons he would sneak a look at a few lines whenever he could. However, Fred was not really that good at sports and by the time he reached high school his sports career was over because he did not make any of the teams. So after graduation from high school, instead of heading for baseball training camp, he headed to college. Bowen graduated from the University of Pennsylvania with a degree in history and headed on to law school at George Washington University in Washington, D.C.

In college, Bowen recalls, "In 1975, I was studying for my law classes and listening to the World Series. The Cincinnati Reds were playing the Boston Red Sox and Carlton Fisk hit a home run. It became painfully obvious that I cared a lot more for baseball than the studying I was doing."[3] Nonetheless, after completing his law degree Bowen began a career that eventually took him to the U.S. Department of Labor.

**20**

The story of how Fred Bowen came to write sports stories for intermediate and middle school readers is really a story of his metamorphosis from a career attorney to an author. Every day Bowen commuted from his Silver Springs, Maryland home to his office, where he read law books and wrote briefs. Gradually, he began to think about writing of a different sort. He tried writing movie reviews as a freelancer where he actually got paid to go to the movies; he also wrote video reviews. This experience helped him learn to write for a general audience. He says, "it also taught me how exciting it is to get something published."

Bowen describes his start in writing children's books: "after my children were born, I didn't have time to go to the movies, so I gave up my movie columns. But I still wanted to write. I tried to write a sports book for young adults, but it wasn't very good. By this time, my son, Liam, was older and I was reading to him. We used to read sports books together. I didn't think the books were very good, so I tried to write my own."[4] Finally, Bowen realized that his love of sports could be combined with his writing. In the late 1980s he began to write about sports during his commutes between work and home and over his lunch hours. "Everyday at 1 o'clock, I pulled out my sandwich, notebook, and pen and pretended to be a kid again." [5]

Bowen's first sports writing resulted in a young adult novel. After several rewrites, he submitted it to various publishers. Although no contract was offered, he did receive positive comments. At the time his son, Liam, an eight year old, advised Bowen, "you know Dad you need more games in this book."[6] That discussion made Bowen aware that "kids like to read about the games, what's happening with the kids."[7] Bowen was determined to get his book published so he took a week off from his job and rewrote the manuscript including a lot more play-by-play action. But the book still did not have a publisher.

In the fall of 1994, Bowen's wife, Peggy Jackson, convinced him to attend a librarian's conference in Baltimore. By chance, Bowen met Pat Quinlin, the sister of Margaret Quinlin, who just happened to be the sister of the president of Peachtree Publishers. Pat Quinlin suggested that Bowen send the manuscript to Peachtree. He did, and in 1996, *T.J.'s Secret Pitch* (Peachtree, 1996) was published. That title became the first book in Bowen's very popular AllStar SportStory series.

As Fred Bowen sits down to write a story he has several goals in mind:

First, "I want to tell them a good story; something that will keep them turning the pages."
Second, "I want to teach kids about the history of the game they play."
Third, "I want to teach readers lessons; lessons that can be learned from sports."[8]

Bowen usually begins a story by outlining the plot and making notes concerning the beginning, the middle, and the end. There must be an idea for the plot or theme, generally 15 scenes, and the games—the action that push the plot. Then there must be a narrative that connects the story. Bowen works on one book at a time adding details to the scenes and chapters as he goes—revising as he writes. Because he writes on the commuter train or at his desk over lunchtime, he writes his stories in longhand in a notebook. Peggy types his writing and serves as the book's first reader and editor. Once Bowen feels his book is ready to be sent to the publisher, both Bowen and Jackson work with the publisher to get the book into its final form.

Bowen has often coached the sports teams of his children, Liam and Kerry, and finds that listening in on the game-bench conversations gives him plenty of ideas for dialogue that he can incorporate into his books. But the action often comes from the games themselves. Bowen's action-filled stories end with a final chapter that he uses to tell readers some of the great stories in sports history. He found that it was a great way to get children interested in reading. Over the years Bowen says, "I've collected a lot of baseball knowledge—quirky facts, player trivia, and historical dates—without even trying."[9] Each of Bowen's books is inspired by pieces of this trivia or a quirky fact.

Bowen draws his plots from real life, just as he draws his characters, especially their names, from his environment. "Some of the names of the parks, coaches, and kids in the books are named after places and people that I know now or knew when I was growing up."[10] At first Bowen used the names of childhood friends and even some of his law-school classmates. One of his friends and classmates, Carl Fink, never did like the referees throughout the 18 years that Bowen and he played basketball together. So Bowen was delighted to include Carl's name on a scorecard in one of his books. On the scorecard Carl is the referee. Several of the names of his female coworkers were included in *Playoff Dreams* (Peachtree, 1997) as the patients of one of the mother characters who is an obstetrician.

Bowen began to look to his reading audience for names when he realized the names from his childhood might be more old-fashioned than those that appeal to present-day readers. Once during a book signing at a bookstore in Alexandria, Virginia, Bowen suggested that those at the signing put their names in a drawing and the two names that were drawn would be included in his next book, *The Final Cut* (Peachtree, 1999). A librarian at Bethesda Regional Library, Diane Monnier, became the referee on page 36 of the same book. The real Greta Pemberton in Bowen's *Off the Rim* (Peachtree, 1999) lives just down the street from Bowen. Although she was not good at basketball, she did play on a team that Bowen coached when she was in the second grade. The name of Greta's real dog, Mingo, was also used in the book. However, one of the people who shows up in Bowen's books had nothing to do with Bowen's efforts. An unexplained quirk came about when *T.J.'s Secret Pitch* was published. Even though the illustrator, Jim Thorpe, had never met Bowen's son, Liam, the boy featured on the cover illustration looked just like him.

Bowen's books have sold in the thousands and he is quickly, according to some reviewers, becoming one of the most popular sports writers for young readers. Now, in addition to writing novels for middle-grade readers, Bowen also writes a weekly sports column for the *Washington Post* and the articles are archived on the newspaper's Web site, <http://www.washingtonpost.com/kidspost>. A year or two after his sports column debuted, Bowen discovered that "my weekly kids sports column for *The Washington Post* keeps me very busy and has all but swallowed up most of my writing time."[11] Once Bowen had been writing a book or two a year but now the pace has slowed down and he is publishing fewer books.

Nonetheless, Bowen says his writing career is on track and he continues to outline and devise chapters for a new book. Throughout his writing career, he has found a way to combine his love of history with his love of sports.

Fred Bowen and Margaret "Peggy" Jackson live with their teenage and college-aged children, Liam and Kelly, in Silver Springs, Maryland. Bowen still works for the federal government and he is still passionate about sports and writing. He has coached his children's sports teams and participated in several programs at the Baseball Hall of Fame in Cooperstown, New York, where he has been given a lifetime membership. For someone like Fred Bowen, it doesn't get much better than that.

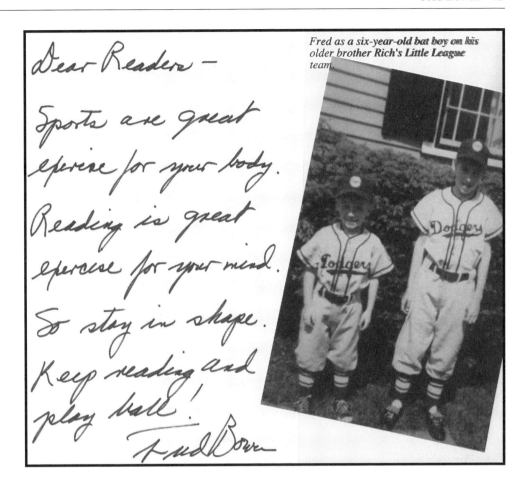

Dear Readers –

Sports are great exercise for your body.

Reading is great exercise for your mind.

So stay in shape.

Keep reading and play ball!

Fred Bowen

*Fred as a six-year-old bat boy on his older brother Rich's Little League team.*

## Book Connections

Each of Fred Bowen's nine tales includes a nugget of history and a bonus historical chapter. But he says that all of his books have some part of his own experiences in them. Bowen was cut from his ninth-grade basketball and baseball teams and that experience became the background for his book *Final Cut.* Bowen recalls that "other books have smaller scenes that happened to me when I was growing up. For example, I used to ride my bike and grab hold of a low tree branch and let my bike go flying just like T.J. does in *T.J.'s Secret Pitch.* And I spent many hours trying to beat my four older brothers in one-on-one basketball games, just like Michael does in *Full Court Fever*."[12]

Bowen has written books about basketball and baseball. Sports figures from history are often mentioned as role models and examples for the young players in the story. In *Final Cut* Bowen incorporated information about famous players, such as Michael Jordan, who did not make their high school basketball team on the first try. In *Full Court Fever* (Peachtree, 1998) Bowen capitalizes on the University of California, Los Angeles (UCLA) men's basketball team's strategy in the 1960s to make up for their team's lack of height. In this book the players locate a *Sports Illustrated* article about the UCLA team and use the information to help their team. *Off the Rim* incorporates information about the six-on-six girls basketball that was played for years in Iowa, until 1993. Another book, *On the Line* (Peachtree, 1998), makes use of the so-called granny shot that was regularly used by NBA star Rick Barry.

Bowen's baseball books zero-in on the Hall of Fame honoree, Honus Wagner, who used a glove with no web and no pocket (*The Golden Glove,* Peachtree, 1996). The stick-to-itiveness of Ernie Banks, who played in the most major league ball games without ever being in a playoff or a World Series, becomes important in *Playoff Dreams.* The secret pitch in *T.J.'s Secret Pitch* comes from the secret "eephus" pitch used by Rip Sewell in the major leagues. Other books are inspired by unique individuals such as the player coach of the Cleveland Indians, Lou Boudreau (*The Kid Coach,* Peachtree, 1997) and Christopher "Christy" Matthewson (*Winners Take All,* Peachtree, 2000), who was so honest that umpires at times asked for his call when their view was obstructed. At the end of each book, Bowen tells about the real team or person that inspired the story and gives a chapter's worth of background.

## Books Written by Fred Bowen

*The Final Cut.* Illustrated by Ann Barrow. (Peachtree, 1999).

*Full Court Fever.* Illustrated by Ann Barrow. (Peachtree, 1998).

*The Golden Glove.* Illustrated by Jim Thorpe. (Peachtree, 1996).

*The Kid Coach.* Illustrated by Ann Barrow. (Peachtree, 1997).

*Off the Rim.* Illustrated by Ann Barrow. (Peachtree, 1998).

*On the Line.* Illustrated by Ann Barrow. (Peachtree, 1999).

*Playoff Dreams.* Illustrated by Ann Barrow. (Peachtree, 1997).

*T.J.'s Secret Pitch.* Illustrated by Jim Thorpe. (Peachtree, 1996).

*Winners Take All.* Illustrated by Paul Casale. (Peachtree, 2000).

## For More Information

### Articles

McElmeel, Sharron L. "Author Profile: Fred Bowen." *Library Talk* 14.1 (January/ February 2001): 20–21.

"Meet Authors and Illustrators." *Children's Literature: Meet Authors & Illustrators.* March 2004. <http://www.childrenslit.com/f_bowen.htm>.

### Web Sites

Bowen, Fred. *Fred Bowen—Sports Writer for Kids—Welcome to My Website.* March 2004. <http://www.fredbowen.com>.

Bowen, Fred. "Column: The Score." *The Washington Post: KidsPost.* March 2004. <http://www.washingtonpost.com/kidspost>. Once you reach this site you will need to search for articles authored by Fred Bowen. The past two weeks can be read without cost but columns over two weeks old must be purchased. The archived columns and transcripts of Bowen's online chats with KidsPost may be accessed directly from a page on Fred Bowen's Web site <http://www.fredbowen.com/columns.htm>, accessed March 2004.

## Notes

1. Fred Bowen, interview with the author, 7 Apr. 2000.
2. Ibid.
3. Ibid.
4. Fred Bowen, letter to the author, 20 Sept. 2002.
5. Ibid.
6. Fred Bowen, *Sports, Kids, and Books,* presented at the Iowa Reading Association Conference, Des Moines, Iowa, 7 Apr. 2000.
7. Ibid.
8. Ibid.
9. Bowen, interview.
10. Bowen, letter.
11. Ibid.
12. Ibid.

# Toni Buzzeo

◆  Folk literature  ◆  Animals

**Dearborn, Michigan**
October 4, 1951

📖  *Dawdle Duckling*
📖  *The Sea Chest*

## About the Author

Toni Buzzeo's closest companions while she was growing up were books and her grandma, Mae. For the first 10 years of her life, Toni was the only child in her family, who lived in a tiny garage home in Dearborn, Michigan. Toni's father and grandfather both worked for Ford Motor Company. Her mother, Jeanne, often took Toni to the library where she spent many hours reading books and imagining things in front of a beautiful dollhouse that was on the second floor.

Toni was "an enormous reader as a child and spent every available summer day of my preteen and teen years at the library or back home reading the books I got there."[1] By then the family had moved to a neighborhood where there were a lot of children. The Cyll family lived next door and Toni became best friends with Mike, "Mikey," who was just a year younger than she. They "became fast friends and spent lots of time together imagining and—our specialty—digging to China in the dirt pile under the big elm tree in my backyard. We really did believe that one day we'd get there!"[2]

Toni says that she and her best friend were very different from one another. "Mike was much more of a dreamer than I was, a guy who thought globally while I was great at the details. . . . Mike was more of a dawdler and I was more of a follow-the-rules type." Their differences, however, did not bother their friendship one bit. Just five blocks from her new home the Dearborn library system built the Snow branch library. To Toni, "that was like having Disney World built in my neighborhood."[3]

By then Toni was no longer an only child. At first her parents, thinking they would not have other children, decided to open their home to a foster daughter. Nine-month-old Marianne lived with the Buzzeo's while awaiting adoption by another family. Soon, however, Toni's mother found out that she was expecting a baby and shortly after that, Marianne was adopted by another family. Just a month after she turned 10, Toni became a sister for keeps when her sister Karen was born. During the next few years Toni would become the big sister twice more when her two brothers, David and Glen, were born.

Toni spent a great deal of time helping her parents care for her three younger siblings. She read and reread favorite books to her siblings. She also spent a lot of time finding and copying poems into her own notebook to create a very personal anthology of favorites.

Books led Toni to her first experience in the life of a librarian or writer. At the age of 16 she got a part-time job as a library page at the Dearborn Public Library. Her experience there led to a full-time job at the "brand new main library—the Henry Ford Centennial Library," where she worked as a library telephone operator and a library aide in the General Information department. She worked full-time while going to college at night. "After a few years, I transferred to the Snow Branch Library as the Children's Department Library Aide and really fell in love with children's books all over again. I began to buy my own copies of them and to pay careful attention to what was published."[4]

During her college years Toni continued to write and some of her poetry was published in the university literary magazines. Poets were among her favorite writers, in fact, her Master's seminar work focused on the poetry of Christina Rossetti. She earned undergraduate and graduate degrees in English language and literature from the University of Michigan.

Toni Buzzeo began a career as a high school teacher and married a childhood friend, Kenneth Cyll, the older brother of her friend Mikey. The couple moved to Maine in 1979 and soon became parents of a son, Christopher. Buzzeo realized that Christopher was a dawdler like his uncle, Mike. "He had an enormous imagination—a large internal life—which was wonderful. But it often prevented him from just doing things I asked him to do, like getting dressed or eating his breakfast."[5]

Chris's imagination was often fueled by the ideas and stories in the many books Buzzeo read to him. "I spent hours and hours everyday reading wonderful children's books to him and once again, familiarizing myself with children's literature." By now the family had moved to Gorham, Maine where they frequented the children's section of the public library. And then, as Buzzeo says, "life presented me with an opportunity that would change my course. I was offered the position of Children's Librarian at the Baxter Memorial Library in Gorham, Maine."[6] This was the same library where Buzzeo and her son spent many hours each week. Buzzeo loved the work and decided to get a second graduate degree, this time in library and information science.

She enrolled in the master's program at the University of Rhode Island at Kingston and on graduation, she became a school library media specialist. In 1995, Buzzio began to think about writing children's books so she devised her own "self-study course on writing for children, reading all of the best guide books, taking notes, joining several online children's writing groups, and focusing my attention exclusively on children's literature."[7]

That year she also made a connection with Jane Kurtz, an author of picture books and novels, who became her mentor. While working on her children's book manuscripts, Buzzeo researched and wrote several resource books for her professional colleagues, including *Terrific Connections with Authors, Illustrators, and Storytellers* (Libraries Unlimited, 1999). But she really wanted to publish in the children's book field. After five long years, in July 2000, a manuscript completed by Buzzeo won the Society of Children's Book Writers and Illustrators' Barbara Karlin Grant for the best picture book manuscript yet unpublished. Five weeks later, Dial Books for Young Readers offered a contract for the manuscript and *The Sea Chest* (Dial, 2002) became Buzzeo's first published book.

The inspiration for *The Sea Chest* was a video Buzzeo viewed about lighthouses that introduced her to a legend that told of a baby that arrived on a lighthouse island in a sea chest. The legend awakened Buzzeo's own childhood memories of becoming a sister, first to her foster sister Marianne and later to three siblings born to her parents. The emotions flooded back and the story soon emerged as a beautiful tale of adoption intertwined with the nineteenth-century legend.

It wasn't long before a second picture book was under contract. When Buzzeo's son Chris graduated from high school, her childhood friend (and now brother-in-law) Mike and his wife came to Maine from Arizona for the celebration. The families took a trip up the coast and were staying at a cabin right on the ocean. It was during a morning walk that Mike saw a family of ducks, one mother and several babies. Later as Mike told Toni about the encounter he talked about the one little duck who wasn't swimming in a straight line like the other ducklings. "[The duckling] was off dawdling until some threat that Mike didn't even see caused every single one of the ducklings to hop on Mama's back, even the little dawdler."[8]

That incident prompted Buzzeo to think about ducks and dawdlers. Buzzeo recalls, "I used all that I knew about dawdlers and dreamers (thanks to Mike and Chris) and all that I knew about poetry to write that manuscript."[9] *Dawdle Duckling* (Dial, 2003) was published in January 2003 and on the dedication page Buzzeo thanks Mike for the story and for a lifetime of friendship.

For many years Toni Buzzeo was a library media specialist at Longfellow School in Portland, Maine, where she shared her own enthusiasm about books and reading. In 1999 she was named Maine's Library Media Specialist of the Year. Today Buzzeo is a full-time writer. Her writing space is in her family home, a 200-year-old colonial farmhouse on a 35-acre site filled with gardens and trees, wild turkeys and black flies. A treasured member of the household is a Belgian sheep dog mix, Indy (short for her full name Indigo Jones, a combination of Indigo Girls and Indiana Jones). Their son Christopher is grown and now maintains his mother's Web site. Buzzeo continues to write and develop picture book manuscripts and she has even started writing novels. Undoubtedly, there will be many more stories that emerge from Buzzeo's vast experience with poetry and story.

## Book Connections

Toni Buzzeo's first two picture books were released within six months of one another. Both were met with rave reviews and accolades. The first, *The Sea Chest,* was named a Junior Literary Guild Selection and the second, *Dawdle Duckling,* was named a Children's Book-of-the-Month selection. More manuscripts are currently under consideration by publishers. *Little Loon and Papa* (Dial, 2004), Buzzeo's third book, tells the story of a little loon and his first diving lessons. Papa Loon plays a pivotal role making the story one that will showcase a father's role in a child's life. Not surprisingly, the pop-

## Toni Buzzeo

Dear Readers,

I am a book person. I always have been. When I was your age, I spent so many hours reading — and walking back and forth to the library in my neighborhood — that the people in the books were as real to me as my friends.

And now, as a grownup, I still love children's books. I am a school librarian who shares that love of children's books with students every day in the library and who writes books for kids to enjoy too.

Why do I think books and reading are so important?

- First, if you are a reader, you exercise your mind everyday. You've heard in Physical Education class how important it is to exercise your muscles. The same goes for your mind. Reading is one great tool to help you do that.

- Second, reading is the key to information. Even if you're in front of the computer screen, looking at a great article you located on mountain gorillas for your endangered species research project, you're going to need to <u>read</u> it to get the information.

- Third, reading expands your horizons. In order to be a well-educated person, you will need to know an enormous number of things. Being a student and listening to your teachers will get you there. Watching educational television and the evening news will get you there. Living a rich and varied life will get you there. And above all, reading will get you there!

Good luck on the journey!

Toni Buzzeo

ularity of *Dawdle Duckling* spawned a fourth picture book, *Ready or Not, Dawdle Duckling* (Dial, 2005).

As with all authors, remnants of Buzzeo's own past experiences and those of the people she knows, family and friends, show up in her books. Those who read *The Sea Chest* will find that it reveals a lot about Buzzeo, "both in my life as a lonely only child and in my love of poetic language and in my home state of Maine."[10] It takes but a spark to ignite memories of the past and bring forth wonderful stories for readers.

## Books Written by Toni Buzzeo

*Dawdle Duckling.* Illustrated by Margaret Spengler. (Dial Books for Young Readers, 2003).

*Little Loon and Papa.* Illustrated by Margaret Spengler. (Dial Books for Young Readers, 2004).

*Ready or Not Dawdle Duckling.* Illustrated by Margaret Spengler. (Dial Books for Young Readers, 2005).

*The Sea Chest.* Illustrated by Mary Grand Pre. (Dial Books for Young Readers, 2002).

## For More Information

### Articles

Garretson, Jerri. *Authors Among Us: Librarians Who Are Authors of Children's & Young Adult Literature—Toni Buzzeo.* March 2004. <http://ravenstonepress.com/buzzeo.html>.

Maine Association of School Librarians. 1999 School Library Media Specialist of the Year. March 2004. <http://www.maslibraries.org/about/awards/1999win.html>.

Waterboro Public Library. *Maine Writers: Toni Buzzeo.* March 2004. <http://www.waterborolibrary.org/maineaut/ab.htm#buzzeo>.

### Web Sites

Buzzeo, Toni. *Toni Buzzeo, Author, Library Media Specialist.* Nov. 2003. <http://www.tonibuzzeo.com>.

## Notes

1. Toni Buzzeo, letter to the author, 22 Sept. 2002.
2. Ibid.
3. Toni Buzzeo, *Toni Buzzeo, Author, Library Media Specialist.* March 2004. <http://www.tonibuzzeo.com/bio.html>.
4. Buzzeo, letter.
5. Ibid.

6. Ibid.
7. Ibid.
8. Ibid.
9. Ibid.
10. Ibid.

# Janie Bynum

◆  Animals  ◆  Rhyming

### Dallas, Texas
October 4, 1951

📖  *Altoona Baboona*

📖  *Otis*

📖  *Too Big, Too Small, Just Right*

📖  *Edna the Elephant*

## About the Author/Illustrator

Janie Bynum was born and raised in Dallas, Texas. Her family includes her parents, Jack and Bea Bynum, and an older sister and brother. Janie's interest in writing began early in her life and she says, "I wrote and illustrated my first book in 6th grade—just because I felt compelled to. It was a morality tale—very, very didactic!"[1]

Over time Janie developed a list of favorites: chocolate ice cream, seafood, and most ethnic foods. She likes all kinds of pets, especially dogs. Her favorite colors include red, purple, olive, cobalt or periwinkle blue, butter yellow and too many more to list![2] Undoubtedly it was Janie's love of color that brought her to a career in graphic design. She earned a bachelor of fine arts degree from the University of North Texas in 1983 and eventually opened her own corporate design studio. She was a graphic designer for 11 years before turning to children's books as a source of creative satisfaction.[3] "I keep working as a freelance designer, but took a couple of children's book illustration classes at the SAIC (School of the Art Institute of Chicago) in 1996 and 1997. I was hooked."[4]

In April 1996 Janie Bynum, in the process of moving to Chicago, was riding a train from Kalamazoo, Michigan to the city. The title of her first book, *Altoona Baboona* (Harcourt, 1999), just popped into her head. She says, "I have no idea why."[5] The title was soon followed by the image of a baboon girl, an image that came along with the singsong line, "Altoona Baboona flicks peas with a spoon-a. She dances all night and sings songs to the moon-a."[6]

Bynum says she "studied the works of Sendak [Maurice Sendak, author of *Where the Wild Things Are*] and others, used Uri Shulevitz's *Writing with Pictures* as my 'bible,' and began writing and dummying my stories."[7] As part of an assignment in one of her children's book illustration classes at SAIC, she created a book dummy for *Altoona*

32

*Baboona.* At about the same time she joined the Society of Children's Book Writers and Illustrators (SCBWI) and learned about the organization's national conference. In 1997 Bynum attended the conference and began to network with other book creators. One of the author/illustrators she met at the conference saw her book dummy for *Altoona Baboona* and offered to forward Bynum's portfolio to her agent, Steve Malk. In a matter of a few weeks, Malk had sold the book for *Altoona Baboona* to Harcourt. It had taken just 16 months from start to contract. It was another 18 months from the time Harcourt bought the book from Bynum until they published *Altoona Baboona* in 1999.[8] From that first spark of inspiration on the train in 1996, it was a total of three years before *Altoona Baboona* grew from idea to reality.

With the success of selling her first book, Bynum decided in 1997 to shift the focus of her artistic work to illustration. She was able to utilize her extensive graphic design skills to help her compose and create the art for her books. Bynum's art is created with a combination of traditional and digital techniques. She creates digital illustrations using such tools as an electronic tablet with a pressure-sensitive stylus. In contrast, a traditional method might use pen and ink, paints, or a graphite (lead) pencil. Bynum draws digitally using a Wacom tablet and stylus. To paint digitally she uses a program called Painter®.

Computer art no longer looks like it is created with pixels. Today digital art is difficult to distinguish from art created with traditional paints and pen. Bynum says that, "digital illustration is very efficient—not necessarily faster."[9] A digital process, according to Bynum, is "stimulating, the chances for do-overs is almost unlimited."[10]

In other words, artists who create images through a digital process can manipulate the elements and components to make alterations in the artwork easily and usually seamlessly. Traditional art is generally considered more spontaneous and unpredictable. Artists cannot accurately predict what reaction will happen when the actual pigment from paints or other art media is introduced to real paper and sometimes the result is a big surprise. In contrast, the element of surprise is not present in digitally-created art.

Bynum uses a Macintosh computer with a large screen, utilizing several software programs in the creative process. She uses a pixel-based painting program, a Vector-based (shape-oriented) art program, image-editing software, and a page-layout program. Some of the programs have drawbacks and Bynum is constantly refining her skills and learning how to manipulate the features of the software to achieve the effects she wants. The quality and permanency of digitally-created art has increased considerably in the recent years. The technology available now makes it possible to print digital art on 100 percent rag watercolor or printmaking paper using 50-year archival-quality inks.

The art for her first book, *Altoona Baboona,* was designed and created as a rough-sketch dummy with one piece of color art and a color cover. Bynum incorporated digital and traditional techniques using Quark Xpress to create the book's layout. With digital art Bynum says that a nice advantage is "you rarely have to re-mix your paint. Once you save a color to your palette, you have it for as long as you need it."[11] On the other hand, different printing techniques might not interpret the colors generated in exactly the same way so proofing the prints is very important.

As Bynum was creating her art for *Altoona Baboona,* she was able to mount the illustrations, in progress, on a private Internet staging site. Her editor could check the progress and the development of the art and make suggestions along the way and the final art was sent to her editor on a CD.

After living in Chicago for a short time, Bynum and her teenage son, Taylor, moved back to Kalamazoo, Michigan where Bynum writes and illustrates children's books as well as continues some work in the graphic design field. In addition to her work as an artist, she often speaks about her digital art at schools and libraries.

## Book Connections

*Altoona Baboona* is the humorous tale of a baboon that delights in flying off in a hot-air balloon to parts of the world unknown. Altoona takes essential items with her on the trip: bananas, a trunk, sunglasses, and a camera, even a friend or two. At the end of the trip she and her friends, a loon and a raccoon, are seen joyously roasting marshmallows over a roaring campfire. In the sequel, *Altoona Up North* (Harcourt, 2001), the three friends board their hot-air balloon and head to the north to visit Altoona's aunt in north Saskatoon-a. There the trio visits with Altoona's auntie, who would really like to be in a warmer place. Auntie takes the friends skiing, ice fishing, and sledding with sled dogs. It takes awhile but eventually, to the friends delight, they find that Auntie has taken them on a surprise voyage. With a rhythmic bouncing rhyme, these two tales are great read-alouds for young learners. Bynum's illustrations enliven not only her own texts but also the books of others. For example, in Frances Minters's *Too Big, Too Small, Just Right* (Harcourt, 2001), the text deals with opposites and it is Bynum's clever pen-and-ink and watercolor art that shows readers the clever concept and humorous aspects of each situation.

Bynum uses images from her own experiences that are important or humorous to her. For example, she says, "on the *Altoona Baboona* dedication page—the aerial view 'snapshot' of the monkey family represents my parents, Jack and Bea Bynum, at their farm house with my son Taylor pushing the wheelbarrow—with his Dallas cousins, Logan and Baron Farmar, riding in the wheelbarrow—all depicted as little monkeys!"[12] Within the book, on the page where Altoona is flicking the peas, Bynum uses the refrigerator to showcase magnets, photos, calendar dates representing people, places, and dates that are important to her. The sketchbook on the bed when Altoona unpacks in her room represents Bynum herself and her art.[13]

Described as cartoon-like with a springtime palette, Bynum's digital pen-and-ink and watercolor illustrations complement the text and aid in the comprehensibility of the text that is being illustrated.

## Books Written and Illustrated by Janie Bynum

*Altoona Baboona* (Harcourt, 1999).

*Altoona Up North* (Harcourt, 2001).

*Otis* (Harcourt, 2000).

*Pig Enough* (Harcourt, 2003).

## Books Illustrated by Janie Bynum

*Too Big, Too Small, Just Right.* Written by Frances Minters. (Harcourt, 2001).

*Edna the Elephant.* Written by Margaret Park Bridges. (Candlewick Press, 2002).

# For More Information

## Articles

Bynum, Janie. "Let's Get Digital." *The Drawing Board for Illustrators.* Nov. 2003. <http://members.aol.com/thedrawing/digital.html>.

Smith, Cynthia Leitich. "The Story Behind the Story: Janie Bynum on *Altoona Baboona.*" *Cynthia Leitich Smith Web site.* June 2003. <http://www.cynthialeitichsmith.com/storybynum.html>.

## Web Sites

Bynum, Janie. *www.janiebynum.com.* March 2004. <http://www.janiebynum.com>.

# Notes

1. Janie Bynum, letter to the author, 5 Sept. 2002.
2. Ibid.
3. Ibid.
4. Ibid.
5. Cynthia Leitich Smith, "The Story Behind the Story: Janie Bynum on *Altoona Baboona.*" *Cynthia Leitich Smith Web site.* <http://www.cynthialeitichsmith.com/storybynum.html>.
6. Ibid.
7. Bynum, letter.
8. Smith, "The Story Behind the Story."
9. Janie Bynum, "Let's Get Digital," *Watercolor,* June 2003, <http://members.aol.com/thedrawing/digital.html>.
10. Ibid.
11. Ibid.
12. Bynum, letter.
13. Ibid.

# Nancy L. Carlson

◆ Animals ◆ Humor ◆ Holidays

**Edina, Minnesota**
October 10, 1953

📖 *Harriet and the Garden*

📖 *Hooray for Grandparents' Day!*

📖 *Louanne Pig in the Perfect Family*

## About the Author/Illustrator

A life-long Minnesota resident, Nancy L. Carlson lives and works in Bloomington, Minnesota where her life is filled with furry animals and all types of art projects. Carlson was born and raised in Edina, Minnesota, with her sister, Susan, and brother, David. Nancy's parents, Louise and Harry Carlson, read to her every night. Nancy recalls, "the first book that I read from cover-to-cover was a biography of Babe Ruth. When I was young, I really loved baseball."[1] She also enjoyed reading comic books and the old Golden books.

After graduating from Edina High School, Nancy entered college and in 1976 she obtained an undergraduate fine arts degree in printmaking from the Minneapolis College of Art. Soon design collectors in both the private and public sectors purchased her art. While working at Minneapolis's Walker Art Center the young artist developed an interest in children's books. In the early 1980s Carlson illustrated two books written by other writers. She says, "I loved [being an illustrator] then my editor talked me into writing my own stories."[2]

Nancy Carlson began to submit her own stories along with her illustrations. By the time her first child, Kelly, was born in 1983, Carlson had introduced her characters Harriet and Loudmouth George to readers. Harriet is a loveable golden retriever and George is a self-confident rabbit. Together the two characters learn from experiences similar to those encountered by young readers—sharing, honesty, how to deal with bullies, and so forth. A golden retriever named Dame, Carlson's first dog, inspired the creation of Harriet who starred in five books before being left behind by other books about other characters. Loudmouth George got his own books and in 1985 Louanne the Pig came on the scene.

During this time Carlson and her husband Barry McCool became parents of two more children: Patrick, born in 1985, and a second son, Michael, born in 1988. Soon

Carlson was writing and illustrating books about bunnies, Arnie, a "top cat," and other animal characters that dealt with anxiety about going away to camp, meeting new kids, friendships, grandparents, and starting school.

Then, almost 20 years after her first book, Carlson returned to writing about Harriet and George. In *Harriet and George's Christmas Treat* (Carolrhoda, 2001) the two pals spend a lot of time trying to avoid the dreaded annual Christmas treat that Ms. Hoozit makes for them. They picture the fruitcake that was used to crack nuts but after arriving at Ms. Hoozit's they realize that this year's treat is something much different. The lesson the two pals learn involves politeness—a lesson taught gently and humorously.

Harriet and George's old neighborhood has stayed pretty much the same in *Harriet and George's Christmas Treat.* Carlson has made Harriet a little more fashionable and the colors of the illustrations are brighter and more exuberant. Harriet, as a character, has her own profile. According to Carlson, Harriet's goal when she grows up is to be a baseball player, ballerina, or an artist. Her favorite foods are hamburgers, hamburgers, and hamburgers. Harriet's greatest fears are recitals and Ms. Hoozit's fruitcake. The things Harriet likes best about herself are her cute golden colored and diamond-shaped ears.[3]

Nancy Carlson says that the work of Maurice Sendak, Steven Kellogg, and Barbara Cooney has influenced her work as an illustrator.[4] The influence for her work as a writer came from books such as *"The Secret Garden, The Borrowers* and the wonderful Betsy-Tacy series."[5]

Among Carlson's favorite things are her pets: Lily, a black mutt; Carmel, her old cat; Curly, a guinea pig; and Steve, a mouse. Once she had a rabbit but it ran away. She also likes candy corn, cookies without nuts, and she loves pasta. Many of her animals show up in her books and no doubt, among Harriet's Halloween candy is Carlson's favorite treat, candy corn. Recipes for some of Carlson's favorite cookie bar treats can be found on her Web site, <http://www.nancycarlson.com>.

Nancy Carlson lives in Bloomington, Minnesota with her husband, their daughter, two sons, and their pets. When Carlson is not writing or illustrating a book, she is most often involved in other art endeavors or some outdoor activity such as hiking, bird watching, running, biking, or swimming. She designs posters, greeting cards, stuffed toys, t-shirts, caps, and other items that her family's company, McCool Limited, Inc., makes and they are available from Carlson's Web site.

## Book Connections

Nancy Carlson's own experiences and those of her children and her husband provide the situations for many of the story plots that she uses for her books. The bully in *Loudmouth George and the Sixth Grade Bully* (Carolrhoda, 1983) was based on a bully who was mean to Carlson when she was in grade school. The story settings are drawn from Carlson's old neighborhood and the characters she invents actually are based on people she knows.

In *Hooray for Grandparents' Day* (Viking, 2000), the librarian is modeled on the librarian in Carlson's son's grade school. However, the star of the book is Arnie, a cat who grows a little older and a little wiser after each everyday experience. The teacher in *Look Out Kindergarten, Here I Come!* (Viking, 1999) was based on the teacher who taught the kindergarten class that one of her son's attended. The house scenes in her books come from Carlson's favorite old television show, *Leave It to Beaver.* Illustrations in other books often include amusing details. For example, Loudmouth George's clothing in *Loudmouth George and the Sixth Grade Bully* features carrot prints, which create a wardrobe just right for the rabbit. In a scene in *I Like Me* (Viking, 1988) Carlson shows a newspaper in the background with the headline, "Minnesota Twins Win!" showing both her interest in baseball and her hometown area.[6]

*I Like Me* is the author's favorite title and the one, of all her books, that she would choose for young readers to read first.[7] *I Like Me* was followed in 1997 by a sequel of sorts, *A.B.C. I Like Me!* (Viking, 1997). The self-confident pig from *I Like Me* frolics through the alphabet sequence with a group of friends. Together these books are awesome, brave, and cheerful; the faces of her characters are filled with expression and the illustrations are bold, cheerful, and colorful.

Although the text in Carlson's books are simple, each carries a positive message without preaching. Typically Carlson writes and rewrites a text as many as 30 times and most of the writing and rewriting, she says, is done by hand.[8] The topics covered in her books vary. Carlson has dealt with a new baby in the family, adoption, blaming others, bullies, self-esteem, honesty, and a myriad of other childhood concerns.

Fear that can be caused by horrific events has not been avoided either. On September 11, 2001, terrorists attacked the United States by flying hijacked airplanes into the World Trade Center's twin towers in New York City and the Pentagon in Washington, D.C. Passengers on a fourth hijacked plane forced it to crash in a field in Pennsylvania rather than let it crash into another building full of people. The following day on September 12, Nancy Carlson began to write and illustrate a book that helped young readers face their own fears. In *There's a Big Beautiful World Out There!* (Viking, 2002), Carlson begins by encouraging young readers to confront and overcome their fears. A brown-haired girl with braids hides under her covers fearing the mean-looking dogs, thunderstorms, and scary stories in the news. She is able to come out from hiding only when she thinks about all the good things that she will miss if she keeps on hiding.

## Books Written and Illustrated by Nancy Carlson

*A.B.C. I Like Me!* (Viking, 1987).

*Harriet and George's Christmas Treat* (Carolrhoda, 2001).

*Hooray for Grandparents' Day* (Viking, 2000).

*How About a Hug* (Viking, 2001).

*I Like Me* (Viking, 1988).

*It's Going to Be Perfect* (Viking, 1998).

*It's Not My Fault* (Carolrhoda, 2003).

*Look Out Kindergarten, Here I Come!* (Viking, 1999).

*Louanne Pig in the Perfect Family* (Carolrhoda, 1985).

*Loudmouth George and the Sixth Grade Bully* (Carolrhoda, 1983).

*My Best Friend Moved Away* (Viking, 2001).

*Smile a Lot!* (Carolrhoda, 2002).

*There's a Big Beautiful World Out There!* (Viking, 2002).

*A Visit to Grandma's* (Viking, 1993).

# For More Information

## Web Sites

Carlson, Nancy. *Nancy's Neighborhood.* March 2004. <http://www.nancycarlson.com>.

# Notes

1. Nancy Carlson, "What It's Like to Be Me!" in the newsletter *Nancy's Neighborhood* 4.1 (2001): 1.

2. Nancy Carlson, letter to the author, 6 Sept. 2002.

3. Nancy Carlson, "Getting to Know Harriet," in the newsletter *Nancy's Neighborhood* 4.1 (2001): 3.

4. Carlson, "What It's Like to Be Me!"

5. Ibid.

6. Carlson, letter.

7. Ibid.

8. Nancy Carlson, presentation at Viking Elementary School, Grand Forks, Nebraska, 12 Apr. 2000.

# Mary Casanova

◆ Adventure fiction ◆ Folk literature ◆ Historical fiction

**Duluth, Minnesota**
February 2, 1957

📖 *Moose Tracks*
📖 *The Hunter*
📖 *Cécile: Gates of Gold*

## About the Author

The fourth child in a family of 10, Mary Casanova was born on Groundhog's Day in Duluth, Minnesota. Her father, Gene Gazelka, was a manager of a State Farm Insurance company headquarters in St. Paul. When Mary was very young, the family moved to Arden Hills, Minnesota where she and her two sisters and seven brothers grew up.

With so many siblings Mary often felt as if she were at camp. The children spent a lot of time outdoors. In the winter they played ice hockey and in the summer they always had a group ready to play tag off the family pontoon boat. Mary grew up water skiing, sailing, camping, and riding the family's horse everywhere she could. As if a family of 12 was not enough, there were also many animals—including a Shetland pony that managed to make his least favorite riders fall off and a Canadian goose that protected his turf by leaving welts on the legs of those who threatened his space.

To Mary, books did not seem adventurous enough to compete with the horseback riding, skiing, swimming, and all the other activities she was able to do. It wasn't until high school that, according to Mary, "I fell in love with the power and magic of words."[1] She says she has been writing regularly since high school when she began a journal to record her observations—paying attention to her surroundings with her five senses.

High school was also the place where she met her future husband, Charles. Mary Gazelka and Charles Casanova graduated from Mounds View High School in 1975. He headed for the University of Minnesota and she headed to Aspen, Colorado where she became a ski bum. To support herself, Mary did maid work and one of her clients was Ethel Kennedy. After a year or so, Mary returned to Minnesota and entered the University of Minnesota to study English. She and Charles became reacquainted and they were married in 1978. Both graduated from the university in 1981 and their love of the outdoors lured them to the north where they made their home near Ranier, Minnesota, close to the Canadian border. From their turn-of-the-century, barn-style house they can observe eagles, otters, moose, black bears, and wolves and they are close enough to the border to see an old bridge that leads into Canada.

The family soon grew to include a daughter, Katie, and a son, Eric. While the children were young, Mary Casanova honed her writing skills. She prepared resumes, taught at Rainy River Community College, and wrote many short articles and poems. She collected so many rejection letters from the publishers that she submitted her work to that she thought about giving up writing and considered becoming a full-time teacher. The year was 1989, her children were seven and four and she was working on a Master's degree. She needed two credits and decided to sign up for a weeklong writing workshop lead by young adult author Marion Dane Bauer. That workshop was the turning point in Casanova's writing career. Up to that point Casanova had not thought about writing for a young audience but Bauer helped her realize how her own emotions could be transformed into a character.

Casanova's successes after the workshop came swiftly. First, she won a medallion and $250 for a short story she submitted at a children's literature conference in Grand Forks, North Dakota. Shortly after that, she received a $1000 grant from the Minnesota State Arts Board. With those successes spurring her on, Casanova decided to write a novel. After reading some of Gary Paulsen's titles of life in the north woods, Casanova felt that she might have her own story to tell. Her goal at the time was not necessarily to get published but rather to just finish a book, even a book of 120 pages. She wanted to write a book that readers could not put down—a book that mattered.[2]

Casanova met several established writers at writing workshops: Marion Dane Bauer, Jean Craighead George, Avi, and Pam Conrad. Each of them read the manuscript, encouraged her, offered critiques, and in general spurred her on during the three-and-a-half years that it took her to write, revise, and rewrite that book. Finally, Casanova had an adventure that would draw readers in and keep them turning the pages. In *Moose Tracks* (Hyperion, 1995), the character Seth Jacobson, a 12-year-old boy, tries to protect an orphaned moose calf from poachers. Along the way, Seth's attitude about hunting begins to change and he has to sort out his relationship with his game warden stepfather. *Moose Tracks* was published in 1995 and earned a spot on several state award lists. The book reflects all those years of growing up with seven brothers who hunted and Nancy's efforts to reconcile hunting with her love of animals.[3]

Soon Casanova was working on a second book. This time the book grew out of labor unrest that occurred in nearby International Falls. The labor dispute resulted in a riot during which over 600 angry men roamed the streets. The actual riot took place in 1989, a turbulent period of time, and when word got out that Casanova was writing a book about the unrest, some people in her hometown threatened to boycott her husband's business. She did not back down and bravely continued with the story of Bryan Grant, a sixth grader who videotapes his father, a union worker, setting fire to the mobile homes of nonunion workers. Bryan's father's anger is fueled when the paper company he works for decided to hire nonunion workers for an expansion at the plant. Bryan struggles with how he should respond to his father's lawlessness and finds his life further complicated when he becomes friends with Chelsia, the daughter of a nonunion worker. Once the book was finished Casanova said her community responded favorably to what they called an account "that handles the event fairly, trying to show both sides."[4] *Riot* (Hyperion, 1996) won Casanova recognition and her first Minnesota Book Award nomination.

The following year *Wolf Shadows* (Hyperion, 1997), a sequel to *Moose Tracks,* was published. Casanova continued the story of Seth Jacobson. This time Seth, who is the son of a northern Minnesota game warden, admires wolves but his friend Matt does not view them so favorably. To Matt, the wolves are animals that kill livestock and he looks with disdain at Seth's admiration of the wolf. When Matt calls Seth a "wolf-lover" and actually shoots a wolf, the boys' relationship is seriously strained. In anger, Seth abandons Matt in the woods. Matt's ability to find his way out of the woods is questionable and because of that his life is seriously threatened. This book, like Casanova's first two, garnered favorable reviews and nominations to regional and state book lists.

Casanova loves horses and as a young girl, she rode her horse everywhere. In her fourth novel, *Stealing Thunder* (Hyperion, 1999), Casanova writes about Libby, a young girl who wants a horse of her own. But for now Libby must be satisfied with riding and caring for her neighbor's horse, Thunder. Later, when her neighbor Mrs. Porter leaves her husband, Libby finds out that the horse is being abused by Mr. Porter. Libby resolves to save the horse and she plots, with a new friend, to rescue the horse by stealing it. Meanwhile, Mr. Porter is planning to set the barn on fire to get the insurance money and to be rid of the burden of owning the stable. The two scenarios come together to present a story that will show what one can do by standing up and voicing an opinion for the right thing. Libby, similar to Casanova who grew up in a male dominated family, seems to struggle to be heard but in the end finds her voice, loud and clear. "As a child in a family of 10 children, it wasn't easy to be heard—writing has become a way for me (and my characters) to have a voice."[5]

Casanova's early books came from her experience in the north woods but her love for history and other places eventually led her to Europe where she conducted research for *Curse of a Winter Moon* (Hyperion, 2002). The book is a departure from Casanova's previous novels. It is set in sixteenth-century France and focuses on a boy whose brother is thought to be a werewolf because he was born on Christmas Eve. In this book Casanova manages to explore superstition, religious persecution, freedom, and the power of books and love.

Yet another book, a picture book, came directly from an exchange student from China who lived with the family. Wu Geng Hui practiced his English by sharing traditional Chinese pencil-sketch stories with Casanova's family. Casanova particularly liked a story about a hunter who was rewarded for a good deed with the gift of being able to understand the language of animals. The only stipulation was that the hunter could not reveal his gift to others or he would sacrifice his own life. Eventually the hunter must choose to keep his life or reveal his gift and save an entire village with information he has learned from the animals. He unselfishly chooses to save the village. Casanova retold the tale in her book, *The Hunter* (Atheneum, 2000), in a framework where the villagers survive a disaster but also learn the importance of listening to one another. Shortly after the publisher, Atheneum, accepted the manuscript, the art editor at the publishing house identified an illustrator, Ed Young, a Caldecott illustrator, who she wanted to look at the manuscript. The only problem was that Young was booked for several years' work. Atheneum sent the manuscript to him anyway. He liked it so much that he agreed to create the illustrations and managed to move the book up in the schedule so it could be published earlier. *The Hunter* was widely acclaimed and was one of the first of Casanova's books to win the Minnesota Book Award. In April, 2002, Casanova was presented with a book award for her young-adult novel, *Curse of a Winter Moon*, and for *The Hunter*, a picture book that won in that category. With these awards, Casanova became the first author in the 13-year history of the awards to win in two categories. Both of these books, *Curse of a Winter Moon* and *The Hunter*, represented Casanova's willingness to take a chance and put her firmly on the path of a full-time writer.

In 2002, Casanova received an honorable mention in the competition for a prestigious McKnight Artist Fellowships for Writers award. That year was also the year that her first book for Pleasant Company was released. *Cécile: Gates of Gold* (Pleasant Company, 2002) was one of the first of five in the publisher's series, Girls of Many Lands. To research this title Casanova returned to France and spent a week "floating on the Grand Canal, exploring the passageways of the palace, and biking along the cobblestone streets." [6]

Sometimes Casanova searches for a story and sometimes the story actually comes to her. *One-Dog Canoe* (Farrar, Straus, Giroux, 2003) is a story that came with a cocker spaniel. During a break while on a writer's retreat, Casanova decided to go canoeing with her friend Phyllis Root. They were halfway across a small bay when Casanova looked back and saw Bror, a small cocker spaniel, following them from the island on which the retreat was held. Casanova and Root pulled over to a rock and let the dog hop aboard. As they paddled around the next bend there was a golden retriever staring at them from the end of a dock. Casanova recalls, "he hung his head and seemed to ask, 'Can I come too?' 'No,' I said aloud, 'it's a one-dog canoe.' I glanced back at Phyllis and said, 'I think there's a story here.' I went back to my cabin and quickly jotted down the ideas. Many drafts later, the story sold." [7]

The love of research is part of Casanova's writing. "More and more, I love the research piece of writing. Though I will do lots of research before I begin writing, I eventually grow impatient and need to start a book. While I write I'm surrounded by books related to my topic, whether it's eagles or 18th Century France." [8]

Mary Casanova usually writes in the morning, "I'm a morning person and prefer writing from about nine A.M. to noon or 1 P.M., five days a week." [9] Early in her career she decided to devote weekends and evenings to her family so she seldom writes at those times. Sometimes she writes in her sunroom where, in the winter, she can watch the snowflakes fall around her house. At other times she writes on her houseboat on Rainy Lake. Her first drafts are written and revised on her laptop computer, sometimes as many as 32 times.

Casanova does most of her writing during two seasons, winter and summer. Traveling to speak to and connect with her readers takes place most often in the spring and fall. However, she says, "I can revise anywhere, although, I am not good at writing new drafts while I'm on the road." To Casanova, being able to travel and hear from readers who tell her that a story touched them or that they couldn't put it down, is "chocolate frosting on chocolate cake." [10]

As a way to relax from her writing Casanova enjoys baking bread, playing the piano, or going for a hike. She says these are activities that give "her brain a rest and [let her] subconscious do its creative brewing." But Casanova quickly adds, "writing is my life's calling." Regarding her preference for writing novels or picture books, Casanova says, "I see myself as a novelist who loves to tinker with picture books between longer projects. Not that picture books are easy." [11]

To you, the reader,

We may not have met before, but through the pages of a book we share a world of experiences and ideas. I'm grateful to see my stories published, yet even more grateful to know that my books find their way into the hands of readers—like you!

Maybe you dream of being an author someday, or maybe you dream of doing something entirely different. Whatever it is, don't wait for others to point your way. Listen to the dreams within you. Pay attention to the world around you. Notice the little things—the small gifts—in everyday. Expect good things ahead. Take risks for things that matter. And keep reading—for stories build bridges between us!

Love, Mary Casanova

Regardless of the book's setting or whether it is a novel or picture book, each story that Casanova writes seems to reflect this thought from her: "Our lives are like fireflies, brilliant flashes of light in the darkness, here and gone. Each life matters. Listen to your dreams and giftings; take risks, live fully, make a difference."[12]

Today Mary Casanova lives with her husband, Charles, and their almost grown son, Eric, and daughter, Kelly, in the so-called Icebox of the Nation. This is where her family has a team of sled dogs, moose is seen regularly, and poaching (illegal hunting) has resulted in some unusual incidents surrounding the poacher's arrests—all of which provide fodder for Casanova's writing.

## Book Connections

Mary Casanova turns to her community and her family for inspiration when writing. In *Moose Tracks,* a young boy attempts to save an orphaned moose calf from poachers. As Casanova was writing the book she recalled the stories her grandpa Eric told her about a bull moose that charged a train as the engine was chugging down the track and another tale about a bull moose that held him captive in a tree for a long time on a cold day. *Riot* is the drama of a family divided by a labor dispute that actually occurred in a paper-mill in Casanova's hometown. *Wolf Shadows* continues the story of the characters in *Moose Tracks* and reflects on the friendship of two young men. In the story, wolves are reestablished in the Minnesota north and some farmers are against it. The character, Seth, and his friend, Matt, find themselves on opposite sides of the debate. Friendship is also a theme in *Stealing Thunder,* a story that involves the characters Jolene and Libby and the horse they both love, Thunder. When Libby realizes that Thunder is being abused, she makes plans to rescue the horse from harm. After featuring a female protagonist in *Stealing Thunder,* Casanova continued to present strong female characters in her books. *When Eagles Fall* (Hyperion, 2002) is about Alexandra, Alex for short, who gets lost with an injured eaglet on the Minnesota-Canadian border. Alex discovers that her survival has everything to do with facing her past.

Casanova first wrote about a female protagonist in *Cécile: Gates of Gold,* in the Girls of Many Lands series. Cécile Revel, as a favor to her father, finds herself in the service of the court of King Louis XIV. She is not sure what to expect and certainly she is not totally prepared for what she finds at court. She has only imagined the court's luxury not the danger that waits there. The *Curse of a Winter Moon* is also set in sixteenth-century France. The character Jean-Pierre is marked with the curse of the Loup garou—the werewolf—because of the circumstances of his birth. When his mother dies, his brother Marius is left to care for Jean-Pierre and to protect him from the community's hysterical campaign to find and destroy enemies of the church.

## Books Written by Mary Casanova

*Cécile: Gates of Gold* (Pleasant Company, 2002).

*Curse of a Winter Moon* (Hyperion, 2000).

*The Hunter* (Atheneum, 2000). Picture book.

*Moose Tracks* (Hyperion, 1995).

*One-Dog Canoe* (Farrar, Straus, Giroux, 2003).

*Riot* (Hyperion, 1996).

*Stealing Thunder* (Hyperion, 1999).

*When Eagles Fall* (Hyperion, 2002).

*Wolf Shadows* (Hyperion, 1997).

# For More Information

## Articles

Grossman, Mary Ann. "Heart of the Child." *Saint Paul Pioneer Press* 17 June 2001: 1E.

Grossman, Mary Ann. "Mary Gazelka Casanova's Books Appeal to the Inner Kid." *Saint Paul Pioneer Press* 5 July 2001: n. pag.

McElmeel, Sharron L. "Author Profile: Mary Casanova." *Book Report* 21.1 (May/June 2002): 40–41. March 2004. <http://www.mcelmeel.com/writing/casanova.html>.

## Web Sites

Casanova, Mary. *Mary Casanova: Author of Books for Young Readers.* March 2004. <http://www.marycasanova.com>.

# Notes

1. Mary Casanova, letter to the author, 20 Sept. 2002.
2. Ibid.
3. Ibid.
4. Mary Casanova, letter to the author, 6 Nov. 2001.
5. Ibid.
6. Ibid.
7. Ibid.
8. Ibid.
9. Ibid.
10. Ibid.
11. Ibid.
12. Ibid.

# Vicki Cobb

◆ Science: informational books

**Brooklyn, New York**
August 19, 1938

📖 *See for Yourself: 100 Amazing Experiments for Science Fairs and Projects*

📖 *I See Myself*

📖 *Dirt & Grime: Like You've Never Seen*

## About the Author

Vicki Cobb has been writing informational books about science for more than 30 years. She's hardly an author that is new to the field of children's literature but readers are just beginning to notice her work. According to her granddaughter, Abby, Vicki "spends her days doing things like blowing toilet paper around and setting tea bags on fire."[1]

Vicki Cobb does these things because she is a science writer. She does "all the experiments so everything I write about is a first-hand experience as much as possible."[2] Vicki was born in Brooklyn, New York, the daughter of Ben and Paula Wolf. She describes her father as "a Renaissance man, lawyer, musician, artist, chess master, and golfer."[3] She was greatly influenced by her parents varied interests and by her experiences at school. Until seventh grade she attended the Little Red School House in New York, a school known for its innovative, hands-on approach to education. Vicki's junior high years were spent at Washington Irving Junior-Senior High School in Tarrytown, New York, however, she only attended through tenth grade. Instead of entering eleventh grade she was admitted to the University of Wisconsin as a Ford Foundation Early Admissions Scholar. She later transferred to Barnard College at Columbia University where she obtained an undergraduate degree in zoology and chemistry and later obtained a graduate degree in secondary school science from the teacher's college at the university. That was the same year, 1960, that she married Edward Scribner Cobb III.

Vicki Cobb's first career, which she started in 1953, was as a researcher at Sloan Kettering Institute and Pfizer & Co. Eight years later, after obtaining her graduate degree, she became a high school science teacher. Her teaching career lasted only three years because she left in 1964 to have her first child. While she was caring for her newborn son, Vicki saw an advertisement for science writers in the *New York Times*. "I figured that if I could

# Vicki Cobb

When I was a kid, I couldn't wait to learn to read. I remember being four years old, standing with an eight-year-old girl looking out at the billboards that decorated New York City rooftops. "Can you read *everything* you see?" I asked her enviously, because I couldn't. Of course she could. But she was so much older than I. How long would I have to wait before I could read everything I saw?

As it turned out, not so long. I was reading at five and I've never stopped. I became the kind of reader who has no awareness of the individual words I'm reading. I don't sound words in my head as I read; I absorb paragraphs. As a child, my nose was always in a book. My mother would pick me up at school and run errands while I kept on reading. I remember looking up, surprised, wondering how I got home. I became so involved in books that I would not answer my parents unless they called me by the name of the heroine in the book I was currently reading. When I was eight, I remember reading a story about a dog who was wounded in a war while crossing enemy lines to deliver messages. I felt the dog's pain so intensely that I actually fainted face down into the open book. Reading is not just about decoding words. It is about experiencing other peoples' lives and ideas. It is listening to the many personalities and voices that tell stories. It is discovering connections to other human beings even if they have lived a very different life from one's own.

Today, when I want to learn something new, I read a kids' book on the subject. In fact, I may read several. I find I like some writes better than others. Some speak to me in an Interesting way while others are boring. I like to get several points of view so I can draw my own conclusions. I also read for entertainment and I read books on lots of different subjects. I feel funny if I don't have a book going at all times. What has happened to me as a result of all this reading? I think I've become an interesting person. I am never bored. I've never stopped
Learning. Old age will not stop me. You, too, can discover this lifelong joy. Just keep on reading!!!

Best wishes,

*Vicki Cobb*

talk about science I could write about it."[4] In 1969 she published her first science book for children, *The First Book of Logic* (Franklin Watts, 1969). She continued writing, almost always focusing on science. Then, in the early 1970s, Cobb wrote and hosted the television show *The Science Game* for a New York cable company. The program showcased experiments children could try at home. For a time she also wrote for the *Good Morning*

*America* talk show, conducted numerous science demonstrations, and even made her own appearances on *Late Night with David Letterman* and *Live with Regis and Kathie Lee*. Her books continued to be published at a steady rate of three or four titles a year.

In 1983, Cobb and her husband divorced. Their two children, Theo and Josh, were teenagers at the time. Vicki Cobb continued to write and while her focus continued to be on science, she also traveled extensively to research information for many of her titles. She wrote about Alaska, the Sonoran Desert, the Andes, the Amazon basin, Australia, Japan, and East Africa. Now when she visits schools, Cobb often shares slides from her trips all around the world where she was in search of material for future science books.

She collaborated with her son, Josh, an optical engineer and senior scientist for research at Kodak, to produce *Light Action! Amazing Experiments with Optics* (Harper-Collins, 1993). Her other son, Theo, an artist and art director, was the book's illustrator.

Because Cobb writes about so many science topics, some might think that her home would be filled with plants and animals. Although those images might seem to fit, Cobb says that she has "no pets, (no living plants either, only artificial that don't need water)."[5]

In 1996, Vicki Cobb married Richard Trachenberg and the couple currently lives in White Plains, New York. Together they have four sons and a daughter: Theo Cobb—married to Rachel and father of Abigail "Abby" (1989) and Lexie (1995); Josh Cobb—married to Judy and father of Jonathan (1998) and Jillian (2000); David Trachtenberg; Eric Trachtenberg—married to Berett and father to Benjamin (1997); and Millie Trachtenberg. One of Cobb's granddaughters, Abby, provided the perspective for a book about her grandmother. That book, *Meet My Grandmother: She's a Children's Book Author* (Millbrook, 2001), is part of Millbrook's series on grandmothers. Vicki Cobb often visits schools where she talks to students, parents, and teachers as a mother, grandmother, and always a science enthusiast.

## Book Connections

Vicki Cobb's science interests are many and varied. She featured projects for science fairs in *See for Yourself: 100 Amazing Experiments for Science Fairs and Projects* (Scholastic, 2001) and has several series dealing with the senses and physical science, dozens of books featuring experiments of one type or another, and books that look at various locations throughout the world through the lens of a scientist.

Cobb has written several books about food including *The Scoop on Ice Cream* (Little, Brown, 1985), *Feeding Yourself* (Lippincott, 1989), and *Science Experiments You Can Eat*, rev. ed. (HarperCollins, 1994). Because she actively investigates all of the topics that are the subjects of her books, it is a good thing that her favorites in terms of food is "all food."[6]

## Books Written by Vicki Cobb

*Blood & Gore: Like You've Never Seen* (Scholastic Books, 1998).

*Dirt & Grime: Like You've Never Seen* (Scholastic Books, 1998).

*Feeling Your Way: Discovering Your Sense of Touch.* Illustrated by Cynthia Lewis. (Millbrook, 2001; paperback 2003).

*Follow Your Nose: Discovering Your Sense of Smell.* Illustrated by Cynthia Lewis. (Millbrook, 2001; paperback 2003).

*I Face the Wind.* Illustrated by Julia Gorton. (HarperCollins, 2003).

*I Fall Down.* Illustrated by Julia Gorton. (HarperCollins, 2004).

*I Get Wet.* Illustrated by Julia Gorton. (HarperCollins, 2002).

*I See Myself.* Illustrated by Julia Gorton. (HarperCollins, 2002).

*Light Action! Amazing Experiments with Optics.* Written with Josh Cobb, illustrated by Theo Cobb. (HarperCollins, 1993).

*Open Your Eyes: Discovering Your Sense of Sight.* Illustrated by Cynthia Lewis. (Millbrook, 2001; paperback 2003).

*Perk Up Your Ears: Discovering Your Sense of Hearing.* Illustrated by Cynthia Lewis. (Millbrook, 2001; paperback 2003).

*Science Experiments You Can Eat,* rev. and updated. (HarperCollins, 1994).

*Secret Life of School Supplies.* Illustrated by Bill Morrison. (Lippincott, 1981).

*See for Yourself: 100 Amazing Experiments for Science Fairs and Projects.* Illustrated by Dave Klug. (Scholastic, 2001).

*Sources of Forces.* Illustrated by Stephen Haefle. (Millbrook, 2002).

*You Gotta Try This! Absolutely Irresistible Science.* Written with Kathy Darling. (Morrow, 1999).

*Your Tongue Can Tell: Discovering Your Sense of Taste.* Illustrated by Cynthia Lewis. (Millbrook, 2001; paperback 2003).

## For More Information

### Books

McElroy, Lisa Tucker, with Abigail Jane Cobb. *Meet My Grandmother: She's a Children's Book Author.* Grandmothers at Work Series. Photographs by Joel Benjamin. Brookfield, CT: Millbrook, 2001.

### Web Sites

Cobb, Vicki. *Home Page: Vicki Cobb's Science Page.* March 2004. <http://www.vickicobb.com>.

## Notes

1. Lisa Tucker McElroy with Abigail Jane Cobb, *Meet My Grandmother: She's a Children's Book Author,* Grandmothers at Work Series, photographs by Joel Benjamin (Brookfield, CT: Millbrook, 2001): 1.
2. Vicki Cobb, letter to the author, 5 Sept. 2002.
3. Ibid.
4. Ibid.
5. Ibid.
6. Ibid.

# Sharon Creech

**South Euclid, Ohio**
July 29, 1945

📖 *Absolutely Normal Chaos*

📖 *Fishing in the Air*

📖 *Love That Dog*

📖 *Walk Two Moons*

## About the Author

Sharon Creech was born in South Euclid, Ohio, a suburb of Cleveland. Her parents, Ann and Arvel, already had four children, Sandy, Dennis, Doug, and Tom. The large rambunctious family enjoyed telling stories around the kitchen table and Sharon learned to embellish and exaggerate her own stories in an effort to keep up with her siblings.

Throughout Sharon's childhood she dreamed of being a writer. She began as a neighborhood reporter and made up outlandish stories and repeated them to her neighbors. Sharon also wanted to be a painter, ice skater, singer, and teacher. She soon realized, however, that she could not paint, skate, or sing, and that she really did not like sticking to the facts as a reporter. Her aspirations toward writing and teaching grew but on many days she could be found climbing trees and riding her bike.

The family often took road trips across the United States through states such as Wisconsin and Michigan. One trip to Idaho to visit Sharon's grandparents inspired her award winning, *Walk Two Moons* (HarperCollins, 1994). The book's resolve and the title, however, came from a message in a fortune cookie, "don't judge a man until you have walked two moons in his moccasins."[1]

A family vacation to a Wisconsin lake when Creech was 12 provided the idea for a picture book, *Fishing in the Air* (HarperCollins/Joanna Cotler, 2000). On this trip, she and her family searched for her father's childhood home but found that it had been torn down. During the car ride, Sharon heard many tales from her father's childhood. She drew on her own memories and her father's reminiscences of fishing to write the story. The story she tells is about a father and his son who go on a fishing trip but end up sitting, relaxing, and talking about the father's childhood home. The title, *Fishing in the Air,* came from a quote in *Walk Two Moons* where the main character, Salamanca Tree Hiddle, describes herself as a "fisher in the air."

Sharon first took a writing class when she was working on her undergraduate degree at Hiram College in Ohio where she was able to study with John Gardner, James Dickey, and John Irving, among others. Those writing courses helped her develop her writing style and develop a stable of characters—all of whom seemed to make journeys to distant lands in order to find themselves.

After receiving her undergraduate degree, Sharon Creech married and moved to Washington, D.C. where she enrolled in graduate school at George Mason University. In Washington, D.C. she worked part-time at Federal Theatre Project Archives and as an editorial assistant at the *Congressional Quarterly.* Both positions involved working with facts, which was something that did not interest Creech too much so she subsequently entered the teaching field.

By this time Creech was a divorced, single mother and she wanted a change. In 1979, she decided to apply for a teaching position at the TASIS American School in England. Her undergraduate degree had been in English and literature not education but she could still teach in a private school. Her application to the American School was accepted and she moved to England where she took her position in the TASIS School outside of London. Her children attended the school where Creech taught English and literature. That same year the head master had hired a new assistant, Lyle Riggs. Creech and Riggs met on their first day at the school when Creech asked to borrow some ice. The two formed a friendship and by the time Riggs was offered the position of headmaster at the school's Swiss boarding school, the two had decided to marry. In 1982, they celebrated their wedding with a party on a riverboat floating down the Thames River. Then, Sharon Creech, her husband Lyle Riggs, and her two children, Rob and Karin, moved to the foothills of the Swiss Alps.

Creech's experiences at this boarding school became part of her book, *Bloomability* (HarperCollins/Joanna Cotler, 1998). In *Bloomability,* a 13-year-old American girl grows to love Switzerland when she is taken to boarding school with her aunt and uncle. The cover of the book includes a collage of photos of Creech's family, friends, and home while she lived in the Swiss Alps. Her daughter, Karin, is shown scaling a mountain in Andermatt and beneath that image is a picture of Creech's brother, Tom. To the right of him is a photo of the family's Swiss home. The hardcover version of this title has even more pictures on the back of the cover. There is a photo of Creech's son and daughter, Rob and Karin, on the slopes of St. Moritz and right beneath them is a picture of her husband.

After two years in Switzerland, the family moved back to England and Riggs took over at the English TASIS boarding school. During this period, after the family's return to England, Creech began to write. It was shortly after the death of her father and she wrote and wrote and wrote.

At first Creech wrote short pieces but when one of her poems won the Billee Murray Denny Poetry Award, sponsored by Lincoln College in Illinois, she was inspired to continue to write more. Creech's first two books were written for adults and published in England. *The Recital* (1990) and *Nickel Malley* (1991) were followed by a play, *The Center of the Universe: Waiting for the Girl* (1992). The budding author received her share of rejection slips along the way but she reached a pinnacle in her success when she turned to books for young readers. Her children's book, *Walk Two Moons,* captured the 1995 Newbery Award.

Another novel, *Absolutely Normal Chaos* (HarperCollins/Joanna Cotler, 1995) was written for adults but the publisher recognized its marketability in the young-adult area. In this book the protagonist, Mary Lou Finney, is 13 years old. Mary Lou has three brothers who coincidentally share the same names as Creech's own brothers although they do not share the same behaviors. Creech's cousin would also visit when she was young and she used her own childhood home's address, 4059 Buxton Road, as Mary Lou's address in the book.[2]

While her family lived at the TASIS American School in the village of Thorpe, Surrey, England, Creech wrote her first five books including *Walk Two Moons* and *Bloomability*. For many years while they lived in England, Riggs and Creech would spend the summers in Chautauqua, New York. During one of those summers, Creech attended one of the annual Highlights workshops held at Chautauqua. At the conference, the other attendees convinced Creech that she could write for children and that it was a noble endeavor. Creech was still living in England when she received news of the Newbery Award for *Walk Two Moons*. It was a cold, gray day early in February when she got a call from the committee chair, Kathleen Horning. The award changed her life and the biggest change was that it gave her freedom to write and not to worry about getting a publisher for her next book or if readers would notice her books.

After nearly 19 years of living in Europe, Sharon Creech and Lyle Riggs moved back to the United States where the couple—their grown son and daughter also live in the states—settled in Pennington, New Jersey. Riggs became headmaster of the Pennington School. Behind their home is a small pond that Creech uses as a retreat when she gets stuck at a spot in her writing. In the summer the couple spend a lot of time relaxing at their small cottage on Lake Chautauqua in western New York state.

Sharon Creech continues to draw on her own life for inspiration for her stories. In the year or so before her family moved back to the United States, she crossed the Atlantic several times to care for her sick mother and finally to attend her mother's funeral. Those numerous trips and another trip undertaken by Creech's daughter brought about *The Wanderer* (HarperCollins/Joanna Cotler, 2000). After Karin, Creech's daughter, graduated from college, she and six male friends embarked on a crossing of the Atlantic and in the process, they almost perished when their small boat was caught in a gale. Creech used those events to create some dramatic episodes in *The Wanderer.*

*Love That Dog* (HarperCollins/Joanna Cotler, 2001) evolved from Creech's experience with literature and with a poem, "Love That Boy" by Walter Dean Myers. She had found the poem on a greeting card and hung the card above her desk. Soon she was contemplating what the boy in the poem might have loved, such as a pet dog. Creech's novel follows the story of the character Jack and tells how he learns to write about his love for his dog, Sky. The book, written in free verse, returned Creech to her beginnings because the first successes she had with writing, before she turned to novels, was with poetry.

*Pleasing the Ghost* (HarperCollins/Joanna Cotler, 1996) was written during the time Creech was teaching Shakespeare's *Hamlet* and the class had been discussing the reasons why ghosts may or may not exist. Nine months after Creech and her children arrived in England her father Arvel had a stroke and for the last six years of his life he could not articulate his thoughts in comprehensible speech. Later, after Creech's father had died, her mother came across a love letter he had written some 50 years earlier. Out of those two incidents came the story of the ghost of Uncle Arvie. In *Pleasing the Ghost,* Uncle Arvie cannot speak clearly and visits his nephew Dennis to get help with three unfinished tasks one of which is a love letter. Lyle Riggs's pride in his school spawned the plot for *A*

*Fine, Fine School* (HarperCollins/Joanna Cotler, 2001). In this book, Creech exaggerated the pride to humorous proportions and created a less than serious look at school life.

Sharon Creech and Lyle Riggs now live in a large three-story neo-Georgian redbrick home on the campus of the Pennington School in New Jersey. The first floor is reserved for official school functions and the second and third stories are the family living quarters. The hall leading to her sunny office is lined with photographs and bulletin boards that contain dummies and sketches for some of her books. In her office are many gifts from friends—many of which are moons.

Creech's ideal writing day would find her in her office by 8:30 A.M. For the first hour she deals with e-mails and then begins to write. Shortly after noon she has lunch, rests, and maybe takes a walk. Later in the afternoon until dinnertime Creech returns to her writing. After dinner, when she is not obligated to attend some school function or a book signing, Creech often returns to her writing desk. Every now and then she might spend a full day responding to letters she has received from readers. Each response takes her approximately nine minutes so the task is a real investment of time. That is one of the downsides of her notoriety as an author, she says. But the positive side is that she now earns enough money that she can be a full-time writer.

Creech's writing is done directly on the computer and every day she rereads and revises what she has written the day before. By the time she has completed the first draft of a story, she has probably revised each page a dozen or more times. Then, after the editor makes her comments, there are more revisions. The names of characters in Creech's stories are often taken from her family and acquaintances.

Sharon Creech and her husband Lyle Riggs live in New Jersey where Riggs continues his work as headmaster of the Pennington School and Creech continues to write books. Both enjoy visits from their son and daughter and now a new granddaughter, Pearl, Karen's daughter.

# Book Connections

When Sharon Creech begins her stories, she has no idea of how the story will evolve. She simply follows the character and each day as she rereads what she has already written, she gets a thread that leads her in the direction the character wants her to go. As Creech was writing *Walk Two Moons,* the character Salamanca eventually let her know that something would be realized once the family reached Idaho. In some ways, journeys are a part of each of Creech's books. Through Salamanca, Creech was able to return to the United States, a place that she missed. When Creech wrote *Chasing Redbird* (HarperCollins/Joanna Cotler, 1997), she longed for the quiet of the woods—the same place she put the character Zinny each day. The woods in the story were actually patterned after the woods on her cousins' farm in Quincy, Kentucky. Quincy was also the prototype for the fictional town, Bybanks, Kentucky, where the character Zinnia Taylor lives and is also the home of Salamanca in *Walk Two Moons.*

The stories Creech writes begin with an idea or a simple event. For example, *Ruby Holler* (HarperCollins/Joanna Cotler, 2002) became a cool and mysterious place for an older couple, Tiller and Sairy, when the couple invites the trouble twins, Dallas and Florida, to come with them on a trip. The idea of a holler came in a letter written to Creech by her aunt. In the letter, her aunt told her a story about her father and she ended the letter by saying that the event had occurred when the family had lived in the holler. Creech hadn't known about the holler until then but she quickly began to imagine her grandparents, her father, and his many siblings living in this intriguing place. In many ways Tiller and Sairy exhibited many of the same traits that Chreech remembers in her grandparents.

Although many of the incidents in Creech's books are deliberate references or scenes consciously based on events in Creech's life, sometimes references or incidents seem to be eerie coincidences. Walter Dean Myers wrote the poem that inspired *Love That Dog* but even Creech was surprised that he ended up as a character in the book. She tried to take him out of the book but she just couldn't do it without leaving a big hole that she could not otherwise fill.

Details from *The Wanderer* are even eerier. Creech remembered several tales her father told and included them in *The Wanderer* as "Bompie and the Car" and "Bompie and the Train." There are more Bompie tales in the book but Creech imagined all the rest. Sophie was a name taken from an English friend and the name Cody came from a young student who attended one of Creech's presentations in the United States. However, the name Bompie had come from Creech's sister-in-law, who used that nickname to refer to her own grandfather. In the book, Bompie's wife's name is Margaret and they have a son named Mo. After *The Wanderer* was published and Creech's sister-in-law read it, Creech learned from her that the real Bompie had a wife also named Margaret and their son's name was also Mo. Two facts Creech had not known before using the names in her own book.

Creech's recent book, *Granny Torelli Makes Soup* (HarperCollins/Joanna Cotler, 2003), takes place entirely in a kitchen and is about an Italian grandmother, her granddaughter, and the boy next door.

# Books Written by Sharon Creech

## Fiction

*Absolutely Normal Chaos* (HarperCollins/Joanna Cotler, 1995).

*Bloomability* (HarperCollins/Joanna Cotler, 1998).

*Chasing Redbird* (HarperCollins/Joanna Cotler, 1997).

*Granny Torelli Makes Soup* (HarperCollins/Joanna Cotler, 2003).

*Love That Dog* (HarperCollins/Joanna Cotler, 2001).

*Pleasing the Ghost* (HarperCollins/Joanna Cotler, 1996).

*Ruby Holler* (HarperCollins/Joanna Cotler, 2002).

*Walk Two Moons* (HarperCollins, 1994).

*The Wanderer* (HarperCollins/Joanna Cotler, 2000).

## Picture Books

*A Baby in a Basket: New Baby Songs.* Illustrated by David Diaz. (HarperCollins/JoannaCotler, 2004).

*A Fine, Fine School.* Illustrated by Harry Bliss. (HarperCollins/JoannaCotler, 2001).

*Fishing in the Air.* Illustrated by Chris Raschka. (HarperCollins/Joanna Cotler, 2000).

# For More Information

## Articles

ACHUKA. "ACHUKA Interview: Sharon Creech." March 2004. <http://www.achuka.co.uk/interviews/creech.php>.

Britton, Jason. "Sharon Creech: Everyday Journeys." *Publishers Weekly* 248.29 (16 July 2001): 153–154.

Creech, Sharon. "Newbery Acceptance Speech." *The Horn Book Magazine* 71.4 (July/August 1995): 418–425.

Hendershot, Judy. "An Interview with Sharon Creech, 1995 Newbery Medal Winner." *The Reading Teacher* 49 (February 1996): 380–382.

Raymond, Allen. "Sharon Creech: 1995 Newbery Medal Winner." *Teaching K-8* 26 (May 1996): 48–50.

Riggs, Lyle D. "Sharon Creech." *The Horn Book Magazine* 71.4 (July/August 1995): 426–429.

## Web Sites

Creech, Sharon. *Sharon Creech.* March 2004. <http://www.sharoncreech.com>.

# Notes

1. Sharon Creech, Newbery acceptance speech at the American Library Association Newbery-Caldecott Banquet, Chicago, 25 June 1995.
2. Sharon Creech, *Sharon Creech,* March 2004, <http://www.sharoncreech.com>.

# Christopher Paul Curtis

♦  Historical fiction

**Flint, Michigan**
*May 10, 1953*

📖  *Bucking the Sarge*

📖  *Bud, Not Buddy*

📖  *The Watsons Go to Birmingham, 1963*

## About the Author

If anyone is responsible for Christopher Paul Curtis's writing success, besides himself, it is his wife, Kaysandra. Curtis's success came after his wife told him that she would support the family for a year so that he could pursue his writing full time. She had encouraged his writing for several years but the gift of an entire year to write brought young readers Curtis's first book, *The Watsons Go to Birmingham, 1963* (Delacorte, 1995), and a few years later *Bud, Not Buddy* (Delacorte, 1999).

So far all of the books Christopher Curtis has written (or is working on) are set in his hometown of Flint, Michigan. Christopher was born in Flint in 1953, the second of five children born to Herman E. Curtis Jr. and Leslie Curtis. His father was a chiropodist and a member of Flint's black professional community. But many of his patients could not pay so three days after Christopher's birth, Herman Curtis quit his medical practice and went to work in the Fisher Body Plant No. 1, an automobile assembly factory, where the pay was much better.

Christopher read a lot as a child, mostly comic books. He particularly enjoyed *Mad Magazine, National Geographic,* and *Sports Illustrated.* At the time, there were not a lot of books for or about young black children so books did not really influence him. Nonetheless, Christopher always had a sense that someday he would become a writer and when he was 10 or 11 he actually told his brothers and sisters that one day he would write a book. At about that same time his father made a great sacrifice and used $300 to buy the family the *World Book Encyclopedia* set. Christopher's father admonished the family that he didn't want to see a pencil or a crayon near the books. His sister would often take Christopher into the hallway and read him his favorite part of the encyclopedias—the dog section.

After graduating from high school, Christopher went to work at the same plant at which his father worked, Fisher Body Plant No. 1. He worked at the plant for 13 years where his job was to hang 80-pound doors on Buicks. Christopher and a coworker would alternate hanging the doors and they soon agreed that if one of them worked at double the pace for 30 minutes the other could have a 30-minute break. Christopher used his 30 minutes to write in a journal. He tried writing fiction but when that didn't work out he just wrote about what was going on in his life. In 1985, Christopher quit his job at the factory. During his time at the factory, Christopher had been attending the University of Michigan at night and on plant holidays. He had been accepted to the university right after high school but he didn't quit his job at the plant because the money was too good. He was just one credit short of his political science degree when he went to work for U.S. Senator Don Riegle in his reelection campaign in the Flint and Saginaw areas. That experience soured him on the idea of working in politics. From that point on, Curtis worked at a number of other jobs. He mowed lawns, was an apartment complex maintenance man, a census taker, a customer service representative for the Detroit Power Company, and he worked on a loading dock and in a warehouse.

Christopher Curtis met Kaysandra Anne Sookram, a native of Trinidad, at a basketball game in Hamilton, Ontario, Canada. During their courtship, Curtis wrote Kaysandra almost every day. They eventually married and in the late 1980s the couple moved to Windsor, Canada. Kaysandra's nursing license was Canadian so the move made it easier for her to work in Windsor and Christopher could easily travel across the bridge to his work at a loading dock in Detroit.

In 1992, Kaysandra suggested that Curtis take a year off to write his book. He had won the Avery Hopwood Prize for major essays and the Jules Hopwood Prize for an early draft of *The Watson's Go to Birmingham, 1963,* which was written while he was attending the University of Michigan. So at the urging of his wife, Christopher Paul Curtis, at the age of 40, began his writing career.

Curtis quickly established a writing schedule that would lead him to success. He starts his day at 5 A.M., a habit that has stayed with him from his Fisher Body Plant days. During the quiet of the morning, he edits what he has written the day before. After a couple of hours he awakens his young daughter, Cydney (named after Curtis's sister), and gets her off to school. By 9 A.M. Curtis is at his usual table in the public library. For the next two hours or so he writes in a yellow legal tablet, writing on both sides. *Bud, Not Buddy* used up 25 legal tablets. By noon, four days a week, Curtis is at the YMCA playing a basketball game.

Eventually Curtis finished *The Watsons Go to Birmingham, 1963* and entered it in two novel-writing contests. One contest was sponsored by Little Brown Publishers and the other by Delacorte. The book did not do well in the Little Brown contest and a Delacorte editor, Wendy Lamb, called to say that his book did not meet the criteria for their contest and could not win. However, Lamb told Curtis that Delacorte wanted to publish the book anyway. They offered him a $4,000 advance. Curtis accepted and the family celebrated with dinner at Red Lobster.

Shortly before *The Watsons Go to Birmingham, 1963* was published, Curtis was typing his name into the library's catalog—just to see how it would feel—and discovered that there was another writer named Christopher Curtis who had written a book about chimney sweeping. To distinguish himself from that writer, Curtis put his middle name in his author moniker and has become known as Christopher Paul Curtis.

*The Watsons Go to Birmingham, 1963* was named to several best books lists and was given two of the highest honors in children's literature: a Newbery honor book and a Coretta Scott King honor book. Soon after the awards announcements were made, Curtis was working in the library on his next book.

It had taken a couple of years for *The Watsons Go to Birmingham, 1963* to be published, so Curtis had gone back to a day job—this time at a warehouse. However, readers soon discovered his book and Curtis began to get invitations to speak. The money he made from one speech was enough to replace one week's salary at the warehouse. Needless to say, Curtis quit his warehouse job and concentrated more on his writing and making himself available to speak at schools and in libraries.

Curtis was sincerely surprised when *The Watsons Go to Birmingham, 1963* received so many honors. Several people had mentioned *Bud, Not Buddy,* his second book, as a contender for the Newbery Award so the Curtis family had hope that it would win. The morning of January 17, 2000, the day Curtis was notified that *Bud, Not Buddy* had won the award, Kaysandra had taken Cydney to school and Curtis was home alone. During the time Kaysandra was gone, the phone rang twice. The chair of the Newbery Award committee and the chair of the Coretta Scott King Award both called to notify Curtis of his awards. When Kaysandra returned home, he asked if she would do the dishes for a year if his book won the Newbery Award. She joked that he would have to win both the Newbery and the Coretta Scott King Award before she would agree to that. Of course, he told her that his book had won both awards, however, Curtis still helps wash the dishes. With those awards he became the first black author to win the Newbery in 30 years and the first black man to ever earn the award. He also became the first person to have a book win both the Newbery Award and the Coretta Scott King Award.

With the success of her husband's books and the demand of his increased travel and speaking schedule, Kaysandra has left the nursing profession. She now works full time as his agent and manager.

Curtis still is most often found writing his books in a library—the Windsor Public Library or the Leedy Library on the University of Windsor campus. He begins writing his books in longhand with a pen and legal pad. Writing on paper helps him slow his pace, to get a better flow, he says, and to think about what he is writing. As he writes and changes his mind about where sentences and paragraphs best fit he draws arrows from one spot to the other. After he gets his basic story drafted, he enters the writing or has it entered onto his computer where he also edits it. Curtis says, "my typing is so bad that I probably would not be a writer without a computer."[1] When he was writing his first book his son, Steven, was living at home and every night he would enter his dad's handwritten pages into the computer. Curtis revises his work many times going over and over it 30 times or more.

When Curtis begins to write, he has only the basic idea for the story. As he thinks about the idea, a character comes into his mind and starts talking to him. Curtis tries to figure out what kind of a history the character has and what is going on in the character's life. Once the character becomes familiar enough to Curtis, the writing comes easier. He does not outline the story but just writes and rewrites—not a very efficient way to write, as he says, "I have to start and restart but eventually I hear the character's voice quite clearly."[2]

Once the character and basic story line is developed Curtis must find the details that will fit the setting. His first book was originally titled *The Watsons Go to Florida* and the family was going to visit relatives. The idea came during a trip Curtis took from Michigan to Florida with his family several years before. He wanted to make the trip in 24 hours and in order to stay awake he started thinking about this family—the weird Watsons of Flint. The story didn't work, however, because the story line came to a dead end when the family arrived in Florida.

One day Curtis's son brought home a school assignment; he was to read "The Ballad of Birmingham" by Dudley Randall. After hearing the poem, Curtis knew he had to change the destination of the Watson family. Instead of a trip to Florida, the Watsons had to travel to Birmingham the summer before the 1963 bombing. That fact focused the book. Curtis had never been to Birmingham and, in fact, only visited the city five years after the book was written. Because of this, he had to research details to make the setting accurate. He read newspapers and books about the events that took place in Birmingham in 1963. Curtis had grown up surrounded by racism in the North during the 1960s. Curtis's father had become the head of education at the Fisher plant and was very active in the Civil Rights movement; he did a lot of traveling with the United Auto Workers (UAW). Curtis's mother graduated from Michigan State University and she often lectured on black history in the Flint Public Schools. His parents took him on NAACP picket lines where the family participated in protests in front of businesses that would not hire black people. So, the Civil Rights movement was very much on Curtis's mind throughout his childhood. The character Kenny Watson grew up in a self-contained black community just like Curtis. Their dentist was black and so were the grocer, the doctor, and the insurance man. Curtis's exposure to white people was similar to Kenny's.

When Curtis wrote *Bud, Not Buddy,* he decided to focus on the 10-year-old character Bud Caldwell, who runs away from an abusive foster home and takes to the road to find his father and hopefully to find a home. Bud's mother died and left him with only a few clues that might help him locate his father. The story is set in 1936 and involves a lot of information about that era. For this story line, Curtis drew heavily on stories that he heard about his grandfathers, who were alive in the 1930s. His mother's father, Earl "Lefty" Lewis, a Pullman porter and union organizer, had been a left-handed pitcher in the Negro Baseball League of the 1930s and even pitched against Satchel Paige. Curtis remembers him as a wonderful man to be around.

His other grandfather died when Curtis was 10 but he had been a bandleader in the 1930s. Herman E. Curtis Sr. was the bandleader of "Herman Curtis and the Dusky Devastators of the Depression!!!!!!" This was most unusual because in the 1930s a band usually had a white bandleader. African Americans in Wyoming and Michigan could not even own property, nonetheless, Curtis's grandfather was a pioneer of sorts. Herman Curtis was the first African American in Illinois to have a pilot's license and he attended the Indiana Conservatory of Music, where he studied violin. During the day he painted cars and had a trucking business. By night he played in his band.

In *Bud, Not Buddy* "Lefty" Lewis, an African American man with the same background as the real "Lefty" Lewis, takes Bud into his home. The jazz musician that Bud thinks is his father is in a band that Curtis called "The Dusky Devastators of the Depression!!!!!!" the same name as his grandfather's band.

Ideas for Curtis's stories come from everywhere. One phrase that Curtis used in *Bud, Not Buddy,* "My eyes don't cry no more,"[3] came from the title of a song by Stevie Wonder, which was one of the songs used to dance the hustle. In *The Watsons Go to Birmingham, 1963* the chapter "Nazi Parachutes Attack America and Get Shot Down by Bryon Watson and His Flamethrower of Death" came right out of Curtis's childhood and his own interest in fire. Just like in the book, his younger sister, Cydney, really did rescue him by spitting on matches lit by his mother, who threatened to teach him a lesson by burning his fingertips. The character Kenny Watson is a composite of Curtis and his brother David. On the cover of *The Watsons Go to Birmingham, 1963,* one of the pictures is of Cydney and another picture is of Christopher's parents.

Often in schools where he visits, girls ask Curtis when he is going to write a book about a girl. One character that Curtis has mentioned as a possibility is Dezamalone, the girl that Bud met in the shantytown in Flint.

According to Curtis, when he accepted the Newbery Award for *Bud, Not Buddy* in Chicago he was probably the first person to accept the award in dreadlocks. Actually, he adds, his hairstyle was not dreadlocks. Dreadlocks, Curtis explained, is a more "organic, much wilder" hairstyle so to be more accurate, his hairstyle should be known as Nubian Locks.[4]

Today, Curtis enjoys reading books. Among his favorites are *Beloved* by Toni Morrison and novels by Jim Thompson, a crime writer from the 1950s. Kurt Vonnegut is another favorite author—Curtis especially enjoyed *Palm Sunday.* When Curtis is asked to do author readings from his own books, he often chooses the opening chapter of *The Watsons Go to Birmingham, 1963.* That is the chapter where the character Byron kisses the car mirror and gets his lips stuck. The chapter he often chooses from *Bud, Not Buddy* is the chapter where Bud is in the soup kitchen line waiting to be fed. That chapter shows that no matter how needy you are you, similar to the family that helped Bud, can always help someone else.

Curtis tries to make a yearly trip to Kenya in an effort to reconnect with his heritage. He has given many gifts and donations to the impoverished people and schools in that country. His dedication to helping the people of Kenya and other African countries has led to grass-roots support for his nomination as Canada's Goodwill Ambassador. In 2001 he received the annual Award for Literary Arts from the mayor of Windsor. In an effort to help raise funds for a charity, he has offered to name a character in one of his next books after the person with the largest donation. His and Kaysandra's support of the public library system in Windsor resulted in the renovated children's section in the Ouellette Avenue branch to be named in honor of Kaysandra and Christopher Paul Curtis.

Christopher Paul Curtis and his wife Kaysandra live in Ontario with their daughter Cydney (born in 1992). Their adult son, Steven, served in the U.S. Navy as a first class petty officer and plans to pursue a law degree. Cydney wrote a song when she was five, which appeared on page 124 in *Bud, Not Buddy* and in the front matter for that book, Curtis credits the song "Mama Says 'No' " to Cydney McKinsie Curtis. Curtis's own interests include a wide range of music including rhythm and blues, old school, soul, jazz, and classical. He has more than 3,000 records of soul music from the 1960s. When he is not writing, Curtis enjoys listening to music, playing basketball—he's six-feet two-inches—swimming with his daughter, and doing things around the house.

## Book Connections

Each of Christopher Paul Curtis's books is set in Flint, Michigan. *The Watsons Go to Birmingham, 1963* begins in Flint and takes the family to Birmingham, Alabama during the summer before the fateful bombing. *Bud, Not Buddy* takes place in the Flint area during the Great Depression of the 1930s. Both of these books end with a male protagonist coming to terms with his own emotions. In *The Watsons,* it is Byron whose emotions flow after saving Kenny. In *Bud, Not Buddy,* it is the man, Herman E. Calloway, who sheds tears once he realizes the true identity of Bud.

In his third published book, *Bucking the Sarge* (Delacorte, 2004), Curtis moved from historical perspectives to write a story set in a contemporary Flint setting. In this book, 15-year-old Luther Farrell is being groomed to take over his mother's rental property business. But she cheats everyone and Luther does not want to have anything to do with being a scam artist. He wants to be a philosopher, even though it won't pay a lot of money. Curtis's roots are in Flint, Michigan and he says that the town has many stories and a rich history.[5] His books are characterized as humorous with some very funny characters that experience some very serious things.

## Books Written by Christopher Paul Curtis

*Bucking the Sarge* (Delacorte, 2004).

*Bud, Not Buddy* (Delacorte, 1999).

*The Watsons Go to Birmingham, 1963* (Delacorte, 1995).

## For More Information

### Articles

Beck, Martha Davis. "Riverbank Review of Books for Young Readers—Christopher Paul Curtis." (Winter 1999/2000).March 2004. <http://www.riverbankreview.com/cpcurtis.html>.

Lamb, Wendy. "Christopher Paul Curtis." *The Horn Book Magazine* 76.4 (July/August 2000): 397–402. March 2004. <http://www.hbook.com/article_curtisprofile.shtml>.

Telfer, D. J. "Portrait: No Mamma, It's Bud, Not Buddy." *The Drive Online* 10 (2001). March 2004. <http://www.thedriveonline.com/article-10.html>.

Weich, Dave. "Christopher Paul Curtis Goes to Powell's—2000." *Powell Book Interviews; April 5, 2000.* March 2004. <http://www.powells.com/authors/curtis.html>.

### Books

Gaines, Ann. *Christopher Paul Curtis.* Hockessin, DE: Mitchell Lane, 2001.

### Web Sites

*Teachers@Random.* "Christopher Paul Curtis." April 2004. <http://www.randomhouse.com/teachers/authors/results.pper/?authorid=6203>.

# Notes

1. Christopher Paul Curtis, interview with the author, 9 July 2000, Chicago, Illinois.
2. Ibid.
3. Christopher Paul Curtis, *Bud, Not Buddy* (New York: Delacorte, 1999) 1.
4. Christopher Paul Curtis, "Newbery Acceptance Speech," American Library Association Conference Newbery-Caldecott Banquet, 9 July 2000, Chicago, Illinois.
5. Curtis, interview.

# Karen Cushman

♦ Historical fiction

## Chicago, Illinois
October 4, 1941

📖 *The Ballad of Lucy Whipple*

📖 *Catherine, Called Birdy*

📖 *The Midwife's Apprentice*

## About the Author

When Karen Cushman was 10 years old, her parents, Arthur and Loretta Lipski, moved their family from Chicago, Illinois to Oakland, California. The family left their midwestern home and Karen left behind her dog, her grandparents, and the public library, which was just around the corner. In California, she had to wait until someone could drive her to the library. Eventually, books helped her adjust to the move.

Karen's favorite book was *Homer Price* by Robert McCloskey. Actually, she read anything she could get her hands on. She enjoyed comic books; Donald Duck, Archie, and Little Lulu; Russian novels; *Mad Magazine;* books about World War II; and she even read cereal boxes. Karen was a reader and really did not think about becoming a writer, in fact, what she wanted to be was a librarian, a movie star, or perhaps a tap dancer.

After high school, Karen studied Greek and Latin at Stanford University and in 1963 earned a bachelor's degree in the classics. It was the early 1960s and few jobs were open to women with a liberal arts degree that didn't include waitressing or secretarial duties—she tried to avoid the latter by refusing to learn to type. At first she worked at the telephone company but soon quit, as she did with several other jobs. Eventually Karen ended up as an assistant-clerk-administrator in the graduate school of a Hebrew Union College in Los Angeles. That is where, in 1968, she met the man she would marry, a rabbinical student, Philip Cushman. The following year they married and moved to Oregon, where their dreams of growing organic corn, apple trees, making blackberry jam, rainy days, and nights before the fireplace all came true. In 1969, while living in Oregon, they even made a beautiful four-by-eight foot dining table out of hardwoods from many places around the world. Their young daughter, Leah, thrived, but life proved costly and teaching jobs for Philip were scarce.

**64**

Faced with economic realities, the couple reassessed their dreams and moved to Berkeley. Karen Cushman tried many different occupations. For a time she was involved with organic gardening and then she was a community arts program administrator. Cushman earned a graduate degree in human behavior from the United States International University in San Diego. She earned her second graduate degree in museum studies from John F. Kennedy University in Orinda, California, where she worked as an adjunct professor in the Museum Studies Department and editor of the *Museum Studies Journal* for 10 years. During this time she also raised their daughter, Leah.

Cushman often had ideas for stories and she shared them with her husband. Finally, in 1989, he decided he had heard enough. When she began to tell him about another idea she had, he interrupted, "you've been telling me ideas for 25 years. I won't listen anymore. Write it down."[1]

So at the age of 49, she sat down to write a seven-page outline of a story. The outline was the beginning of *Catherine, Called Birdy* (Clarion, 1994), a book set in the Middle Ages and featuring a freethinking girl, Catherine, as its main character. Catherine cleverly avoids marrying a man of her father's choosing.

While Cushman's first book garnered critical notice and a Newbery Honor Award, it was her second book, *The Midwife's Apprentice* (Clarion, 1995), also set in the Middle Ages, that changed her life when it was named the 1996 Newbery Award book. Suddenly she was recognized as a distinguished author and her financial situation improved.

In her work, Cushman strives to show the similarities between life in a historical period and life in the present day. Once she has an idea for a story she spends a lot of time exploring the setting and the historical period. Even the names of the characters are drawn from her research. She finds the names in letters, legal documents, and other papers of the time. For her first book she thought the character would be named Katherine. But later she found that the French version of the name would more likely be spelled Catherine.

Cushman had long been interested in the Middle Ages and she had always enjoyed the music and pageantry associated with the time period. She tried to imagine what it would have been like to be a young girl growing up during that time. How did the poor people cope and keep a sense of their own worth? How did they survive with such a lack of power? Because Cushman wanted to write about an ordinary girl living in the medieval days, she studied everything she could about the daily customs, holidays, celebrations, traditions, clothing, food, and dress.

Cushman says *The Midwife's Apprentice* was an enjoyable book to write because she had already done much of the research for *Catherine, Called Birdy*. For these two books Cushman learned all she could about bee keeping, shearing sheep, ointments, remedies, and superstitions that were prevalent during the Middle Ages. She researched the clothing young people wore, and the food they ate. She discovered that people living at that time even used words that modern day readers might consider cursing.

Cushman wanted the ordinary everyday information about the times and she found it in the Oakland Public Library. She read books that had information about English domestic and cultural history and she also found a couple of books with good bibliographies and used interlibrary loan to get the titles on those lists. She scoured bookstores to find paperback reproductions of several useful books, including *Housekeeping in the 14th Century* and *Daily Living in the 12th Century.*

When Cushman sat down to write *Catherine, Called Birdy,* she wrote and rewrote her manuscript. The first page alone had 27 drafts. Catherine's story is often told through her diary, the entries of which begin with feast days such as "Feast of Saint

Mawnan, an Irish bishop who kept a pet ram." Cushman found that the Oxford Dictionary of Saints provided her with plenty of names to use in the book. It was also relatively easy to become a saint in the Middle Ages; one just had to be a good person and die or be martyred.

Cushman also used books such as a book of manners to help her research the customs of the time. When she read the etiquette rule that said one should not blow their nose on the tablecloth, Cushman knew that the common people were probably doing just that. Another rule advised dinner guests not to chew off a bone and then throw it back in the pot. The author even discovered the rules for sharing a bed in an inn. Those who wanted to stay at the inn paid their coins and got one-third of a bed to sleep in for the night.

Cushman's third novel, *The Ballad of Lucy Whipple* (Clarion, 1996), differed from her previous books in that it was set in the days of the California gold rush. Cushman drew on the emotions that she experienced when she moved to California as a child to shape how the character Lucy felt when she was uprooted and taken to California with her mother. But Cushman did not have a lot of background knowledge about the days of the gold rush. In many ways the research for this book was more difficult than that for the Middle Ages. Cushman was able to uncover quite a bit of information about the miners, doctors, and businessmen that came to California during the gold rush but little information about the women or children who accompanied them. To complicate things, the gold rush was only a period of six or seven years so it was a rather short period in California history.

Cushman returned to the Middle Ages in her fourth novel, *Matilda Bone* (Clarion, 2000), which is set in England. Cushman had become intrigued with the information she uncovered about Medieval medicine when she was researching her first two books. Not surprisingly, Cushman had been interested in Medieval England since she was 23, when she read English historical fiction and decorated her walls with such items as fifteenth-century illuminated manuscripts. Even though her own heritage is Polish, German, and Irish, Cushman found that the English appealed to her, especially because she could read a lot of sources without having to learn another language.

Cushman's fifth book, *Rodzina* (Clarion, 2003), is set in America during a period of history between 1854 and 1929 when orphans were sent West on the orphan trains. Rodzina is a 12-year-old Polish-American girl who boards an orphan train in Chicago fearing what lies ahead—a life filled with work with no pay.

Cushman's manuscript for *Catherine, Called Birdy* ended up in the hands of Dorothy Briley, the editor-in-chief at Clarion books. Cushman had sent the manuscript to an agent friend of hers who lived in New York City. It happened that Cushman's agent-friend happened to live in the same apartment building as Briley and the deal for the book was made while both were riding in the elevator. Briley asked Dinah Stevenson to edit the book and Stevenson has worked with Cushman ever since. Stevenson provides suggestions for tightening up the story and making the manuscript more consistent. That big table the Cushman's made early in their marriage now serves as the place where the old pages, the new pages, all the intermediate pages, scissors, tape, and yellow stickie pads are laid out while Cushman uses the different versions to dummy up a new manuscript before putting it back into the computer. Her first drafts are relatively brief—50 or 60 pages long. As she rereads the story she begins to enrich the details and expand on the story; each draft becomes richer and more complex. Sometimes researching a particular word takes Cushman an entire day in the library. It took her three-and-a-half years to finish *Birdy,* nine months to finish *The Midwife's Apprentice,* and 18 months to write and research *The Ballad of Lucy Whipple. Matilda Bone* came on the heels of the Newbery

Award and with all the distractions of the award and some health problems, it took four years for that book to be ready for the publisher.

Karen Cushman and her husband Philip live in Oakland with a cat and a dog. When she is not writing, Karen enjoys reading, especially the medieval mysteries of Peter Ellis and books by Patricia MacLachlan. Their daughter Leah is grown and lives in northern California. While Leah was growing up, the family had several dogs, cats, rats, hamsters, guinea pigs, birds, fish, and a rabbit.

## Book Connections

Cushman has always been interested in Medieval Europe, not particularly the Kings and Queens, but the common citizens. She is interested in how they lived and what they did, so writing about that era is a natural interest for her. Even though the stories involve topics not usually written about in children's books, they have been of enormous success. In *The Midwife's Apprentice,* Alyce is a poor homeless girl who works for Jane, a mid-wife. Not only does Jane seem to give her the menial jobs, the villagers do not give her much respect either. But after avenging herself, Alyce leaves with her cat and works at an inn. In the end, she decides she should return to work once again for Jane as the mid-wife's apprentice. Catherine in *Catherine, Called Birdy* writes in her diary because her brother, a monk, tells her that she should. During the Middle Ages girls were often married off to a suitor selected by the girl's father. Catherine objects to this practice and she decides she wants to marry for love.

Cushman's fourth book, *Matilda Bone,* is also set in the Middle Ages, but rather than being a book that was quick to write, it took Cushman over four years to get it to a publishable form. The book tells the story of Matilda Brown, an apprentice to a bonesetter in the medical quarter of a medieval town.

Cushman's third book came about when she came across a random fact that 90 percent of the people involved in the gold rush were men. Cushman began to wonder about the other 10 percent—the women and children who were, for the most part, brought West by men. Unlike other children of the time, Lucy Whipple comes to California with her mother who plans to operate a boarding house. *Rodzina,* a book about the orphan trains in America during the nineteenth century and the early twentieth century, brought about another set of research.

Each of Cushman's books conveys a strong sense of setting and character. Each of the protagonists seems to be, in some way, searching for the place they belong. Catherine, Alyce, Lucy, Matilda, and Rodzina all find their place in the world after much struggle and soul searching. And whether by accident or by design, each of Cushman's stories features a strong female protagonist. Cushman uses these characters and their circumstances to help readers think about home and family and to learn about the importance of books and reading.[2]

## Books Written by Karen Cushman

*The Ballad of Lucy Whipple* (Clarion, 1996).

*Catherine, Called Birdy* (Clarion, 1994).

*Matilda Bone* (Clarion, 2000).

*The Midwife's Apprentice* (Clarion, 1995).

*Rodzina* (Clarion, 2003).

# For More Information

### Articles

Cushman, Karen. "Newbery Acceptance Speech." *The Horn Book Magazine* 72.4 (July/August 1996): 413–419.

Cushman, Philip. "Karen Cushman." *The Horn Book Magazine* 72.4 (July/August 1996): 420–424.

Elliot, Ian. "Karen Cushman: Pursuing the Past." *Teaching K-8* 28.5. (February 1998): 42–45.

Hendershot, Judith. "Interview with the Newbery Medal Winner: Karen Cushman." *The Reading Teacher* 50 (November 1996): 198–201.

Rochman, Hazel. "The Booklist Interview: Karen Cushman." *Booklist* 92.19–20 (June 1996): 1700–1701.

Williams, Karen. "For Award-Winning Author, the Story Comes First." *Christian Science Monitor* 88.212 (26 September 1996): B2.

"Writing from the Heart: Karen Cushman Interview." *Cricket Magazine* 24.10 (June 1997): 42–47.

### Web Sites

Cushman, Karen. *Author Karen Cushman's Tribute Home Page.* Nov. 2003. <http://www.karencushman.com>.

# Notes

1. Karen Cushman, Newbery acceptance speech, American Library Association Conference, Newbery-Caldecott Banquet, 7 July 1996, New York, New York.

2. Ibid.

# Katie Davis

◆ Animals ◆ Humor ◆ Family stories

**New York, New York**
January 4, 1959

📖 *Who Hops?*

📖 *Who Hoots?*

📖 *Mabel the Tooth Fairy and How She Got Her Job*

## About the Author

Katie Davis says she wrote and illustrated throughout her "whole life but it never occurred to me that maybe I could do this as a job!"[1] However, in 1996 she attended a writing conference and has been selling her stories ever since.

Katie was born in New York City, the older of two children. Until she was four, her family lived on 86th Street and Riverside Drive on the Upper West Side. Then the family moved to Los Angles but after two years the four of them moved back to New York. The first thing Katie remembers writing is a story about her Papa Louie, who made her laugh by taking out his false teeth. Katie also often told stories through her art. She says her pictures were narrative in nature. She even has memories of posing for a photograph at the age of five with a painting she had made. Katie was very proud of her artwork.

Another thing Katie remembers from her childhood is the time her brother's snake got loose for several weeks. One day they heard a loud shriek from the upstairs. Their father had slid his foot into a slipper in his closet—and had found the snake. Little did she know but that snake would reappear years later.

When Katie was in first grade, the family moved to Edgemont, New York where she attended Seely Place Elementary; later she graduated from Edgemont High School. After high school, Katie attended the American College of Paris and she finished her undergraduate degree at Boston University. Although she would eventually earn her living as an illustrator, Katie did not attend art school.

After college Katie worked in the field of public relations and advertising and she had several jobs in that industry before figuring out that she really would rather work for herself. In 1986 she started a hand-painted ceramics business that she playfully dubbed Dirty Dishes. During this time she also developed Scared Guy™—a character who would be scared for a child who was frightened by what was happening. Katie came up with the idea for Scared Guy while volunteering for the Starlight Children's Foundation, a worldwide organization that grants wishes to children who are ill. One young child was frightened of his treatments so Davis drew a guy with a face full of frazzled fright. She told the child that Scared Guy would be frightened for him so he wouldn't have to be. Scared Guy now shows up on t-shirts, cards, and all sorts of merchandise. According to Katie, he did "pretty well, especially in Asia."[2]

By this time, Katie had married Jerry Davis and they had become the parents of two children: Ben (1993) and Ruby (1996). Davis was also working on writing and illustrating children's books but she was only collecting rejections from publishers. Her husband encouraged her to attend a workshop sponsored by the Society of Children's Book Writers and Illustrators (SCBWI). After the workshop, Davis reworked her ideas and by 1998 her first book, *Who Hops?* (Harcourt, 1998), was released.

Davis ultimately joined the SCBWI and made connections and learned how to rework her story ideas so that they were more marketable. Then, in what she describes as "an incredible stroke of luck," she met Peggy Rathmann, the illustrator of the Caldecott Award winning, *Officer Buckle and Gloria* (G.P. Putnam, 1995).[3] Rathmann introduced Davis to her agent who agreed to represent Davis. The agent sent Davis's books to different publishers and Harcourt accepted *Who Hops?* This same agent has helped her sell each of her subsequent books.

Davis's exuberance for life is certainly evident in her books. She says "I love all food! But I especially love savory foods, with lots of flavor, and anything can be on that list from smooey (old family recipe of cream cheese, blue cheese, garlic and a splash of milk . . . )—it's really more than a sum of it's parts . . . and best eaten with celery, to my favorite candy, Hot Tamales." Davis's illustrations are splashy, a riot of colors. She says her favorite color is "red. No purple. No, make that cornflower blue. No, golden yellow. I know! Fuchsia!"[4] In the end, Davis can't decide what color is really her favorite.

Davis says that she "loves to go camping but never does, loves to play tennis which she occasionally does, and loves to eat Hot Tamales candy which she always does."[5] Her family has several pets: a chocolate lab, Millie; an albino aquatic frog, Lil; and a guinea pig, Milton.

Katie Davis, her husband, film animator Jerry Davis, and their two children live in New York state, where she continues to write and illustrate new books.

## Book Connections

Katie Davis's books are deceptively simple. Although *Who Hops?* began as a game that she played with her young children, she had to do extensive research to write the text that finally ended up in the book. For the swimming section she wanted to use an animal that doesn't or won't swim. When she couldn't think of one, she contacted 45 zoos to find out if any one who worked with the animals could help her find one that would work in her book. Some of the zoo workers suggested monkeys, apes, or other primates but Davis didn't want to use them because they didn't seem funny enough. Eventually someone suggested an anteater and that was the one she chose to use in the book.

Each of Davis's books is illustrated with bold energetic characters that bounce off the pages. Interestingly, she has used a variety of media to create her illustrations. In her first book, *Who Hops?* the illustrations were created with gouache—a kind of opaque, chalky watercolor that resembles poster paint. The illustrations for *I Hate to Go to Bed* (Harcourt, 1999) were made with acrylics. *Who Hoots?* (Harcourt, 2000), a companion title to *Who Hops?,* features digitally created pictures.

Davis's books feature neon-colored animals in combinations that are just weird enough to be funny and exciting. In *Who Hoots?* There is a purple alligator with green teeth and pigs that fly (well, no, they don't). Each illustration is more gleeful than the last. There are animals in pink, red, kelly green, purple, red-orange, and goldenrod yellow.

When her book *Party Animals* (Harcourt, 2002) was released, Davis threw a big party in her community. There were balloons, book signings, face paintings, and all sorts of other fun things. *Party Animals* featured barnyard animals by the dozen, everything from one blue ant and two purple frogs to a dozen baaing black sheep. Children reading Davis's books will delight in the tangerine ducks, turquoise cows with purple snouts, and the monsters and the electric-blue girl-eating dogs.

## Books Written and Illustrated by Katie Davis

*I Hate to Go to Bed* (Harcourt, 1999; pb. 2002).

*Mabel the Tooth Fairy and How She Got Her Job* (Harcourt, 2003).

*Party Animals* (Harcourt, 2002).

*Scared Stiff* (Harcourt, 2001).

*Who Hoots?* (Harcourt, 2000; board book, 2002).

*Who Hops?* (Harcourt, 1998; board book, 2002).

## For More Information

### Articles

Smith, Cynthia Leitich. "Interview with Children's Book Author-Illustrator Katie Davis." March 2004. <http://www.cynthialeitichsmith.com/author-illKatie Davis.htm>.

### Web Sites

Davis, Katie. *Katie Davis: Children's Author and Illustrator.* March 2004. <http://www.katiedavis.com>.

## Notes

1. Katie Davis, letter to the author, 6 Sept. 2002.
2. Ibid.
3. Cynthia Leitich Smith, "Interview with Children's Book Author-Illustrator Katie Davis," March 2004, <http://www.cynthialeitichsmith.com/author-illKatieDavis.htm>.
4. Davis, letter.
5. Ibid.

# David Diaz

◆ Biography ◆ Contemporary fiction

---
**New York, New York**
1959
---

📖 *Smoky Night*

📖 *Wilma Unlimited: How Wilma Rudolph
Became the World's Fastest Woman*

## About the Illustrator

It sounds simple. David Diaz met his wife in a high school art class, they married, and he
became a freelance artist. Together the couple produced a thank-you book for one of the
people who had hired Diaz to do some artwork. That person invited him to illustrate a
children's book, which led to his illustrating Eve Bunting's *Smoky Night* (Clarion, 1994)
and the book earned Diaz the prestigious Caldecott Award in 1995. Many reviewers
thought Diaz had arrived from nowhere to win the award but in truth, Diaz's story is not
simple. He arrived from Fort Lauderdale, Florida and had spent more than a decade
establishing himself as an artist. His reputation came first in the area of commercial
design and art; he entered the field of children's books later.

David Diaz was born in New York in 1958 (some sources say 1959) and very soon
afterward his family moved to Fort Lauderdale, Florida, where he grew up. David's
mother died when he was just 16 years old and his art became his emotional outlet.

During his junior year in high school, Diaz met his future wife, Cecelia, in a ceramics class. The two of them exchanged sarcastic remarks and angled for one another's
attention. The following year they found themselves together again—this time in a weav-
ing class. Soon they were sweethearts.

When it came to art, David was a natural. Despite the fact that he never worked on
his assignments in class, he managed to earn a scholarship.[1] His art teacher happened to
be friends with the renowned hyper-realistic sculptor, Duane Hanson, and she arranged
for David to work as an apprentice to Hanson. This experience helped David develop his
art style and led to a friendship that lasted until Hanson's death. However, David credits
Cecelia with teaching him about color. "She," he says, "opened my eyes to vivid color,
and I began to use it."[2]

David entered the Fort Lauderdale Art Institute and on his graduation, David and Cecelia packed their bags and headed to California. They arrived in San Diego in January 1979 with very little money. David Diaz's first job was at a Fotomat kiosk—a drive-up film-developing booth. But soon he landed an illustration job with the *San Diego Reader,* which paid him $25—a cause for celebration. Diaz had a car that he and Cecelia had to coax into starting and after dark they would cruise their neighborhood for fallen avocados or lemons. Their diet consisted mostly of peanut butter and honey, tortillas, rice, beans, and salsa.[3]

But the couple survived and soon Diaz was receiving more commissions. He worked for several graphic design firms until he established his own design and illustration business, Diaz Icon. Over the next decade, his persistence in showing his portfolio resulted in over five thousand editorial and design projects. His work appeared in advertisements for Pepsi, Perrier, Snapple, and in magazines such as *Atlantic Monthly* and on the covers (and a few interior illustrations) for books including Gary Soto's *Neighborhood Odes.*

During this period, David and Cecelia often created and assembled limited edition books that they gave to business clients as thank-you gifts. One of those books, *Sweet Peas,* went to Diane D'Andrade at Harcourt Brace as a thank-you for the illustrative work she had asked him to do for Soto's book. When D'Andrade saw the work Diaz did on *Sweet Peas,* she asked him to read Eve Bunting's manuscript for *Smoky Night.*

The summer before, while on a trip with his brother floating down the Amazon River in Brazil, Diaz developed a sketching technique that inspired the photographic collages he created and photographed to create the illustrations for *Smoky Night.* His challenge was to achieve a balance between text, design, painted illustrations, and collage backgrounds. Diaz decided to use the same color palette for all of the characters in the book. The intent was to avoid any ethnic or racial implications—he wanted the characters' personalities to speak for themselves.[4]

David Diaz was asleep when the phone call came telling him that he had won the 1995 Caldecott Award. The message that was left on the answering machine was heard first by Cecelia. She woke David and, she says, "we jumped up and down the hallway till we woke up the kids."[5]

Since that morning Diaz has continued to make his mark in the world of children's literature. A year later his second book was released, *Wilma Unlimited: How Wilma Rudolph Became the World's Fastest Woman* (Harcourt Brace, 1996) written by Kathleen Krull. It too was widely acclaimed. His bold black outlined characters have been compared to the work of John Steptoe, another Caldecott artist.

Today, Diaz continues to create commissioned work and illustrate children's books. David and Cecelia live in Rancho La Costa, California. They have three children: Gabrielle, Jericho, and Ariel. Their youngest son, Ariel, was five at the time Diaz won the Caldecott but all three are now approaching adulthood. In fact, Jericho has codesigned a college course manual cover with her father and Cecelia is often involved in photographing the artwork.

## Book Connections

David Diaz's work is characterized by bold colors, strong lines, and always-striking innovations. The illustrations for his first picture book, *Smoky Night,* are unique. Strong, brilliantly colored acrylic paintings are framed with photographic collages. Each collage frame was created from remnants of other art projects including fragments of pottery and other diverse items such as cloth, matches, cardboard, and cereal. Thematically, the collages are tied to the paintings they frame. For example, cereal is used in the frame that surrounds the painting of the looting of Mrs. Kim's store.

Diaz created the illustrations for *Wilma Unlimited* by framing each image with a sepia photograph appropriate to the interior illustration. The frame around the illustration of Wilma and her mother riding a bus to a Nashville hospital shows a bus wheel in the frame. The illustration of children walking to school is surrounded with a frame of a white wooden fence with peeling paint. A shadow of a chain link fence surrounds the picture of Rudolph bursting ahead in the relay race and an American flag frames the image of her receiving her third gold medal with the Star-Spangled Banner playing.

David Diaz even created a typeface, or font, for that book called Ariel after one of his sons. The typeface is designed to give the illusion of running. For example, the word "Wilma" has long V shapes and there are notches and blocks to the letters that create light and dark spots, which provide the illusion of movement.

Diaz's illustrations for another book written by Bunting, *December* (Harcourt Brace, 1997), are filled with stars, roses, feathers, and angels. In this book Diaz also uses varied colors for the newsprint included in the design.

As a hobby, Diaz collects objects from the Arts and Crafts Era at the turn of the century. He admires Gustav Stickley as well as the more recent work of Friedrich Hunderwasser and Gustav Klimt. He often puts images of Arts and Crafts Era tiles, vases, and lamps as well as Stickley's functional furniture into his illustrations.

Diaz continues to experiment with a variety of media and styles. He used vibrant computer art to illustrate Nancy Andrews-Goebel's *The Pot That Juan Built* (Lee and Low, 2002). This book is a visual biography and a tribute to Juan Quezada, a renowned Mexican potter.

## Books Illustrated by David Diaz

*The Christmas House.* Written by Eve Bunting. (Harcourt Brace, 1997).

*December.* Written by Eve Bunting. (Harcourt Brace, 1997).

*Going Home.* Written by Eve Bunting. (HarperCollins, 1996).

*Jump Rope Magic.* Written by Afi Scruggs. (Scholastic, 2000).

*The Pot That Juan Built.* Written by Nancy Andrews-Goebel. (Lee and Low, 2002).

*Smoky Night.* Written by Eve Bunting. (Harcourt Brace, 1994).

*Wilma Unlimited: How Wilma Rudolph Became the World's Fastest Woman.* Written by Kathleen Krull. (Harcourt Brace, 1996).

## For More Information

### Articles

Cary, Alice. "Fast Book to Honor World's Fastest Woman." *BookPage Review:* Wilma Unlimited: How Wilma Rudolph Became the World's Fastest Woman. April 2004. <http://www.bookpage.com/9605bp/childrens/daviddiaz.html>.

Diaz, Cecelia. "David Diaz." *Horn Book Magazine* 71.4 (July/August 1995): 434–435.

Diaz, David. "Caldecott Medal Acceptance Speech." *Horn Book Magazine* 71.4 (July/August 1995): 430–433.

Peck, Jackie, and Judy Hendershot. "Conversation with a Winner—David Diaz Talks about *Smoky Night*." *The Reading Teacher* 49.5 (February 1996): 386–388.

## Notes

1. Cecelia Diaz, "David Diaz." *Horn Book Magazine* 71.4 (July/August 1995): 434.
2. David Diaz, Caldecott Medal Acceptance Speech given at the American Library Association Newbery/Caldecott dinner, 25 June 1995, Chicago.
3. Diaz, Cecelia, "David Diaz," 435.
4. Diaz, David, Caldecott Medal Acceptance Speech.
5. Diaz, Cecelia, "David Diaz," 435.

# Kate DiCamillo

◆ Contemporary fiction ◆ Family stories

**Merion, Pennsylvania**
March 25, 1964

📖 *Because of Winn-Dixie*
📖 *Tale of Despereaux: Being the Story of a Mouse, a Princess, Some Soup, and a Spool of Thread*
📖 *The Tiger Rising*

## About the Author

Kate DiCamillo was five when she, her mother Betty Lee, and her older brother Curt moved from Philadelphia to Clermont, Florida, a small town 30 miles west of Orlando. The move was an effort to help Kate's chronic pneumonia. Her father, an orthodontist with a thriving practice in Philadelphia, was going to follow in a few months but he never did. He came to Florida every once in a while to visit but never to stay.

Kate says she and her brother Curt spent a lot of time digging when they were young, adding, "I am not sure what I was digging for."[1] When she was eight years old she unearthed a big white rock from underneath a huge magnolia tree. The rock had an indentation just the size of a thumb. Kate thought it was something special and showed her brother. Curt was not impressed, "that's not ancient, it's not even a rock—it's a bone." Although Curt was apathetic, Kate's 10-year-old friend Beverly thought it might be a "magical bone." So Kate put her thumb in the bone and wished for a pony. She could almost see herself on a pony and actually, she says, she did get to ride on her neighbor's pony. Kate explains, "I had to conjure something from nothing. That's what writing is about."[2]

Kate grew up in Clermont and she and her friend, Beverly, attended Clermont Elementary School (now Cypress Ridge Elementary). Kate often played in her backyard where they had a tree house that was home to their book-club meetings. After high school Kate attended Rollins College, worked at Disneyland, and then headed to the University of Florida in Gainesville. After earning an English degree, she returned to Clermont and worked several entry-level jobs. In school Kate had been told that she was a talented writer and although becoming a famous writer was a goal, she admits that she thought her talent would be rewarded automatically so she "just sat around for the next seven or eight years."[3]

For a time Kate committed to running 25 minutes a day. It became a passion. Then because of a knee injury she had to quit running but the experience taught her that she could do something if she committed to it.

In 1994 Kate moved to Minneapolis. She was in a long-term relationship that was not progressing so when her best girlfriend decided to move back to her home state of Minnesota, Kate told her boyfriend that she had decided to move with her friend. She thought the suggestion of her moving would encourage him to make a commitment to her but instead he offered to help her rent a U-Haul truck.

Kate's pride would not let her change her mind so she moved. She arrived in Minneapolis totally unprepared for the weather but was thrilled with the social climate. People seemed concerned about the environment, valued literature and the arts, and displayed social tolerance. She had come with no socks and the climate was cold but she loved where she was.

Kate DiCamillo started various odd jobs but finally ended up as a picker in a book warehouse. She, of course, had to read the books she was handling and many were for young readers. Meanwhile, she decided that if she was ever going to be a writer she would have to commit to writing. At first, she set her goal to write for an hour each day. But often she would get up from her desk without having written a thing. DiCamillo adjusted her goal—to write two pages a day. Soon she began submitting her writing and collected at least 470 rejection letters from various publishers. She set her alarm clock for 4:00 A.M. and each day she wrote before going off to work at the book warehouse.

A colleague at the warehouse suggested DiCamillo join his wife's writing group. She did, and gained friends who encouraged her to keep writing. She signed up for a workshop led by author Jane Resh Thomas. Thomas immediately recognized DiCamillo's talent when she heard her read her manuscript to the class. Thomas encouraged DiCamillo to persist, even when DiCamillo was feeling that perhaps she wasn't going to succeed in the writing world.

Then, a publisher's representative who called on buyers at the warehouse got to know of DiCamillo's writing. He offered to take her manuscript to an editor he knew at Candlewick Publishers. The first manuscript DiCamillo sent to that editor was a picture book and it was rejected.

After some much needed financial support from a competitive grant from the McKnight Foundation, DiCamillo wrote another book, *Because of Winn-Dixie* (Candlewick, 1999). The first draft of the book did not include a dog but during a particularly cold winter in Minneapolis DiCamillo was missing Florida and missing having a dog. "One night I was just going asleep and I hear this little girl's voice say 'I have a dog and his name is Winn-Dixie.' "[4]

DiCamillo sent that book off to Candlewick too and it landed in the slush pile in an employee's vacated office. One day, staff members found DiCamillo's novel while they were cleaning out the office. Kara LeRue became her editor and offered her a contract, which DiCamillo signed and mailed back to Candlewick in Boston. When her editor called and said they were ready to begin the rewriting process, DiCamillo thought, "Oh. No. I've rewritten it six times." But she did not want to return the $5,000 advance so she rewrote it, even though she didn't want to.[5]

Fortunately, the revision made the book better. Shortly before publication, DiCamillo began to be concerned about using the name Winn-Dixie in her book. Winn-Dixie is actually the name of a large grocery chain with headquarters in the South. There are approximately 2,000 stores in the chain. The attorneys for Candlewick composed a disclaimer for the book that they assured DiCamillo would make using the name okay. But DiCamillo thought it was only a matter of time before someone at the store caught up with her.

One day after the book was published, DiCamillo received a letter written on engraved stationery. The letter was from a Ms. Flo Davis, the widow of one of the founders of the Winn-Dixie stores. When she opened the letter, DiCamillo was pleasantly surprised. It turns out that Ms. Davis is involved in many philanthropic projects and just "wanted to know what she could do to help this little girl."[6]

Ms. Davis decided to sponsor a series of author visits for DiCamillo in several Florida schools and to distribute her book throughout Florida. *Because of Winn-Dixie* won a Newbery Honor Award and sold over 345,000 copies, a resoundingly successful entry into the world of books for young readers. Shortly after her honor award was publicized, DiCamillo fielded many phone calls including one from her childhood friend, Beverly Jones Cunningham, that 10 year old who helped her find her "magic bone."

After living several years in a tiny apartment, DiCamillo's success with her first book enabled her to purchase a little red house in southwest Minneapolis and to buy her first new car. She was also able to quit her book warehouse job and concentrate on her writing. Doing so made it possible for her to get up at a more conventional time of day. DiCamillo does maintain her writing schedule—writing a minimum of two pages a day, five days a week.

DiCamillo's second book, *The Tiger Rising* (Candlewick, 2001), is more serious than *Because of Winn-Dixie*. It began because a single character from a short story that DiCamillo previously wrote still haunted her. That character, Rob Horton, would not leave her head. Kate explains, "I finally asked him what he wanted and he said he had found a tiger."[7] The conversation with Rob came after DiCamillo's mom told her about a newspaper story about a tiger that had escaped from a circus. *The Tiger Rising* became a National Book Award finalist.

DiCamillo's third book, *Tale of Despereaux: Being the Story of a Mouse, a Princess, Some Soup, and a Spool of Thread* (Candlewick, 2003), was a major departure from her previous two books. *Tale of Despereaux* left the realistic world and entered the world of fantasy. The main character is Despereaux Tilling, a mouse with big dreams who leaves the world of mice and enters the world of people and rats and learns that even a tiny mouse can be as brave as a knight.

The story came about during a trip to St. Louis where DiCamillo visited her best friend's family. Luke, her friend's eight-year-old son, asked DiCamillo if she would write a story for him but she responded that she did not usually write stories on command. Luke explained that he was sure that it would be a story that she would like to tell because, he said, "it's about an unlikely hero. He has exceptionally large ears."[8] When DiCamillo asked what happened to the hero Luke informed her that, that is why he wanted her to write the story, so they could find out what happened to the hero. It took DiCamillo three years to write *Tale of Despereaux* and get it published but when it was published in 2003 it won rave reviews and was awarded the 2004 Newbery Medal.

DiCamillo is single with "no children and (alas) no pets."[9] She does date and often has dinner with her girlfriends. Since her writing success, invitations to visit schools and libraries have come in numbers that exceed her ability to fulfill the requests. Among her favorite things are pizza, dogs, and the color green. Her brother, Curt, is a writer and expert on British and Irish country houses—a passion he has had since his adolescence. Her mother still lives in Clermont not too far from DiCamillo's childhood friend Beverly.

DEAR YOUNG READER,

REMEMBER THIS...

EVERY DOOR IN EVERY
UNIVERSE WILL OPEN TO
YOU IF YOU CONTINUE
TO READ.

WITH ALL BEST WISHES,

Kate DiCamillo, at home in Minneapolis, continues to enjoy the popularity of her writings. If that popularity diminishes she says, "I can always go back to work."[10]

## Book Connections

*Because of Winn-Dixie* and *The Tiger Rising* are both set in Florida and deal with a similar theme—the loss of a parent. Although both Opal (from *Because of Winn-Dixie*) and Rob (from *The Tiger Rising*) must deal with the loss of their mother, DiCamillo links the theme to the fact that her father abandoned their family when she was five. During her childhood, friendships such as the one she had with Beverly Jones Cunningham were her "saving grace."[11] Friendships allow the characters (and DiCamillo) to mitigate the sorrow suffered with the loss of their parent.

In fact, early in 2002 the British Council/East Jerusalem planned to distribute an Arabic edition of *The Tiger Rising* to schools and mental health centers on the West Bank and in the Gaza Strip. The literacy project manager felt that this book had much to offer as a help to the tens of thousands in the area who must deal with death on a daily basis. In each of her books DiCamillo slipped in some personal history. In *The Tiger Rising,* Rob has a terrible rash on his legs. DiCamillo had a similar rash when she was young—a bad case of eczema. In *Because of Winn-Dixie,* Otis brings a huge bottle of pickles to the party. This was an inside joke for DiCamillo's friends who know how much she dislikes pickles.

Members of DiCamillo's writing group, including friends Jane Resh Thomas and novelist Alison McGhee, have described DiCamillo's third book, *Tale of Despereaux*, as "different, daring, and funny."[12] Even though the book is indeed a departure from the southern realism of her first two novels, each of DiCamillo's first three titles deal with a sense of loss (or potential loss) and universal themes of friendship, courage, and perseverance.

## Books Written by Kate DiCamillo

*Because of Winn-Dixie* (Candlewick, 2000).

*Tale of Despereaux: Being the Story of a Mouse, a Princess, Some Soup, and a Spool of Thread.* Illustrated by Timothy Basil Ering. (Candlewick, 2003).

*The Tiger Rising* (Candlewick, 2001).

## For More Information

### Articles

Habich, John. "Prize-Winning Novelist Kate DiCamillo Depicts Joys, Pains of Kids' Lives." *Minneapolis-St. Paul Star Tribune* 24 Feb. 2002: 11D.

Pate, Nancy. "Clermont's Kate DiCamillo Wins Literary Awards, Kids' Hearts." *Orlando Sentinel* 28 Sept. 2001: books section.

## Notes

1. Kate DiCamillo, "How I Got Here Today and It Wasn't by Limousine," presented at the Festival of Children's Books, 3 Nov. 2001, University of Iowa, Iowa City.
2. Ibid.
3. Ibid.
4. Kate DiCamillo, "Ten Commandments of Writing," presentation given for the Coe College Author Residency, 6 Nov. 2001, Coe College, Cedar Rapids, Iowa.
5. Ibid.
6. Ibid.
7. Ibid.
8. Kate DiCamillo, "A Fairy-Tale Ending: For DiCamillo, Desperate Times Meant 'Despereaux' Measures," *Washington Post,* 26 Jan. 2004: C14.
9. Kate DiCamillo, interview with the author, 23 Dec. 2002.
10. Ibid.
11. DiCamillo, "Ten Commandments of Writing."
12. John Habich, "Prize-Winning Novelist Kate DiCamillo Depicts Joys, Pains of Kids' Lives," *Minneapolis-St. Paul Star Tribune,* 24 Feb. 2002: 11D.

# Marianne J. Dyson

♦ Science, informational books

## Canton, Ohio
### December 24, 1954

📖 *Space Station Science*

📖 *Home on the Moon: Living on a Space Frontier*

## About the Author

The Football Hall of Fame and the McKinley Monument share with Marianne J. Dyson their hometown of Canton, Ohio. Marianne was born there on the day before Christmas 1954. She lived most of her childhood in Ohio where she attended school and eventually graduated from Glenwood (now Glenoak) High School.

After her parents divorced when she was 11, Marianne and her brothers and sister spent the school year with their father and stepmother. During the summers they lived with their mother and stepfather in several towns in Ohio, Pennsylvania, and North Carolina. Marianne read science fiction and watched "Star Trek." Even then, science and space fascinated her. After reading Robert Heinlein's book, *Starman Jones,* she decided she wanted to navigate a spacecraft—to be an Astrogator.[1]

In high school Marianne took typing classes instead of physics. Becoming a scientist was not really a career goal at that time. After high school, Marianne entered the University of Athens in Ohio. She planned to major in math but also enrolled in an introductory freshman physics class. A professor there encouraged her and suggested she consider a career in science. Marianne was the only female in the class. After one year at the University of Athens she transferred to the University of North Carolina at Greensboro, where she graduated cum laude with an undergraduate degree in physics with minors in math and psychology.

Marianne accepted a graduate fellowship at Rice University in Houston, Texas where she studied space physics and astronomy. During this year she met her husband, Thorton E. Dyson, and they married in the Rice University Chapel. After spending a year in graduate school, Marianne Dyson left to work for a corporation under contract with the National Aeronautics and Space Administration (NASA). She also applied to work at

NASA. After five months, NASA hired Dyson as a flight controller and she became one of the first 10 women to work in mission control. She worked for the first five space shuttle missions—three in 1981 and two in 1982.

In 1984, after five years, her NASA career ended. Dyson comments, "I left NASA when my first son was a year old and [I] worked part-time for Hernandez Engineering as an aerospace consultant, helping the Germans and Italians prepare for the space station program."[2]

After deciding to stay home with her children, Dyson found herself making up games, stories, and activities to share her interest and knowledge of space and science with them. One day at the grocery store, she picked up a flier about a correspondence course for writers from the Children's Institute of Literature and decided to take the course.

Dyson says some of her early stories were "horrible."[3] Her instructor encouraged her to use her science background to write nonfiction. After her second son was born, she completed the course and got her first sale. Dyson was paid $100 for a nonfiction article on how to get a job at NASA.

Today Dyson writes informational books. The facts must be accurate and the research must support those facts. Dyson calls herself a hands-on learner and she often uses her personal experiences in her writing. Shortly before she wrote *Space Station Science* (Scholastic, 1999) she toured a factory in Dallas that was producing the radiator panels for the space station. The panels were enormous white towering structures that stretched across the giant warehouse. "Humans," Dyson said, "were not just docking a few modules together in space; they were building the 8th wonder of the world! That sense of awe is a piece of me that couldn't help but come through in my writing of that book."[4]

Dyson was also able to take the photo of the robotic arm's end effector that is shown on page 89 of *Space Station Science*. The engineer who was working on the project "patiently rotated it open then closed, open then closed until I had one of those 'ah ha' moments."[5] At that moment Dyson knew how she could make a model of the effector from toilet paper tubes and rubber bands. She later sent one of the models to the engineer as a thank you and the engineer told Dyson she was planning to use the model to explain to her own mother what she worked on.

Dyson's association with NASA experts is a valuable asset to her writing. When she wrote the book *Home on the Moon* (National Geographic, 2003), she wrote about NASA's plan to build a station at L1, a place between the Earth and the moon where the gravity of the two bodies balance each other. Initially she interpreted the information she found to mean that trips to the moon could only happen twice a month when the moon was in the plane of the Earth's Equator. She'd also said that the latitude of the launch site on Earth limited the landing choices on the moon. However, during a discussion with fellow members of the National Space Society, a senior engineer who had worked on the space shuttle Apollo told her that those constraints did not exist. Only a handful of people would have known that she had misinterpreted the data she had found but it was important to her to have her text correct. By the time she was able to confirm the correct interpretation of what she had written, the book was at the printer. However, the book had not run on the press yet so the publisher called the plates back from the printer and Dyson fixed the section. She had just one day to rewrite a three-page section and the new information had to fit exactly into the pages that were to be removed. No headers or artwork could be changed at this point in the process.[6] Dyson was able to accomplish that task and when the first copy of *Home on the Moon* rolled off the press, its accuracy was a tribute to her continuing attention to detail and to her connections with science and space experts.

Several events in Dyson's life came together for a cover story she wrote for an anthology, *Girls to the Rescue #7* (Simon & Schuster, 2000). Dyson and her husband own a small plane and have flown all over the United States. Once, before Dyson knew how to fly, her husband was piloting a plane and had to make an emergency landing. That experience prompted Dyson to think about what would happen if he had not been able to land the plane. Afterward she decided to take flying lessons so she could take over if it was ever necessary. While working at mission control, Dyson learned that the way to overcome failure was to focus on what one could do rather than focusing on what one could not do.

The main character in the story she wrote for the *Girls to the Rescue #7* book was modeled after a neighbor's daughter. The character in the book realizes that in order to survive she must get the help of the plane's only passenger, a young burn victim. The patient's burns are from washing her hair with gasoline—a true story Dyson heard from an Angel Flight pilot who flew a burn patient home from Oklahoma.[7]

Dyson's first book, *Space Station Science,* won the Golden Kite Award, an award given by the Society of Children's Book Writers and Illustrators (SCBWI). It also made Booklist's Top 10 Youth Science Book and the National Science Teachers Association (NSTA)/Children's Book Councils (CBC) Outstanding Trade Book list. The book sold out its first printing of 40,000 copies but after her editor at Scholastic moved to National Geographic, the new editor at Scholastic rejected Dyson's proposal for a sequel, *Moon Base Science.* Dyson was told the book did not have enough "commercial potential."

For a few weeks Dyson contemplated returning to the aerospace industry thinking that her first book was a fluke and that she probably would not succeed as a children's book writer. However, during the SCBWI convention where she picked up her Golden Kite Award, other writers encouraged her to try again. They said it was her science background that made her books special.

Dyson returned home, reworked the proposal, and submitted the new book proposal, now titled *Frontier Moon,* to her former editor, now at National Geographic. The editor offered her a contract for the book and suggested the title be changed to *Home on the Moon* so readers would realize the book was about living on the moon rather than a fiction book about the old West. In the acknowledgments for the book, Dyson thanks her SCBWI colleagues and the editor and staff at National Geographic.

Marianne Dyson and her family live in Houston, right down the street from NASA. She describes their house as a "suburb version of Sleeping Beauty's castle with vines grown completely over it!"[8] As a full-time writer Dyson is continually sending proposals to publishers, researching, and writing. At any one time she has several proposals at various stages of production. Her forté is science-based writing, both fiction and nonfiction. While science is certainly a favorite topic to write about, Dyson has many other favorites: potato chips, artichokes, rare steak, sole, strawberries, and chocolate top her foods list and turquoise is a favorite color. The family has several pets—a cat named Charming, a dog named Floppy, and "three silly goldfish, Larry, Curly, and Moe."[9] There's also a family of squirrels that live in the vines that cover an upstairs window of her home.

## Book Connections

Marianne Dyson uses her science background to explore science topics in her nonfiction titles as well as in her fiction books. She also has written a book aimed at helping young researchers locate information on the World Wide Web. Her book, *Homework Help on the Internet* (Scholastic Reference, 2000), is filled with references to online sources

Dear Reader,

Did you know that you can get oxygen from rocks? That time depends on speed? I learned these things through reading. And believe me, what you know is way more important than what you look like. Looks fade, but the information stored in your brain lasts a lifetime. You may use it to build factories on the moon or spaceships to the stars. Whatever happens, as a reader, you will be <u>read</u>y for the future! Ad Astra!

Marianne J Dyson

based on activities and assignments in many school texts. That book came about because Dyson found that the Internet search engines were not precise enough for finding useful information for homework assignments. Dyson continues to propose nonfiction books to publishers but she is also beginning to apply her science background to fiction stories.

## Books Written by Marianne Dyson

*Girls to the Rescue #7.* Edited by Bruce Lansky. (Simon & Schuster, 2000).

*Home on the Moon: Living on a Space Frontier* (National Geographic, 2003).

*Homework Help on the Internet* (Scholastic Reference, 2000).

*The Space Explorer's Guide to Stars & Galaxies* (Scholastic, 2004).

*Space Station Science: Life in Free Fall* (Scholastic, 1999).

# For More Information

### Articles

Simonson, Scott. "Spotlight on Marianne Dyson." *Houston Chronicle* 20 Aug. 2000: 3F.

### Web Sites

Dyson, Marianne. *Author Marianne Dyson's Home Page.* March 2004. <http://www.mariannedyson.com>.

# Notes

1. Scott Simonson, "Spotlight on Marianne Dyson," *Houston Chronicle* 20 Aug. 2000: 3F.
2. Marianne J. Dyson, interview with the author, 6 Sept. 2002.
3. Ibid.
4. Ibid.
5. Ibid.
6. Marianne Dyson, "The Write Space," newsletter, 18 Jan. 2003: 4.
7. Some may wonder why anyone would wash their hair with gasoline but many people have done this as a home remedy believing that gasoline is an effective delousing agent. Those who do use this method are often injured or killed by burns caused when a single spark sets their hair on fire.
8. Dyson, interview.
9. Ibid.

# Denise Fleming

◆  Animals  ◆  Concept books

| Toledo, Ohio |
| --- |
| January 31, 1950 |

📖 *Alphabet Under Construction*

📖 *The Everything Book*

📖 *In a Small, Small Pond*

## About the Author/Illustrator

Denise Fleming and her younger sister, Rochelle, grew up in Toledo, Ohio in a middle-class home. Their father, Frank, was a realtor but his hobby was building furniture in his basement workshop, where the girls also had a place to create. They often put on plays, complete with commercials, for the other children in their neighborhood. They used refrigerator boxes as spook houses and puppet stages and they performed a variety of shows. The girls' mother, Inez Campbell Fleming, who was very active in the local theater group, always suggested that the girls require a button or straight pins as admission to their performances.

By the time Denise was in the third grade she was enrolled in classes at the Toledo Museum of Art. Her illustrations were characterized by strong colorful images not unlike the paintings of other children. After high school Denise enrolled in Kendall College of Art and Design in Grand Rapids, Michigan, where she met her husband David Powers. Both entered the world of art by working for a company as staff artists, drawing what they were asked to draw or paint. A year after graduation, the two married and soon afterward started to work as freelance artists. After their daughter, Indigo, was born in 1979, Denise found that she was drawn to picture books.

Early in her illustrative career, Denise Fleming created detailed illustrations and drew licensed characters such as Care Bears. Then, curiosity led Fleming and her sister to take a papermaking course. Fleming's fascination with the possibilities of papermaking encouraged her to take a more advanced course. After experimenting with the process, she developed an illustration technique that involved making her own paper and using hand-made stencils. She used that technique when she began to write and illustrate picture books. Fleming creates paper pulp and uses it much like other artists use paints or colored pencils. Squeeze bottles filled with different colored pulp become her brushes. "The whole process is wet, messy and wonderful," she says, "I haven't picked up a brush or a colored pencil since I discovered papermaking."[1] Fleming enjoys the art-making process and the surprises that she gets by using pulp as her painting medium. She says there is a certain amount of bleeding between colors and blending of fibers that she cannot completely control.

When Fleming created her first book, *In the Tall, Tall Grass* (Henry Holt, 1991), she says she did not necessarily strive for a realistic look. She says, "I take photographs if I want an illustration to be realistic."[2] The idea for the book came from several summer afternoons that she spent with her daughter in the woods and fields near their home. She used a lot of yellow to set the mood of a very warm and sunny day and blue clear skies. On every page Fleming put in a caterpillar to provide scale to the rest of her illustrations. She added drones of bees in the grasses, birds in the berry bushes, and grasshoppers and crickets. Color helped her establish mood, place, and time. The text is terse verse that shows her love of alliteration.

In addition to writing and illustrating her books, Fleming also designs the book's layout. In that role, she is able to decide where the text will be placed on the page and how large the font should be. All of these things are important to the books and the children who will read them.

After the success of *In the Tall, Tall Grass,* Fleming began to think about writing a sequel. She and her daughter, Indigo, planted flowers and plants in their backyard—plants that attracted butterflies and hummingbirds. They also built a pond in the yard and stocked it with fish. With a little coaxing, they managed to train the fish to eat out of their hands. All they had to do was to wiggle their hands in the water and the fish would come to eat. It wasn't long before raccoons found the pond and wiggled their paws in the water. But the raccoons were not there to feed the fish—they were there to eat the fish! Needless to say, the next group of fish stocked in the pond were not taught to eat when summoned. The pond gave Fleming the idea for *In a Small, Small Pond* (Henry Holt, 1993). Fleming's pond had attracted a frog and that frog appears on every page of this book. Fleming loves how a frog completely changes form from tadpole to frog. Whirligig beetles, a type of pond insect, also appear in the book because, Fleming recalls, " 'Whirligig' is one of my favorite words."[3]

As a young girl, Fleming longed to live on a farm. She finally got a chance to go to a country farm when she wrote and illustrated *Barnyard Banter* (Henry Holt, 1994), a story in which she shows a goose chasing a butterfly. Fleming explains that because "I am a vegetarian he never catches it." Some critics have pointed out that there are not many people in Fleming's books but in her mind there are several people. For example, the rooster in *Barnyard Banter* is, she says, "a guy I dated in high school."[4]

Fleming loves cats. She once had a Mama Cat (Gigi) and a Papa Cat (Samson) and their offspring Isabelle. Sometime later, Gigi and Samson had four more kittens, Hissy, Sparky, Callie, and Mr. Darcy. The kittens made their presence known by their little meows. Three of the little kittens were very active but their brother was often sleeping. *Mama Cat Has Three Kittens* (Henry Holt, 1998) tells Mama Cat's story but instead of four kittens Fleming changes the number to three focusing on three of everything—three kittens, three butterflies, and so forth. A tiny mouse appears throughout the book, which provides a point of comparison for scale.

Near the Fleming/Powers home is a small field that the nearby residents wanted to make into a pocket park, which did not happen. So Fleming immortalized the area by creating *Where Once There Was a Wood* (Henry Holt, 1996). She was able to use a lot of natural material in her paper. "Fall is my very favorite season. For a long time I've wanted to do a book about fall and about bears and hibernation."[5] In the book's illustrations, acorns on the ground establish scale and *Where Once There Was a Wood* became her fall book. *Time to Sleep* (Henry Holt, 1996) became her bear and hibernation book.

*The Everything Book* (Henry Holt, 2000) is a book for a new baby. In this book Fleming did include people. On one page she features the faces of four babies. Then there is a picture of her blond editor, Laura, as a young girl. The last baby face is that of her daughter. There is also a guinea pig named Earl. (Fleming's husband came home from a business trip and found a pig named after him—Earl is his middle name.) Fleming pays homage to her own favorite picture book, *A Chair for My Mother,* by Vera Williams with the image of a small child peeking out from behind a flowered chair—a chair that calls to mind the chair in Williams's book. In *The Everything Book,* Fleming was even able to include a silhouette of singer Lyle Lovett.

Part of Fleming's love for words comes from her mother, who loved language. She particularly likes arranging her words on the page—arranging them the "way they should be read."[6] Picture books give her the freedom to express story elements that she hasn't written with words.

When Fleming begins a book, she usually has only a rough idea of the story. With the story in the back of her mind, she begins to create sketches and then revises her text as the visuals develop.

Denise Fleming's artist husband, David Powers, and their daughter, Indigo, sometimes get involved in Fleming's work. Her husband often helps tote the pulp and large buckets of water to the vats where the pulp and color are mixed. He also assists with hand mixing the pulp and color and helps Fleming make the screens necessary for her painting process. Indigo often becomes the first reader of her mother's words, pictures, and ideas for a new book.

Denise Fleming says she loves to write and illustrate children's books. She is also very fond of cats, in fact, she lives with seven of them. The cats exist harmoniously with the one old and sometimes cranky dog, Warfy, who also lives with the family. Fleming especially enjoys the summertime, filled with her favorite foods: corn-on-the-cob, S'mores, tomatoes with basil, and her daughter Indigo's wonderful homemade lemonade. The family lives in Fleming's hometown, Toledo, Ohio, where they work together to design and plant gardens that attract wildlife and where Fleming and her husband build things including furniture, rooms, and hideaways.

## Book Connections

The first book created by Denise Fleming with the pulp painting technique was *In the Tall, Tall Grass.* Fleming chose strong vibrant colors to convey the mood and movement that she wanted present in the book. *In the Tall, Tall Grass* was widely acclaimed and was included on the American Library Association's Notable Book list. Another book that followed, *In the Small, Small Pond,* also received much acclaim and was named a 1994 Caldecott Honor Book.

Fleming creates her artwork at 130 percent of the size that she wants it to appear in the book. In most, if not all, of her books she puts in an animal or object that helps the reader determine the scale of the other objects and characters in the book. She has used, for example, a caterpillar, a frog, and an acorn.

Fleming creates her illustrative work in her studio, which is populated by a cockatoo that loves to sing and coo while Fleming makes paper. Once when Fleming was on a trip, her husband taught the bird to whistle, so now the cockatoo sings, coos, and even whistles while Fleming works.

# Books Written and Illustrated by Denise Fleming

*Alphabet Under Construction* (Henry Holt, 2002).

*Barnyard Banter* (Henry Holt, 1994).

*Buster* (Henry Holt, 2003).

*Count!* (Henry Holt, 1992).

*The Everything Book* (Henry Holt, 2000).

*In the Small, Small Pond* (Henry Holt, 1993).

*In the Tall, Tall Grass* (Henry Holt, 1991).

*Mama Cat Has Three Kittens* (Henry Holt, 1998).

*Pumpkin Eye* (Henry Holt, 2001).

*Time to Sleep* (Henry Holt, 1997).

*Where Once There Was a Wood* (Henry Holt, 1996).

# For More Information

## Books

Cumming, Pat, compiler. *Talking with Artists. Vol. 2: Conversations with Thomas B. Allen, Mary Jane Begin, Floyd Cooper, Julie Downing, Denise Fleming, Sheila Hamanaka, Kevin Henkes, William Joyce, Maira Kalman, Deborah Nourse Lattimore, Brian Pinkney, Vera B. Williams, and David Wisniewski.* New York: Simon & Schuster, 1995.

Fleming, Denise. *Maker of Things.* Illus. by Karen Bowers. Katonah, NY: Richard C. Owens, 2002.

## Web Sites

Baltimore County Public Library. *BCPL KidsPage Denise Fleming Papermaking.* March 2004. <http://www.bcplonline.org/kidspage/kids_flem_papermaking.html>.

Fleming, Denise. *Online Home of Children's Book Author/Illustrator Denise Fleming.* Nov. 2003. <http://www.denisefleming.com>.

# Notes

1. Denise Fleming, "In My Backyard," presentation at the Beginning Reading Conference, 12 Apr. 2002, Cedar Falls, University of Northern Iowa.

2. Ibid.

3. Ibid.

4. Ibid.

5. Ibid.

6. Denise Fleming, interview with the author, 12 Apr. 2002.

# Robert Florczak

◆ Folk literature ◆ Nature

**Washington, D.C.**
November 22, 1950

📖 *Birdsong*
📖 *The Rainbow Bridge*

## About the Illustrator

Before Robert Florczak was a painter he was a musician and recording artist. He hung out with his musician friends including Jeff Barry, Tom Jans, Nino Tempo, Jim Croce, Harry Nilsson, and Paul Williams. He performed in nightclubs and in concert halls from New York City to Aspen to Beverly Hills. For two years, he toured with Liverpool, a pre-Beatlemania musical review. While composing the soundtrack for the motion picture *Roar,* he lived—surrounded by over one hundred lions, tigers, leopards, cheetahs, and two elephants—on a one hundred acre private wildlife preserve on the African Savannah. Florczak performed the score for the motion picture in London with The National Philharmonic Orchestra and he also played in the video of the movie's title song. But this accomplished musician is also a talented visual artist and eventually he turned his full attention to painting.

Robert Florczak was born in Washington, D.C. and grew up in New Jersey with four younger brothers. After his early education, he earned an undergraduate degree in fine arts from the Cooper Union in New York City. At Cooper Union, he studied painting under Will Barnet and went on to become artist-in-residence at Widener University. Later he taught painting at the Art Institute of Philadelphia.

When Florczak was involved most heavily in the music industry he lived on the John Barrymore estate in Beverly Hills. But he always kept his interest in painting and throughout the past two decades he has enjoyed a successful career as a commercial artist. His work is in the private collections of Michael Jackson, Whoopi Goldberg, and Paul Allen, as well as in the collections of several corporations. Talk radio host and Jewish theologian Dennis Prager considers Florczak and his wife Amy among his best friends in southern California.

Florczak's art reflects his interest and love of historical drama and romance and his work is informed by his understanding of the classical paintings of the old masters. His paintings have been compared to those created by the artists of the Hudson River School.

For many years Florczak dealt with the commitments of a commercial artist. Those commitments kept him from accepting offers to illustrate a children's book. However, in 1980 he created the cover art for *The Sword and the Satchel* by Elizabeth Boyer (Ballantine, 1980). Despite many other invitations, he continued to concentrate on his painting until finally, in the early 1990s, Harcourt offered him an opportunity to illustrate *The Rainbow Bridge,* a book authored by Audrey Wood (Harcourt, 1995). That offer convinced Florczak to take the plunge because the book appealed to his interest in the historical and the imaginative. The contemporary retelling of a Chumash Indian legend allowed Florczak to authentically render depictions of the Native American Chumash tribe while visually portraying the storyline in a more mythic manner. Florczak and the author, Audrey Wood, actually traveled by boat to the Channel Islands off the coast of southern California where the story takes place. During their boat trip, they saw many dolphins, which are an important part of the story, and on the islands they were able to bring together images that were also part of the story. The two of them also researched images and facts in museums in the Santa Barbara area. Florczak hiked through Chumash country familiarizing himself with the terrain so that he could render the images of the area more authentically. Native Americans posed for him in his studio. Once he had thoroughly researched the land and people and immersed himself into the environment, Florczak began to create the oil paintings for the book. It took him two-and-a-half years to create 16 large oil paintings on canvas. Those paintings became the art for his first picture book, *The Rainbow Bridge.*

His second book, *Rough Sketch Beginning* by Jamaican poet James Berry (Harcourt, 1996), depicts an artist's thoughts and visions as he goes from sketch to painting. Florczak selected drawings from his personal sketchbooks to accompany Berry's poetic imaginings. A four-page gatefold painting brings the book to a stunning conclusion.

Florczak's third book was his second collaboration with Audrey Wood. *Birdsong* (Harcourt, 1977) identifies birds from across the United States. Florczak selected a horizontal format to provide an expansive panoramic view of each bird's environment. Borders and color schemes unique to each double-page spread add dimension and the effect of either sound or silence. In the borders of each scene, Florczak placed the state flowers that correspond to the bird depicted. He also incorporated Victorian design elements into the illustrations, which give the book a vintage look. Neighborhood children modeled for the illustrations of children throughout the book and many of their homes became the basis for the houses he painted. Florczak used the locations and architecture of homes in his neighborhood as well as houses he had sketched and observed during his many travels. His research on the birds and their habitat took him to several Museums of Natural History and the Los Angeles Audubon Society. It took Florczak a year to finish the paintings for this book.

Florczak went on to illustrate several other books including other titles by Audrey Wood. His realistic and majestic paintings for Shirley Climo's *The Persian Cinderella* (HarperCollins, 1999) feature rich images from an ornately beautiful land. Framed in detailed borders, the text is Climo's fourth retelling of a cultural version of the Cinderella tale. Florczak's extensive research helped him to authentically portray the exotic botanical flowers and trees in the Middle East with stunningly realistic, exotic, and beautiful illustrations.

Another title, *The Magic Fish-Bone* (Harcourt, 2000), was authored by one of his heroes—Charles Dickens. Florczak says, "it includes some of my best work in picture books."[1] As serious as Florczak seems to be about his art, he is not above having a little fun with his illustrations. In *The Magic Fish-Bone* alert observers will find depictions of his two children, Lukas and Lily, included in the illustrations. In some of his other books, he slips in an illustration from a previous book, often as a picture hanging on the wall.

Robert Florczak has illustrated a wide variety of books from folklore to tales of the wild west such as *A Cowboy Christmas: The Miracle at Lone Pine Ridge* (Simon & Schuster, 2001). He is a musician, a performer, an artist, and an illustrator. His interests are as varied as his talents. At six-foot-five inches tall, his favorite pastime was once basketball. Now his favorite things include: Deli food, Italian, and seafood; Abyssinian cats; and the color forest green. Florczak and his wife Amy live in southern California with their son, Lukas (1994), and their daughter, Lily (1999).

## Book Connections

Robert Florczak's illustrative technique has been compared to that of the pre-Raphaelites—grand and majestic. He uses light and shadows to cast a magical aura over his slightly surreal oil paintings. Florczak paints with oil, layering translucent glazes one on top of the other. Each of his illustrations show realistic details especially his depictions of the plants and flowers that are native to each setting. His illustrations add to the narrative information in each book. For example, in *Birdsong* he not only depicted the birds in a very accurate manner but also placed indigenous flowers and animals in the background frames. In *The Persian Cinderella* some of the most stunning illustrations are the beautiful Pomegranate trees and the many flowers, including the Jasmine flower. *The Magic Fish-Bone* shows a blend of romanticism and contemporary influence. Silhouettes definitely give the illustrations the contemporary flare while his depiction of a Victorian-era family set against detailed backgrounds demonstrates the romantic influence. This interpretation of a classic folktale is as softly colored as the early nursery rhymes of the 1880s.

## Books Illustrated by Robert Florczak

*Birdsong.* Written by Audrey Wood. (Harcourt, 1997).

*A Cowboy Christmas: The Miracle at Lone Pine Ridge.* Written by Audrey Wood. (Simon & Schuster, 2000).

*The Magic Fish-Bone.* Written by Charles Dickens. (Harcourt, 2000).

*The Persian Cinderella.* Written by Shirley Climo. (HarperCollins, 1999).

*The Rainbow Bridge.* Written by Audrey Wood. (Harcourt, 1995).

*Rough Sketch Beginning.* Written by James Berry. (Harcourt, 1996).

*Yikes!* Written by Robert Florczak. (Blue Sky Press, 2003).

# For More Information

## Web Sites

Florczak, Robert. *Welcome to Robert Florczak.com.* March 2004. <http://www. robertflorczak.com>.

Wood, Audrey. "Florczak." *Children's Book Authors and Illustrators Don and Audrey Wood's Clubhouse.* March 2004. <http://www.audreywood.com/mac_ site/friends_clubhouse/florczak/florczak_page/florczak.htm>.

# Note

1.  Robert Florczak, interview with the author, 26 Sept. 2002.

# Debra Frasier

◆ Nature ◆ Word play/visual play

**Vero Beach, Florida**
April 3, 1953

📖 *Miss Alaineus: A Vocabulary Disaster*

📖 *On the Day You Were Born*

📖 *Out of the Ocean*

## About the Author/Illustrator

For generations, Vero Beach, Florida has been home to Debra Frasier and her family who came before her. Her great-grandfather helped to survey the original streets in the early 1920s and her grandmother taught school in Vero—rowing a boat to a one-room school on an island every Monday morning and returning by boat on Friday evening. Debra Frasier's mother was born in Vero and that is where Debra was born and where she attended school.

When Debra was just five years old her parents bought a strip of beachfront along the Atlantic Ocean, near her grandmother's old school house, and set about building a home from salvaged lumber. This is where Debra and her brother grew up. After returning home from school—they were the last bus stop—the two of them would often go down to the beach. Debra, her brother, and two stepsisters, spent hours and days swimming in the ocean and exploring the beach. They often found treasures to collect, which Debra often transformed into pieces of art. When she was eight years old she found a driftwood piece of packing crate that had Japanese writing on it. At that moment she felt a connection with someone from Japan—someone from a faraway place. Her life had suddenly expanded beyond her horizon and extended across the ocean and beyond.

Sometimes Debra's mother went along on those beach excursions. Together they searched for interesting things on the beach and they sometimes sent messages in bottles. Interestingly, 28 years later, a man found one of those messages and contacted Debra's mother, who was still living in the family's home on the beachfront. Many of the projects Debra made from her treasures were influenced by the fact that her mother was a "scrapbook person."[1] That influence can still be seen in Frasier's artwork.

**94**

Once Debra completed high school, she entered Florida State University where, in 1976, she earned an undergraduate degree in design. She continued on to attend the Penland School of Crafts in North Carolina where she learned to make large scale costume puppets—some as long as 60 feet, requiring 8 people to make them move. Later she used those skills to create large wind sculptures of sailcloth framed with steel cables and Debra was awarded several commissions from various cities to build these sculptures. One project, Windwalk Environment, was installed in Pittsburgh and consisted of thousands of cloth strips mounted on cables so that they would swing in the breeze along a planned route. Those walking through Windwalk Environment could also stop and pick up writings about wind written by Pittsburgh students or quotes found by Debra. The project was a successful melding of her artistic vision and the printed words.

Up to this time Debra had not really thought about writing a book even though her friends, who were often the recipients of one of her letters, often questioned her about why she did not write books.

By 1984, Debra Frasier married photographer James Henkel and the couple established their home in Minneapolis, Minnesota. For Frasier, the change was drastic. First of all, the climate was much colder in the Midwest. She had to learn about snow shovels, boots, and all sorts of related snow items. Snowflakes brought a new experience to Frasier, who also came to appreciate the warmth of wood burning in the fireplace. She missed the palm trees and more tropical climate of the South, so she returned often to visit.

Frasier concentrated on her career as a freelance artist until her daughter, Calla, was about to be born. Because of health issues during the end of her pregnancy, Frasier had to limit her activities and she even had to be hospitalized for a time. While she was in the hospital, she began to write down all the things on our earth that would welcome her baby daughter. After Calla was born in 1988 Frasier turned her collection of words and scribbled drawings into the book that became *On the Day You Were Born* (Harcourt, 1991).

Frasier was not looking specifically to publish the book but a friend, Bart Schneider, who was in her studio one day happened to see some of the illustrations that she was creating. He asked if he could use some of them in the *Hungry Mind Review,* an online news tabloid published by a bookstore in St. Paul, Minnesota. The publication of her art caught the attention of an editor at Harcourt. It was not long after that Frasier was offered a contract and began working with editor Allyn Johnston to polish and revise the text and its accompanying illustrations into the book, *On the Day You Were Born.* The book was published in March of 1991; it had taken a little over three years from beginning concept to published book.

A second book, *Out of the Ocean* (Harcourt, 1998), took a full five years to complete. First, Frasier gathered the photographs that she used to help make the collages in the book. She managed to drop two cameras into the ocean while taking photographs of the rising sun, waves, pelicans, and other ocean views. The last entry in the "Ocean Journey" section of *Out of the Ocean* was completed on April 25, 1995—the day her mother called to tell her that a buyer had been found to buy the family's house in Vero Beach.

After several more books dealing with nature and our respect for the world around us, Frasier turned to writing a humorous book. One day her daughter, Calla, who was nine years old at the time said, "Mom, today I figured out that Miss Alanieus is not a person."[2] That comment made it's way into Frasier's journal and was the beginning for her next book, *Miss Alaineus: A Vocabulary Disaster* (Harcourt, 2000). *Miss Alaineus* is a humorous look at the process of learning the meaning of new words and includes a vocabulary parade with the character Sage as "Miss Alaineus, Queen of all Miscellaneous Things." Next year Sage declares she will be "Miss Sterious, Investigator of All Things Mysterious!"[3] A couple of years later Frasier revived the characters from *Miss Alaineus* to make a play about water in *The Incredible Water Show* (Harcourt, 2004). The illustrations she created for this book include many water bubbles outlined with a blue marker. Frasier used up eight blue markers before she finished the illustrations and was left with eight boxes of new markers all of which were missing the blue marker.

Frasier "captures ideas for books in a tiny little journal" that she carries around wherever she goes.[4] Her art and her writing have always been project oriented and while her daughter is at school, Frasier works on her illustrations. Usually the writing is done early in the morning and the art comes later in the day. There's also the business side of being a freelance writer and illustrator. Frasier must plan and organize, spend time with her journal, respond to letters and business agreements, and design her Web site, which helps others learn about her work and the activities that naturally stem from the books and their content.

Debra Frasier divides her time between her own family homes in Minneapolis and Vero Beach. In Minnesota she has a new studio on the third floor of a large brick building in St. Paul, just over the line from Minneapolis. During the school year Frasier lives in Florida where Calla attends school. At times, the family will "slip away to the mountains of North Carolina."[5] Meanwhile, wherever Frasier is, she has her "tiny little journal," ready to catch yet another book idea.

## Book Connections

Frasier uses a collage technique to create illustrations. Interspersed throughout most of her work are photographs that she has taken with a simple point and shoot hand-held 35 mm camera. The film is then developed commercially and Frasier cuts and manipulates the photographic images among other items and objects she finds such as shells and driftwood. Her first book developed from three pages of sketches that she made while she was confined to her hospital bed during her pregnancy. Later, after her daughter's birth, she was able to parlay those sketches into *On the Day You Were Born,* which, in just three months, became third on the *Publisher's Weekly*'s children's bestsellers list. In the first 10 years of its publication, the book sold over a million copies and The Heart of the Beast Puppet and Mask Theatre in Minneapolis developed the text and illustrations into a play. More than 30,000 children and adults saw the play during a yearlong tour. In 1995 the Minnesota Orchestra commissioned a symphony based on Frasier's book.

To celebrate the book's tenth anniversary, Harcourt published a companion book, *On the Day You Were Born: A Photo Journal* (Harcourt, 2001). The journal was based on the original book but it allowed parents to record information about the day of a child's birth. Harcourt publishers and Frasier have also developed dozens of curricular-related activities to accompany each of her books.

## Books Written and Illustrated by Debra Frasier

*The Incredible Water Show* (Harcourt, 2004).

*Miss Alaineus: A Vocabulary Disaster* (Harcourt, 2000).

*On the Day You Were Born* (Harcourt, 1991).

*Out of the Ocean* (Harcourt, 1998).

## Books Illustrated by Debra Frasier

*In the Space of the Sky.* Written by Richard Lewis. (Harcourt, 2002).

## For More Information

### Articles

Stan, Susan. "New Textures in Children's Book Art: Connecting Cultures Using Collage." *Publishers Weekly* 239.9 (15 Feb. 1991): 61–64.

### Web Sites

Frasier, Debra. *FrasierBooks.Com.* March 2004. <http://www.frasierbooks.com> or <http://www.debrafrasier.com>.

## Notes

1. Debra Frasier, interview with the author, 5 May 2002.
2. Ibid.
3. Quoted from the book *Miss Alaineus: A Vocabulary Disaster* (San Diego, CA: Harcourt, 2000), n. pag.
4. Frasier, interview.
5. Debra Frasier, letter to the author, 14 June 2002.

# Barbara Diamond Goldin

◆  Folk literature  ◆  Historical fiction

**New York, New York**
October 4, 1946

📖  *A Mountain of Blintzes*

📖  *Cakes and Miracles*

📖  *Fire! The Beginnings of the Labor Movement*

## About the Author

Barbara Diamond was born in New York City on October 4, 1946 and soon became the big sister to two younger brothers: Robert and Bert. Their father often found places for the children to explore—even in the city. Railroad workers, who tended gardens in the middle of New York City in their spare time, allowed the Diamond family to pick produce and they carried large brown bags of radishes, tomatoes, and cucumbers home to their fifth floor apartment. Sometimes the family went to upstate New York to pick blackberries and explore the woods.

Barbara's father enjoyed writing and he occasionally wrote poems and stories before and after the children were born. Their mother read a lot of books to the children and whenever Barbara encountered a problem while she was learning to read, her mother helped by teaching her the alphabet, phonics, and how to blend the sounds. Because of this, Barbara learned to read better and to love books and stories.

When Barbara was eight, the family moved to Philadelphia where her father had obtained a new job. She was in third grade and entered the new school midyear. All that year Barbara felt different—she was the new kid. Reading books helped her deal with the change and a move to a new neighborhood brought her new friends and plenty of others to play with. Barbara's dad still enjoyed exploring with the children but now they found new discoveries in the Amish communities that filled the Pennsylvania Dutch countryside. Barbara continued to read any book she could get her hands on and enjoyed writing: writing in a journal, writing letters, and researching topics that she was interested in.

The Diamond family was very active in their small synagogue where all the families knew one another and the children attended after-school Hebrew classes. When her grandfather made his first visit to their new home in Philadelphia, Barbara made a gift for him. It was a book of Hebrew words and she was very proud of it. Barbara did not understand why he wasn't very interested in her gift.

In 1968 Barbara Diamond entered the University of Chicago and obtained her undergraduate degree in psychology. The same year she married her high school sweetheart, Alan Goldin. Together, they traveled in Europe and Canada during the summers and taught during the school year in the Gloucester, Massachusetts's area. Later, Goldin took additional courses to earn a teaching certificate from Boston University and a Montessori certificate. She also did some work in school library media at Western Washington University.

After living in Massachusetts, the couple traveled to Montana where Alan studied forestry. Alan stayed in Montana while Goldin spent a year in Michigan and Ohio where she earned her Montessori teaching certificate from the American Montessori Society. She then returned to Montana where she opened a Montessori preschool and a bookstore, which she owned with a friend. Soon, though, the couple moved again, this time to Washington state where Goldin worked as a children's librarian and taught preschool on an Indian reservation. When she taught preschool, she told a lot of stories.

"I really began as a storyteller—first when I babysat, and later when I taught preschool. I loved making up my own stories and telling them to children."[1] However, whenever Goldin was asked to tell the story again she found that she could not remember it. She realized that she would have to write the stories down.

After a move within Washington state, Goldin volunteered in a Head Start program but she started searching for stories as well and drew her ideas from everywhere. She began her writing in earnest while living in Bellingham. One of her first stories developed from that childhood incident with the Hebrew notebook that she gave to her grandfather Joe when she was just nine. Her grandfather spoke Yiddish so when Goldin presented him with the notebook of Hebrew words, he did not react the way she thought he would because he could not understand it. That became the basis for one of her first published stories, "Ketsele's Gift," published in the April 1989 issue of *Cricket Magazine*. Writing that story gave Goldin an opportunity to have the little girl create a notebook of Yiddish words. With this new notebook, the story could have a different ending than the one that Goldin actually experienced.

The stories Goldin writes often are inspired by her family or the experiences she has had living in various parts of the country. She says, "my books that took place in Eastern Europe, such as *Just Enough Is Plenty* [Viking, 1988] and *Cakes and Miracles* [Viking, 1991], were inspired by my grandparents who came from the Old Country." Goldin wanted to learn more about her grandparents lives in Russia and Poland so, because they were no longer living, she turned to memoirs to find out about life in those areas during the time her grandparents would have lived there. The setting for *A Mountain of Blintzes* (Harcourt, 2001) is the Catskill Mountains where her father was born. "All the names in the book are the names of people in my father's family. I have fun that way putting in the names of people I know into my books." Goldin has pictures of the farmhouse where her father was born—pictures that were taken when her family revisited his birthplace during her teenage years. She was able to give that information through her editor to the illustrator, Anik McGory, and McGory was able to base her drawings of the town in the book on the little town, Liberty, New York, which was close to Goldin's father's farmhouse. "Anik McGrory drew wonderful characters in this humorous tale about a family that tries to save up money for a special holiday meal. I especially love the chickens that fly about the farmyard. The story is funny and lively and there's a good moral as well!"[2]

*Fire! The Beginnings of the Labor Movement* (Viking, 1992) was inspired by Goldin's mother's father, who had worked in the garment district. In this story, Goldin writes about the Triangle Factory Fire in the Lower East Side that took place in a shirt-waist factory. Goldin's mother grew up in that neighborhood but to make sure she had the names of the streets correct and other information accurate Goldin went to the Lower East Side to check for herself.

Since childhood Barbara has been fascinated with stories of Elijah. "Every year at Passover we would open the door for the Prophet and watch to see if the wine in his glass lowered."[3] She found hope in the stories about Elijah—a person who helped people in times of trouble. Her fascination with the stories is part of the reason she wrote another book—*Journeys with Elijah: Eight Tales of the Prophet* (Harcourt, 1999). Elijah was a hero, sacred figure, and mystery man all rolled into one and there are hundreds of stories about him. For her collection Goldin was able to choose just eight of these stories. Goldin has written many books during her writing career and many of them are Jewish stories or legends. For that body of work, she was awarded the Sydney Taylor Body-of-Work Award from the Association of Jewish Libraries.

Although many of Goldin's books are inspired by her family, others come from her experiences. She lived in the northwest for 14 years and became fascinated with Native American life. She volunteered on the Lummi Indian Reservation and told stories to the children who were in the Head Start program. In searching for stories to tell the children Goldin was able to identify two stories that she wanted to write: *Coyote and the Fire Stick* (Harcourt, 1996) and *The Girl Who Lived With the Bears* (Gulliver, 1997). "Some of my books are original stories like *Just Enough Is Plenty* [Viking, 1988] and some are retellings of wonderful stories that I find elsewhere than in my own imagination. But then I get to rework them and add my own imagination to them."[4] During the early days of Goldin's writing career, she took classes in writing books for children at Western Washington University. That was about the same time that her daughter, Josee, was born so Goldin planned her writing times around Josee's nap times. As Josee grew older, Goldin took more writing courses. One of those courses was with Jane Yolen, a writer whose work Goldin had long admired. Yolen gave practical advice and taught the group how to critique each other's writing. Goldin met regularly with a supportive group of people. One of the other members of the group was Nancy White Carlstrom, who became a very good friend of Goldin's.

In addition to her job as a children's librarian, Goldin conducts writing workshops and speaks about being a writer to school and library groups all over the country. She often talks about her book *Fire! The Beginnings of the Labor Movement.* The book is "historical fiction about a girl named Rosie whose sister works in the garment factory where the fire takes place." Goldin says "students find the book very exciting. Maybe it's the fire that draws their attention and the drama around that. But the students also learn a lot of history and the way people lived in the early part of the 1900s."[5]

After living in the northwest for 14 years, Barbara and Alan Goldin moved back east to Northampton, Massachusetts. Alan eventually moved yet again with another job but Barbara stayed in Northampton, teaching preschool and working as a children's librarian. Her children, Josee (1980) and Jeremy (1982), are grown now and entering their own careers. Goldin continues to write. Her life is filled with her favorite things with books and stories at the top of the list. Among her favorite foods is a "hamburger with barbecue

Hello!

Reading was so important to me growing up. My 4th grade teacher Mrs. Clombeau had a wonderful little classroom library + that is where I started to read for fun + to lose myself in books. Trips to the library, especially weekly ones in the summer, meant lots of books to lose myself in. I loved Enid Blyton's <u>Castle of Adventure</u>, <u>Ship of Adventure</u>, etc. Now I'm the children's librarian in a small public library. So many have changed so much. Videos, CD Rom games. Computers. But that set of Enid Blyton's adventure books are still on the shelf — even here in Easthampton, MA + so are lots of other books filled with fantasy, reality, faraway places, people dealing with too-close problems, biographies, history, jokes, sports.

And I still lose myself in books + write them too!

Happy reading!

Barbara Steward Yolden

sauce, lettuce, tomato, and onion on a yummy bun." She also likes "Chinese food—all kinds, or a good seafood meal served on the beach."[6]

## Book Connections

Barbara Diamond Goldin has written picture books with original holiday stories and has also collected stories for older readers. She has retold Native American legends, Jewish tales, and explored Jewish customs and traditions. Goldin usually works on more than one project at a time so often on her desk will be, in various stages of publication, several picture books and perhaps a novel or two.

## Books Written by Barbara Diamond Goldin

*Cakes and Miracles: A Purim Tale.* Illustrated by Erika Weihs. (Viking, 1991).

*Coyote and the Fires Stick: A Pacific Northwest Indian Tale.* Illustrated by Will Hellenbrand. (Harcourt, 1996).

*Fire! The Beginnings of the Labor Movement.* Illustrated by James Watling. (Viking, 1992).

*The Girl Who Lived with the Bears.* Illustrated by Andrew Plewes. (Gulliver Books, 1997).

*Just Enough Is Plenty: A Hanukkah Tale.* Illustrated by Seymour Chwast. (Viking, 1988).

*A Mountain of Blintzes.* Illustrated by Anik McGrory. (Harcourt, 2001).

*Night Lights: A Sukkot Story.* Illustrated by Laura Elizabeth Sucher. (Union of American Hebrew Congregations, 2002).

*Red Means Good Fortune: A Story of San Francisco's Chinatown.* Illustrated by Wenhai Ma. (Viking, 1994).

## For More Information

### Articles

Stan, Susan. "New Textures in Children's Book Art: Connecting Cultures Using Collage." *Publishers Weekly* 239.9 (15 Feb. 1991): 61–64.

### Web Sites

Goldin, Barbara Diamond. *Barbara Diamond Goldin: Children's Author.* March 2004. <http://www.barbaradiamondgoldin.com>.

# Notes

1. Barbara Diamond Goldin, letter to the author, 15 Oct. 2002.
2. Ibid.
3. Ibid.
4. Ibid.
5. Ibid.
6. Ibid.

# Matthew Gollub

◆ Animals ◆ Poetry ◆ Word play/visual play

**Los Angeles, California**
September 29, 1960

📖 *Cool Melons—Turn to Frogs!*
📖 *Gobble, Quack, Moon*
📖 *The Jazz Fly*

## About the Author

Matthew Gollub is one of those rare authors who seems to have broken all the rules of conventional publishing. In the early years of children's books, authors and illustrators submitted their work to a publisher as a unit but that is certainly not the way it is generally done today. Today an author is asked to submit their manuscript and then if the publisher wishes to publish the manuscript the art director at the publishing house selects the artist to create the illustrations for the book. Sometimes the author and illustrator never meet and if they do it is after the book has been published. Gollub's first book, however, was created in collaboration with a famous Mexican artist after they met while Gollub was on a trip to Mexico.

Another convention that Gollub successfully changed is the taboo against self-publishing. Not only does self-publishing demand a substantial cash outlay but also the marketing is very difficult. In addition, it is not easy to get a self-published book reviewed in the major publications such as *Publisher's Weekly*. However, when Gollub submitted his book, *The Jazz Fly* (Tortuga Press, 2000), to publishers they were interested but did not want to include a CD, which Gollub thought was important to the book. In fact, it was so important to him that he decided to start his own publishing house to produce the book with a CD. He established Tortuga Press and promptly published *The Jazz Fly,* which became a success.

Matthew Gollub was born in Culver City, California, near Los Angles on September 29, 1960. His father, Irving Gollub, was an accountant but he passed away when Matthew was only 10. Matthew's mother, Lorraine Gollub, raised Matthew and his two older sisters. His mother was an attorney who specialized in family law. Matthew says he was not particularly bookish but by the time he was in fifth grade he knew he wanted to be a writer. One of his teachers took the time to type stories written by each member of the class and make the collection of stories into a book for each student. Others found Matthew's story humorous and the young author enjoyed the attention. "I liked writing silly stories, the more outrageous the better. I had discovered the joy of eliciting guffaws from my peers and next to shooting baskets on the playground, writing was the activity for me."[1]

Because he grew up in the Los Angeles area, Matthew was able to listen to jazz radio stations 24 hours a day and he often went to sleep with his radio playing jazz. He soon found rhythm as a drummer in the school band where he played a snare drum, then a bass drum, and finally the crash cymbals.

After Matthew finished ninth grade, he had an opportunity to spend the summer with a family in Quito, Ecuador. During that summer he spoke Spanish, traveled to the Galápagos Islands, and took bus trips into the jungle. These experiences sparked his interest in travel and other cultures.

When Matthew was 17 he entered the University of the Pacific. Sophomores at the university were encouraged to study abroad and Matthew assumed he would study in a Latin American country. But then he met some students who had just returned from their year in Japan and he discovered that he could actually spend one semester living and working with a group of Japanese drummers. He would have to learn to play the Japanese barrel-shaped drum, the *taiko*. That sounded very interesting to Matthew and he was undaunted by the fact that the other players would only speak Japanese. He immediately enrolled in a beginning Japanese course and his morning jogs began to include the chanting of Japanese numbers: ichi, ni, san, shi, and so forth.

Gollub's year in Japan influenced him to major in international studies and the Japanese language. He says, "throughout high school and college, I assumed that I would be a journalist."[2] After graduation he applied for an English-language newspaper job but when he found out that he would have to spend the first six months working as a proofreader, he withdrew his application. He then talked his way into a job as a copywriter for an advertising company where he translated operation manuals for toaster ovens and tractor ball bearings. He also, eventually, worked as a newscaster and even toured with the same drumming troupe he had toured with as a student.

All of Gollub's translation experience eventually helped him in his career as a children's book author. He says:

> I credit my nieces and nephews piquing my interest [in writing children's books]. My two nephews [now teenagers] used to tie on pillowcases as capes and leap off their bunk beds while dramatizing stories that I'd make up for them on the spot. Often, these stories were set in distant counties where I had traveled. My nieces, who live in Florida, once walked with me through a redwood forest not far from my home in northern California. Every time we came to the burnt out hollow of a tree trunk, we'd duck inside and think up a story. We'd then use a pen to scratch a few words from each story onto fallen leaves. To their minds, we were writing books and, in a sense, we were. By the time my own son was born, I had published several books and was very keen to delve deeper into children's literature.[3]

When Matthew Gollub met the Mexican artist, Leovigildo Martinez, in 1990, they formed a collaborative partnership that produced illustrated tales based on folk stories from Martinez's native Oaxaca, Mexico. Publishers referred to their books as picture books—that is, says Gollub, "when we realized we had entered the field of children's literature."[4] The pair was able to publish three books with William Morrow Publishers, then Gollub teamed up with illustrator Kazuko Stone and produced two more books.

By this time, Gollub was an established author and decided to submit a manuscript for a sixth book, *The Jazz Fly*. This book was written in response to his concern for immigrant children who are faced with the challenges of understanding a second language and with his frustration with lawmakers who think that it is a good idea to create an

English-only law in the United States. *The Jazz Fly* was a way for him to present the idea that learning to speak more than one language is advantageous. Gollub dedicated the book to "children who have learned to speak a second language."[5]

Matthew Gollub is a successful writer and publisher. He, his wife, and son live in Santa Rosa, California, which is also the home of his publishing house, Tortuga Press. Among Gollub's favorite foods are sushi, Indian food, and gourmet veggie burgers. Other favorites include green, the corporate color of his publishing company, and of course, jazz.

## Book Connections

Matthew Gollub's first three books were created with Mexican artist, Leovigildo Martinez, and his next two with illustrator, Kazuko Stone. One of the books created with Stone was *Ten Oni Drummers* (Lee and Low Books, 2000), which had it's start with those Japanese numbers Gollub recited during his early morning jogs. His years spent in Japan as a translator contributed to his efforts to translate haiku by a Japanese poet and to tell that poet's life story. The picture book, *Cool Melons—Turn to Frogs!* (Lee & Low Books, 1998) was the result of those efforts.

By 1997 Gollub had launched Tortuga Press in order to publish *The Jazz Fly* with a companion CD. He worked with a first time artist, Karen Hanke, who as Gollub said, "directed herself. [She] not only illustrated my intent but added scores of her own tasty embellishments filling out the nightclub, the jazz bugs' costumes, the design of the CD, even the endpapers."[6] Gollub gives Hanke credit for the inspiration to present the animal characters for *The Jazz Fly* in black and white and to use color sparingly. As a result of this technique, a review in *School Library Journal* mentioned that the book had a feel of jazz. That comment gratified Gollub because he felt the reviewer actually understood their intent—and their efforts.

*The Jazz Fly* was honored with a Benjamin Franklin Award and was given the Writer's Digest national Self-Published Book Award. Since that time Gollub has continued to publish books and audio CD packages that present his stories with music and drama. Matthew Gollub says:

> All my books are based in some way on my life experiences—traveling in Mexico, playing taiko drums in Japan, and so forth. But one major occurrence in my childhood, I think, gave me the sensitivity to write *Cool Melons—Turn to Frogs!* My father, to whom I felt very close, passed away. With this early encounter with life's fragility, I felt empathy with the poet Issa and the incredible sadness he endured. Every insect, flower, bird and human being is a miracle and a wonder, which, in the end cannot last. That was Issa's perspective that I tried to weave throughout the book.[7]

## Books Written by Matthew Gollub

*The Baby Chronicles* (Tortuga Press, 2003).

*Cool Melons—Turn to Frogs! The Life and Poems of Issa.* Illustrated by Kazuko G. Stone. (Lee & Low Books, 1998).

*Gobble, Quack, Moon.* Illustrated by Judy Love. Book and CD. (Tortuga Press, 2002).

*The Jazz Fly: Starring the Jazz Bugs, The Jazz Fly, Willie the Worm, Nancy the Gnat, Sammy the Centipede.* Illustrated by Karen Hanke. Book and CD. (Tortuga Press, 2000).

*Jazz Fly 2* (Tortuga Press, 2004).

*The Moon Was at a Fiesta.* Illustrated by Leovigildo Martinez. (Tambourine Books, 1994; Rev. ed. Tortuga Press, 1998).

*The Phantom Musician* (Tortuga Press, 2004).

*Ten Oni Drummers.* Illustrated by Kazuko Stone. (Lee & Low Books, 2000).

*The Twenty-Five Mixtec Cats.* Illustrated by Leovigildo Martinez. (Tambourine Books, 1993); *Les Veinticinco Gatos Mixtecos* (Tortuga Press, 1997).

*Uncle Snake.* Illustrated by Leovigildo Martinez. (Tortuga Press, 1996); *Tio Culebra* (Tortuga Press, 2002).

## For More Information

### Articles

Templeton, David. "Speaking in Tongues: Author and Publisher Matthew Gollub Introduces Kids to a Wide World of Culture." *The Sonoma County Independent* (13–19 Apr. 2000): 20–21.

### Web Sites

Gollub, Matthew. *Meet Matthew Gollub: Trilingual Story Performer and Children's Book Author.* June 2003. <http://www.matthewgollub.com>.

## Notes

1. Matthew Gollub, interview with the author, 7 Sept. 2002.
2. Ibid.
3. Ibid.
4. Ibid.
5. Matthew Gollub, *The Jazz Fly* (Santa Rosa, CA: Tortuga Press, 2002): verso of title page.
6. Gollub, interview.
7. Ibid.

# Dan Gutman

◆ Fantasy ◆ Historical fiction ◆ Sports fiction

**New York, New York**
October 19, 1955

### Baseball Card Adventure Series

📖 *Honus & Me*

📖 *Mickey & Me*

📖 *The Million Dollar Shot*

## About the Author

Dan Gutman's writing career began in 1978 but he did not begin writing books for young readers until 1993. In the past decade, he has become well known to intermediate-aged readers as the author of exciting sports stories that intertwine fact with fiction. Today's readers turn to his books for fast-paced, interesting stories laced with sports action and sports heroes. Some readers have even discovered valuable hints for sports success within the pages of his books. For example, while writing *The Million Dollar Shot* (Hyperion, 1997) Gutman interviewed Dr. Tom Amberry, the all-time free-throw champion. Amberry was able to sink a basketball in 2,750 attempts without any misses. So in *The Million Dollar Shot,* Gutman, through one of his characters, tells readers Amberry's secret of successful free throw shooting. But Gutman does not always write sports books and when he was growing up, he didn't even think about becoming a writer. In fact, he had set his goal on being a photographer.

Dan Gutman was born in New York City but he grew up in Newark, New Jersey, where he enjoyed playing Little League baseball. His mother raised him and his older sister, Lucy, after his father abandoned the family when Dan was 12 years old. Of his childhood, Dan says, "it was pretty uneventful until June 1, 1968, when I came home . . . and found that my dad had suddenly abandoned my mom, my sister Lucy, and me. It was pretty traumatic, as you can imagine, but we all survived."[1]

As a child, Dan did not like to read and wasn't very good at it. But his mom bought him comic books and *Mad Magazine* and in the fourth and fifth grades, he found he liked sports books. It was those books that got him to read.

Perhaps it was his father's abrupt departure and Dan's efforts to understand the reasons why that led him to study psychology. After high school, Dan entered Rutgers

**109**

University in New Brunswick, New Jersey, where in 1977 he graduated with a degree in psychology. He entered graduate school and languished there for a few years before realizing that psychology was not what he wanted to do. He decided that he wanted to be a writer. He wanted to write humor—to be entertaining in the same way Erma Bombeck and Art Buchwald entertained their readers. Gutman did manage to get some articles published and he framed the first $15 check he received and hung it over his writing desk. He also did some photography work and published a few of his photographs. He wrote articles and screenplays and received hundreds of rejection letters. He also wrote a few adult books and in 1982 he started a video game magazine, *Video Games Player,* which was later renamed *Computer Games.* Gutman needed an artist to draw some illustrations for the magazine so he hired illustrator Nina Wallace. Not only did Nina turn out to be a good employee but Dan liked her enough to ask her to marry him and in 1983 Dan Gutman and Nina Wallace were married. The magazine survived for two more years but in 1985 it went out of business. By then, Gutman had established a reputation as a computer expert and he began to write articles about computers. He says he really wasn't an expert with computers but his resume included his time with *Computer Games* magazine and that was enough to convince others to give his computer articles a try.

Eventually, Gutman began to stretch out into other topics and he sold many articles to different magazines. It wasn't until he tried his hand at writing about sports that he began to come close to knowing what he really wanted to write about. His first sports book, *It Ain't Cheatin' If You Don't Get Caught* (Penguin, 1990), was about baseball and for adults, not children. None of Gutman's adult books were big sellers but he wrote a few more before he thought about writing for children. He says, "my son was born in 1990, and suddenly I was reading a lot of children's books. My career writing for grownups was going nowhere, so I decided to give children's books a try."[2]

Gutman turned to writing children's books in 1993 and has been going full steam ahead since that time. His first children's book, *Baseball's Biggest Bloopers* (Viking Children's Books, 1993), detailed a dozen of the most dramatic mistakes made in baseball history. Soon after he wrote the book, *Baseball's Greatest Games* (Viking Children's Books, 1994), which he calls "my best non-fiction baseball book for kids."[3]

Gutman set out to be a different kind of writer for young readers because he wanted to be sensitive to children who are reluctant to read In an effort to appeal to that group of readers, he consciously moves his books along with fast paced dialogue and action. He wants to write books that children want to read. One of his most popular titles, *The Million Dollar Shot,* has a main character that Gutman says is "basically me as a child. I always wanted to be a great shooter. I could throw Frisbees and bowl but I could not play basketball."[4]

Dan Gutman is a prolific author. He has written more that 42 books, both fiction and nonfiction, most of them for young readers, and many of them involving sports in some way. He has written several books detailing the greatest baseball games, the biggest bloopers, and so forth. In one book he even had a group of aliens visit earth and demand to be taught the game of baseball. That book, *They Came From Centerfield* (Scholastic, 1995), was a great success. Gutman says he wanted to write something similar to the books written by Matt Christopher—only wackier. Most readers who read *They Came From Centerfield* would agree that he succeeded.

Almost any incident might give Gutman an idea for a book. An article in the *New York Times* about Vicki Van Meter, a 12 year old who was about to fly a plane across the

Atlantic Ocean, sent Gutman on a mission to interview her and write a book about the event. *Taking Flight* (Viking Children's Books, 1995) wasn't very successful but Gutman was undaunted. After reading about the attack on Nancy Kerrigan on January 6, 1994, he turned his attention to ice skating and wrote a book about the sport. He even interviewed Tara Lipinski, who later became an Olympic star.

One of Gutman's most popular series began with *Honus & Me* (Avon, 1997). In this story, a boy is cleaning out an older woman's attic and finds a very valuable baseball card—a 1909 Honus T. Wagner T-206. The card has the power to transport him back to 1909 where he meets Honus and has a great adventure. Gutman submitted the manuscript to seven publishers and all of them liked the premise of the book but managed to find fault with the logic and credibility of the story. Nonetheless, Gutman had faith in the book and continued to send the manuscript to publishers. Finally HarperCollins offered a contract and the book became very popular. It was nominated for 11 state children's choice awards and reviewers gave the book many positive reviews.

*Honus & Me* was so popular that Gutman's editor suggested he might want to write another time travel book using the baseball card concept. He wrote a second book, *Jackie & Me* (Avon, 1999), featuring Jackie Robinson during his rookie season with the Brooklyn Dodgers in 1947. The next book in the series, *Babe & Me* (HarperCollins, 2000), took the main character, Joe, back to 1932 where he observes for himself whether Babe Ruth called where he would hit the ball for the record-breaking home run. Shoeless Joe and the 1919 Black Sox scandal was the focus of the fourth baseball card adventure book, *Shoeless Joe & Me* (HarperCollins, 2002) and *Mickey & Me* (HarperCollins, 2003) was Gutman's fifth book in the series. In *Mickey & Me* most readers assume that the featured ball player is Mickey Mantle but readers are in for a very big surprise when the hero is revealed.

Gutman has used a pseudonym for two of his books. He wrote a book, *Jackie Robinson* (Aladdin, 1999), that was released the same year as *Jackie & Me*. *Jackie Robinson* was a biography in the publisher Aladdin's ongoing series, Childhood of Famous Americans. Gutman did not want the two books to be confused so he wrote it under the name of his good friend from college, Herb Dunn. This is also the name Gutman regularly slips into his other books. Readers will find Herb Dunn as the name of minor characters in several of Gutman's books.[5]

In a departure from his sports titles, Gutman wrote a story about the Wright brothers, *Race for the Sky* (Simon & Schuster, 2003), which took more research time than any of his other books. The book began when Gutman discovered that one of the witnesses of the Wright brothers' first flight in 1903 was a young boy, Johnny Moore. *Race for the Sky* is written in diary form, as if Johnny had written it, and details the story of the Wright brothers and their first flight.

In another departure, Gutman wrote a book that could be classified as an early reader. He stayed with the sports theme in *Babe Ruth and the Ice Cream Mess* (Aladdin, 2003), a story based on an incident in Babe Ruth's childhood. When Babe was young, he stole some money from his father's saloon and treated the neighborhood kids to ice cream cones. The story reflects Babe's personality—generous and sometimes impulsive.

Gutman says he can usually write a book in two to four months, including the research that he must do to give him the necessary facts to create his settings. His writing schedule is fairly predictable. He says, "I get up around 7 and get my son and daughter off to school. If the weather permits, I'll usually take a bicycle ride."[6] Because Gutman

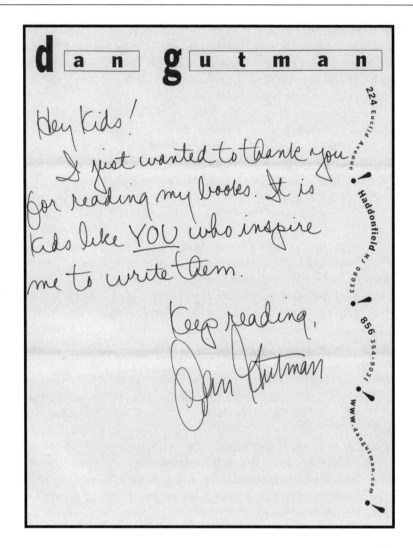

feels that he does his best writing in the morning that is when he tries to schedule most of his writing time. The time after lunch is when he attends to details involved in other aspects of his writing career. He answers e-mail messages, returns phone calls, writes letters, and spends time researching material for his next book. When his two children, Sam and Emma, come home from school Gutman quits for the day but because his office is in his home he sometimes goes back to his office to work after dinner and after the children are in bed.

Gutman now spends a lot of time visiting his readers in schools all across the country. He says "visiting with those who read my books has been the most satisfying thing I've done in my career."[7] The children he meets tell him that his books make them laugh, which is what Gutman wanted to do back at the very beginning of his writing career before he figured out the best way to do it.

Dan Gutman lives in Haddonfield, New Jersey where his wife Nina, and their two children, Sam (1990) and Emma (1995), share their home with a pet cat, Scrumpy.

# Book Connections

Dan Gutman has written books for two series, the Baseball Card Adventure Series and Tales from the Sandlot, as well as books with sequels, nonfiction, and fiction for adults and young readers. *The Kid Who Ran For President* (Scholastic, 1996) was followed in 1999 with its sequel *The Kid Who Became President* (Scholastic, 1999). Two of his books feature the character Qwerty Stevens. Gutman featured Qwerty Stevens in a series of Edison Mystery books, which includes *Qwerty Stevens, Back in Time: The Edison Mystery* (Simon & Schuster, 2001) and *Qwerty Stevens, Stuck in Time with Benjamin Franklin* (Simon & Schuster, 2002). *The Edison Mystery* has a boy digging in his backyard only to find a machine invented by Edison more than 150 years earlier—a machine so revolutionary that Edison had not revealed it to the world. *Stuck in Time with Benjamin Franklin* is a sequel where Qwerty and his friend use the Anytime Anywhere Machine to bring Benjamin Franklin into the future. Then the two of them accompany Franklin back to 1776 where they are able to observe some of the events surrounding the creation of the Declaration of Independence.

In 2004, Gutman launched the My Weird School series. The first title, *Miss Daisy Is Crazy* (HarperCollins, 2004), features a second grade teacher, Miss Daisy. All the grownups in this school are crazy. A second book, *Mr. Klutz Is Nuts* (HarperCollins, 2004), features the principal of this school and another title, *Miss Roopy Is Loopy* (HarperCollins, 2004), features the school librarian. An intermediate fiction book, *The Get Rich Quick Club* (HarperCollins, 2004), is about five friends who vow to get rich quick. They spend the summer creating a fake picture of a UFO and trying to sell it to the tabloids.

Gutman is a versatile and prolific author who uses humor to tell stories set in the present and in the past. He is a researcher who thoroughly presents, in an interesting manner, the topics in his several nonfiction titles.

# Books Written by Dan Gutman

Baseball Card Adventures Series: *Honus & Me* (Avon, 1997); *Jackie & Me* (Avon, 1999); *Babe & Me* (HarperCollins, 2000); *Shoeless Joe & Me* (HarperCollins, 2002); *Mickey & Me* (HarperCollins, 2003).

*Babe Ruth and the Ice Cream Mess* (Aladdin, 2003).

Edison Mysteries: *Qwerty Stevens, Back in Time: The Edison Mystery* (Simon & Schuster, 2001); *Qwerty Stevens, Stuck in Time with Benjamin Franklin* (Simon & Schuster, 2002).

*Jackie Robinson.* Written by Herb Dunn. (Aladdin, 1999).

*Joe DiMaggio.* Written by Herb Dunn. (Aladdin, 1999).

*The Million Dollar Kick* (Hyperion, 2001).

*The Million Dollar Shot* (Hyperion, 1997).

My Weird School Series: *Miss Daisy Is Crazy* (HarperCollins, 2004); *Mr. Klutz Is Nuts* (HarperCollins, 2004); *Miss Roopy Is Loopy* (HarperCollins, 2004).

*Race for the Sky* (Simon & Schuster, 2003).

# For More Information

## Articles

Lesesne, Teri S. " 'LAF-ing' about Books: An Interview with Dan Gutman." *Teacher-Librarian* 29.5 (June 2002): 46–48.

## Web Sites

Gutman, Dan. *Dan Gutman Homepage.* March 2004. <http://www.dangutman.com>.

# Notes

1. Dan Gutman, "Dan Gutman About Page," *Dan Gutman Home Page,* March 2004, <http://www.dangutman.com/pages/about.html>.
2. Dan Gutman, letter to the author, 12 Sept. 2002.
3. Dan Gutman, interview with the author, 24 Apr. 2002.
4. Ibid.
5. Ibid.
6. Ibid.
7. Ibid.

# Wendy Anderson Halperin

◆ Contemporary fiction ◆ Family stories ◆ Humor

**Joliet, Illinois**
April 10, 1952

📖 *Once Upon a Company*
📖 *When Chickens Grow Teeth*

## About the Author/Illustrator

Wendy Anderson Halperin was born in Illinois and was raised on a "land that was forever flat and the sky was everywhere."[1] Wendy grew up in a family of four children. Her father was an attorney and her mother was an artist. As a youngster she once made clothes for a crawfish for a 4-H show and painted rocks that she helped collect along the shores of Lake Michigan. Wendy, her brother, and her sister would transform the rocks into cars and a variety of other objects that they then sold at a local art fair. By the time she was 14 years old Wendy was attending "Oxbows," a summer artist's colony and school for the arts in Saugatuck, Michigan. It was there that she discovered figure drawing and realized that drawing was not just something one learned but something one felt.

After Wendy graduated from high school, she entered Syracuse University and later she attended Pratt Institute. She worked in Chicago and then in New York until 1979 when she moved to the San Francisco, California area to study drawing at the California College of Arts and Crafts and also to study privately with David Hardy.

In the middle 1980s Wendy Anderson married David Richard Halperin and during their marriage they became parents to three children, Kale (1984), Joel (1985), and Lane (1989). Halperin began working as a freelance illustrator and occasionally studied at the American Academy in Chicago.

When her children were young, Halperin worked as a freelance fine arts painter. She was first introduced to creating children's books when she was asked to illustrate a book by Janet Taylor Lisle, *The Lampfish of Twill* (Orchard Books, 1991). Two years later her illustrations for Tres Seymour's *Hunting the White Cow* (Orchard Books, 1993) earned more attention and soon she had more contracts with Orchard Books and also Candlewick Press, Atheneum, Simon and Schuster, and Dial Press. She illustrated *The Full*

**115**

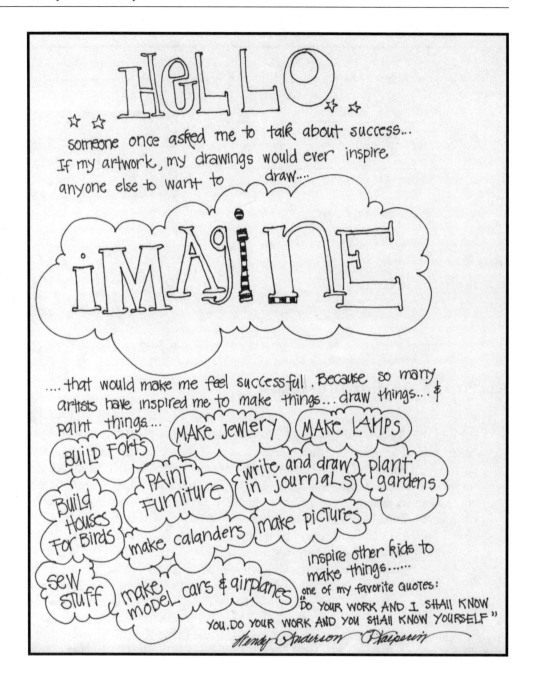

*Belly Bowl* by Jim Aylesworth (Atheneum, 1998) and that same year she and her children created a company to earn money for the children's college tuition. The children used boughs of evergreen trees left over from a friend's tree farm to create wreaths to sell. The business resulted in a spin-off peanut butter and jelly sandwich business for the summer months. The business also spawned the idea for a new book.

The book, *Once Upon a Company* (Orchard Books, 1998), told the story of a seven-year-old boy (Joel) and his sisters who started a wreath-making business that over a period of six years netted the trio more than $16,000. In the book, the business gets off the ground and is a great success with the help of grandparents, classmates, friends, and local townspeople. The success of the Wreath Company brought about another seasonal business, the Peanut Butter & Jelly Company. The children's grandparents offer support and suggestions. In real life, the children's grandparents live on the same street as the Halperin family in South Haven, Michigan.

Currently Halperin illustrates books, conducts workshops for author/illustrator visits, and speaks at schools and conferences for librarians, teachers, and other educators. Sometimes Halperin appears at school or conference programs with her friend, John Mooy. Halperin and her three children live in South Haven, Michigan and also spend time in their second home in Interlochen, Michigan.

# Book Connections

Wendy Anderson Halperin's pen and ink and watercolor illustrations are filled with details that illuminate the text. In *Love Is* (Simon & Schuster, 2001) Halperin portrays people acting without love—bickering, ignoring homeless people, and so forth. On the facing page the scene is exactly the opposite. People are acting kindly, delivering meals to shut-ins, and, in general, caring for others. Some of the panels tell a continuing story. For example, one panel shows a house becoming more and more dilapidated as time goes on. Another panel shows a sculptor creating a sculpture. Readers will delight in finding favorite storybook characters such as Cinderella, the Little Engine (from *The Little Engine that Could*), and Pinocchio.

Halperin's first books were illustrated for Orchard Books where she became acquainted with the editor Richard Jackson, who encouraged her to write her own books. *Once Upon a Company* and *When Chickens Grow Teeth* (Orchard, 1996) resulted from his encouragement but Halperin remains best known for the illustrations she creates for books written by other authors.

Those illustrations regularly feature characters based on people in her life—family and friends. Sometimes Halperin will invent entirely new characters and sometimes the characters are people she's met and the settings are places she has visited. Some of the illustrations Halperin created for Marsha Wilson Chall's *Bonaparte* (Dorling Kindersley, 2000) were developed from images gained when Halperin visited schools in France. The Wee Small Man in Jim Aylesworth's *The Full Belly Bowl* is actually the gym teacher, Mr. Swaggerty, that taught Halperin's children.

In 1998, Halperin's illustrations appeared in a series of books by Cynthia Rylant. The series, The Cobble Street Cousins, chronicles the everyday events of three nine-year-old cousins, Lily, Rosie, and Tess. The three girls live with their Aunt Lucy and many of their adventures focus on the girls' relationship with their aunt. The girls bake and sell cookies, write poetry, and sing songs. They also try to encourage a romance with one of their former customers and they help their aunt and her boyfriend, Michael, prepare a special winter solstice dinner. The girls plan a going away party when it is time to leave their Aunt Lucy's but all three of them return to their aunt's house to help her plan the perfect wedding.

## Books Illustrated by Wendy Anderson Halperin

*Bonaparte.* Written by Marsha Wilson Chall. (Dorling Kindersley, 2000).

Cobble Street Cousins series: *In Aunt Lucy's Kitchen* (1998); *Let's Go Home* (2000); *A Little Shopping* (1998); *Some Good News* (1999); *Special Gifts* (1999); *Wedding Flowers* (2002); and *Summer Party* (2001). All written by Cynthia Rylant and published by Simon & Schuster.

*The Full Belly Bowl.* Written by Jim Aylesworth. (Atheneum, 1998).

*Love Is.* Adapted from the Bible by Wendy Anderson Halperin. (Simon & Schuster, 2001).

*Once Upon a Company.* Written by Wendy Anderson Halperin. (Orchard, 1998).

*The Secret Remedy Book.* Written by Karin Cates. (Orchard, 2003).

*Turn! Turn! Turn!* Written by Pete Seeger. (Simon & Schuster, 2003).

*The Visit.* Written by Reeve Lindbergh. (Dial, 2004).

*When Chickens Grow Teeth.* Retold by Wendy Anderson Halperin. (Orchard, 1996).

## For More Information

### Web Sites

Halperin, Wendy. *Children's Book Author/Illustrator: Wendy Anderson Halperin.* March 2004. <http://www.wendyhalperin.com>.

## Note

1. Wendy Anderson Halperin, interview with the author, 28 Oct. 2002.

# Anna Grossnickle Hines

◆ Family stories ◆ Poetry

**Cincinnati, Ohio**
July 13, 1946

📖 *Winter Lights: A Celebration of Poems and Quilts*

📖 *Pieces: A Year in Poems and Quilts*

## About the Author/Illustrator

From the time she was about seven years old, Anna Grossnickle Hines knew she wanted to make books for children. She just didn't always have a clear idea of how she was going to go about it.

Anna was born in Cincinnati, Ohio and grew up in rural Ohio. Her first home was in Wilmington, where her father attended school on the GI Bill. After her father completed school, the family moved to Red Lion and then to Harveysburg where he worked as a teacher for a time. Later, the family moved to Blanchester, where her grandfather, Joe Putman, was principal of the elementary school, which was later named for him.

When Anna was 11 her parents divorced but later the entire family—her mother and three siblings and Anna's father and her stepmother—all moved to Los Angeles, California. After arriving in California three more siblings were brought into the blended families making Anna the oldest of seven children. The rest of Anna's childhood was spent in California where she was encouraged in her endeavors by both of her parents. She graduated from Verdugo Hills High School and then headed off to San Fernando Valley State College. In college, she found little support for her interest in making children's books. Her college teachers thought it was a waste of time to even think about it. So, after three years of taking basic art courses and a class or two related to children and children's literature, she left college to study on her own.

Anna Grossnickle Hines married and become a mother of two daughters, Bethany (1968) and Sarah (1971). She began working with preschoolers in Los Angeles City Children's Centers and also regularly visited the library and checked out stacks of books to read with her children. Hines also began to write—poetry at first and later narratives that she envisioned as picture books.

**119**

Hines's marriage did not endure and after divorcing her husband she decided that going back to school to earn teaching credentials would help her as a single parent support her daughters. She attended Pacific Oaks College in Pasadena from 1974 to 1978 where she earned an undergraduate and a graduate degree. After earning her degrees, she taught third grade for three years in Columbia, California and married a forest ranger, Gary Hines. Together they became the parents of Hines's third daughter, Lassen (1979). At first Hines stayed at home thinking she would concentrate on her writing but she got waylaid, planting a garden and doing the interesting things home life can bring when one is happy and secure. Still, she knew she wanted to create children's books and, at 28 years old, she realized that she must make writing and illustrating a top priority or she would just be another person who wanted to write children's books.

At first Hines struggled with where to send her manuscripts and how to present them to editors but after attending a Society of Children's Book Writers' conference she met some mentors and received some needed direction. Soon she was making time to write but during the next eight years and four months she collected over one hundred rejection letters, eighteen of which were from Susan Hirschman at Greenwillow Publishing. But Hines also had collected rejection slips from James Cross Giblin at Clarion and Ann Durrell at Dutton Publishers. Although the rejection slips were sometimes difficult to receive, Hines says she learned from each one of them.

Finally, on November 13, 1981 Hirschman contacted her. This time the contact was a phone call to let Hines know that her first manuscript for publication, *Taste the Raindrops* (Greenwillow, 1983), had been accepted. Hines was so surprised by the call that she forgot to ask if Hirschman also wanted her to illustrate the book. In a later conversation she asked and Hirschman did, in fact, want Hines to illustrate it. Nonetheless, she continued to get more rejection letters—including more from Hirschman. A year after *Taste the Raindrops* sold, Hines sold a second book, *Come to the Meadow* (Clarion, 1984), to James Giblin. That same year Ann Durrell bought *Maybe a Band-Aid Will Help* (Dutton, 1984). Since then, Hines has created over 50 books. Most of the books were written and illustrated by Hines but she has also illustrated at least three books written by Gary Hines, her husband, six by her daughter, Sarah Hines Stephens, and eight by other writers. Once in a while another illustrator has been asked to illustrate a book Hines has written.

Anna and Gary Hines lived in the Sierra Nevada Mountains in California for 17 years, not too far from Yosemite National Park. In 1990, Gary's job took the family to Milford, Pennsylvania. It was in Pennsylvania that Hines became interested in making quilts. Her mother had always made beautiful quilts and Hines had made each of her daughters quilts when they were young. Quilts had already found their way into many of Hines's illustrations. In *Taste the Raindrops* she used pen and ink to sketch a quilt for one of the beds. In other books she uses watercolor, acrylic paints, or colored pencils to create her illustrations and in many of those illustrations she included quilts. Sometimes Hines took the quilts off her daughters' beds to use as models for her illustrations. The character in *Keep Your Old Hat* (Dutton, 1987) is named after Hines's second daughter, Sarah, but the quilt shown is one she created for her youngest daughter, Lassen. The quilt was created with the printed fabric that was originally intended to be the pages of a cloth book but instead, Hines used the alphabet pages as the blocks for the quilt.

Hines's interest in quilting took a giant leap when she and her family members decided to create a memory quilt for her mother's birthday. Members of the family each created one or more quilt squares for a very special quilt and by the time Hines and her family members had put the squares together Hines was hooked on quilting.

A result of Hines's interest in quilting came when she proposed illustrating a book of poetry with miniature quilts that she would sew. At first her editor at Greenwillow thought the project too ambitious. But Hines persisted and finally got the okay to create the book. Each poem was illustrated with a quilt pieced with very small squares and so exquisitely reproduced on the page that readers want to feel the texture of the quilted illustration. *Pieces: A Year in Poems & Quilts* (Greenwillow, 2001) won many awards and was given much recognition. Even though it was Hines's first book of poetry and the first book she had illustrated with fabric, the book earned her the coveted 2002 Lee Bennett Hopkins Award for Children's Poetry. Hines used fabric appliqué to create the illustrations for a second book, *Whistling* (Greenwillow, 2003), written by Elizabeth Partridge. Miniature quilts are also used in the illustrations for *Winter Lights: A Celebration of Poems and Quilts* (Greenwillow, 2004), Hines's third book illustrated with fabric.

In November 2001, Gary Hines retired from his position as a U.S. Forest Ranger and became a full-time writer. With that change, the couple decided to move back to California where their daughters had established their own families. Their daughter, Bethany, is an avid mountain biker but uses her artistic talents to create store displays for Nordstrom's department store in the Santa Cruz area. Her daughter, Sarah, cofounded a small book packaging company in Oakland, California and has also authored several books and ghost written several other titles including some in the Curious George series. Lassen graduated from the Rhode Island School of Design in New York and returned to the Bay area where she is establishing her career.

Early in Hines's career it was her children who provided inspiration for her books and often modeled for the rosy checked youngsters that populated her illustrations. Today it is her two grandsons that provide inspiration for ideas. She says, "Jacob Albert Mann, now just about 7 years old [was] the inspiration for *My Grandma Is Coming to Town* [Candlewick, 2003]"[1] The story is of a long-distance relationship between a young boy, Albert, and his grandmother. At the time, Hines lived in Pennsylvania and Jacob was in California.

Gary and Anna Grossnickle Hines live in a rustic area 145 miles north of San Francisco near the Redwood forests. Hines spends her days making quilts, cloth dolls, knitting, reading, and of course, writing and illustrating new books. But don't ask her to name her favorites, as she says, "I hate picking favorites because I like variety. And I don't like leaving others out. Maybe this is partly due to being the last one picked for sports activities in my childhood!"[2]

## Book Connections

Anna Grossnickle Hines uses a variety of media for her many books but most recently she has been using fabric. Earlier she used pen and ink, acrylic paints, and watercolor. Each medium Hines uses has different characteristics and demands different skills.

She used watercolors to create the illustrations for *Flying Firefighters* (Clarion, 1993), *The Day of the Highclimber* (Greenwillow, 1994), and *Bouncing on the Bed* (Orchard, 1999). Because watercolors are transparent, new layers can be added but the images underneath show through and also become part of the illustration. These layers can add shadows and create different colors.

Hines used colored pencils for illustrating *Big Like Me* (Greenwillow, 1989), *Moompa, Toby and Bomp* (Clarion, 1993), *Gramma's Walk* (Greenwillow, 1993), *What Joe Saw* (Greenwillow, 1994), and the Bean Books series (*Bean* [Harcourt, 1998]). Similar to watercolor, the pencils don't cover what is underneath so an illustrator must be pretty sure of what the final picture will look like before beginning with the illustration. Colored pencils were also used for *Rumble Tumble Boom!* (Greenwillow, 1992, o.p.) and *When the Goblins Came Knocking* (Greenwillow, 1995, o.p.), however, these illustrations were created on black paper not white.

Acrylic paints were used for *When We Married Gary* (Greenwillow, 1996, o.p.) and *Miss Emma's Wild Garden* (Greenwillow, 1997, o.p.). Acrylic paint is very forgiving and if Hines makes a mistake she is able to paint right over the part she wants to change. Because the paint is opaque it covers up the mistake underneath. Sometimes Hines uses a combination of media as she did for *Big Help!* (Clarion, 1995, o.p.) and *Grandma Gets Grumpy* (Clarion, 1988, o.p.).

Some of Hines's books have taken just a few days to write while others have consumed several years. Once a manuscript has been accepted for publication, it generally takes Hines about a year to create the illustrations. She starts by making the sketches, sending them off to the art director at the publisher, sending samples of the finished art, and then once the work has been given an okay, she must create the finished art for each illustration. The amount of time it takes for Hines to create a finished illustration depends on the detail and medium she is using. A watercolor illustration might take her a morning or afternoon to finish or sometimes the entire day. Colored pencils with layers and layers of color and a lot of detail can take several days to complete. Acrylic paintings take even longer—a week or more on the average.

Making her illustrations often involves setting up a scene in real life and taking pictures or using the set-up as a model for the illustration. When her daughters were young, they often served as models for the children in her books. Now that they are grown Hines searches through her photo albums for appropriate scenes. She also is beginning to use her grandchildren as models in her photographs.

The inspiration for many of the designs for her books that are illustrated with fabric came from her mother who has made many beautiful quilts. Fabric illustrations are very demanding because if a process or stitch is not just right the seam must be taken out and redone until it is just right.

## Books Written and Illustrated by Anna Grossnickle Hines

*Bean* (Harcourt, 1998).

*Got You!* A Rookie Reader®. (Children's Press, 2001).

*Not Without Bear* (Orchard, 2000).

*Pieces: A Year in Poems and Quilts* (Greenwillow, 2001).

*Winter Lights: A Celebration of Poems and Quilts* (Greenwillow, 2004).

## Books Written by Anna Grossnickle Hines

*My Grandma Is Coming to Town.* Illustrated by Melissa Sweet. (Candlewick Press, 2003).

*Which Hat Is That?* Illustrated by LeUyen Pham. (Harcourt, 2002).

*Whose Shoes?* Illustrated by LeUyen Pham. (Harcourt, 2001).

## Books Illustrated by Anna Grossnickle Hines

*Bean Soup.* Written by Sarah Hines-Stephens. (Harcourt, 2000).

*Soup Too?* Written by Sarah Hines-Stephens. (Harcourt, 2000).

*Soup's Oops!* Written by Sarah Hines-Stephens. (Harcourt, 2000).

*Whistling.* Written by Elizabeth Partridge. (Greenwillow, 2003).

## For More Information

### Articles

Smith, Cynthia Leitich. "The Story Behind the Story: Anna Grossnickle Hines on *Pieces: A Year in Poems & Quilts.*" *Cynthia Leitich Smith: Children's Literature Resources.* March 2004. <http://www.cynthialeitichsmith.com/storyhines.html>.

### Web Sites

Hines, Anna Grossnickle. *Anna Grossnickle Hines_Children's Author and Illustrator.* March 2004. <http://www.aghines.com> or <http://www.annagrossnickle hines.com>.

## Notes

1. Anna Grossnickle Hines, letter to the author, 10 Sept. 2002.
2. Ibid.

# Will Hobbs

◆ Adventure fiction

**Pittsburgh, Pennsylvania**
August 22, 1947

📖 *Down the Yukon*
📖 *Ghost Canoe*

## About the Author

Will Hobbs's adventures and travels began in Pittsburgh, Pennsylvania where he was born, the third son in the family. By the time he was six months old, the family was on a boat headed to Panama where his father, an engineer in the Air Force, would be stationed. Because of the military, the family often relocated. Will entered school in Falls Church, Virginia and by the time he was in the middle grades he was living in Alaska, then California, and on to high school in San Antonio, Texas. After moving back to California, Will graduated from high school and later earned an undergraduate degree at Stanford University.

The first three children in the Hobbs family were boys—their ages pretty close together. Will's younger sister was born four years after him and his younger brother was born nine years after him. Will's father grew up in Florida and he loved the outdoors as much as Will does now. Will's mother was raised in Pittsburgh and she was also as adventurous as her son; when she was 73, she went down the Grand Canyon on a motorized raft.[1]

Because he was the new kid in many schools across the country, Will learned to turn to books and reading. Two books by Marguerite Henry, *Misty of Chincoteague* and *King of the Wind,* were among his favorites along with the adventure titles by Jim Kjelgaard, the Hardy Boys books, and science fiction titles by Jules Verne.[2]

As a teen, Will hiked in the Sierra Mountains and took a two-week canoe trip in Minnesota's boundary waters. During his college years he spent his summers as a guide and camp director on the Philmont Scout Ranch in New Mexico. Will's love for animals began with the bears he saw while his family was living in Alaska and his fascination also was encouraged by his sixth-grade teacher after he moved to California. Will even caught snakes for the class terrarium.

Will Hobbs married Jean in 1972 and after graduating from college they taught school, mostly in Durango, Colorado, where the two of them have lived since 1973. Hobbs spent 17 years as a reading and English teacher, 3 of which were in high school and 14 in seventh and eighth grades. His career as a classroom teacher ended in 1990, shortly after his second novel was published. In 1989 when Hobbs was still working as a classroom teacher and also a fledgling writer, he was fortunate enough to meet author Richard Peck. Peck and Hobbs began a friendship that has endured to this day and that has encouraged Hobbs as a writer.[3]

Hobbs's writing schedule is fairly regular—from 9 to 5. Of course, there are the usual refrigerator breaks and trips to the mailbox but sometimes if his book is going well he might return, in the evening, to his writing study and his blueberry iMac. Most of his books are written over a period of one year but he often spends six months of the year traveling, speaking at conferences, and having outdoor adventures of his own.[4]

As with many writers much of Hobbs's ideas come from his own life experiences and the remainder from his imagination. The actual writing takes a lot of practice and perseverance. Hobbs says, "my biggest breakthrough came when I learned to write with the five senses. I had to help the reader imagine the scenes I was writing about through all five senses: hearing, seeing, tasting, touching, and smelling."[5]

Hobbs spends a lot of time rewriting and revising his stories. He once wrote 10 chapters for the book *Beardance* (HarperCollins, 1993) and then realized that the book should start in the mountains and not on the character Walter's ranch—so the 10 chapters were thrown away and Hobbs had to start over.

Hobbs's first book, *Changes in Latitude* (HarperCollins, 1988), came about after Hobbs saw a photograph of a sea turtle swimming in the sea. He later took two trips to Mexico over spring break and the photograph and the two trips brought together the ideas for the book. The title was borrowed from Jimmy Buffett's song by the same name and just as the lyrics reflect a change of attitude during the course of the song, the character Travis changes his attitude about what life is all about during the course of the novel. At the beginning of the novel, Travis is very much concerned only with himself. By the end of the novel, he has learned to care a lot more about his family and vicariously he learns to care about the endangered sea turtles that his brother cares so much about. During a five-day period to research information for the book, Hobbs was able to work with the leatherback sea turtle project, where he observed turtle hatchlings heading out to the sea. He described this event in his book with Travis's observation that the baby turtles looked like wind-up toys.[6]

Hobbs says his books are usually inspired by an image he has seen or an event or incident he has experienced. Research provides the substance of the setting and events that he puts into the adventure. For instance, *The Big Wanderer* (HarperCollins, 1992) was inspired by the story of Everett Ruess, an adventurer who explored the Sierra Nevada, the California coast, and the desert wilderness of the southwest between 1930 and 1934. During his travels, he sent many letters home and kept diaries and journals. In 1934, Ruess—then 20 years old—disappeared in the Escalante River Canyon in Utah. *The Big Wanderer* takes place in 1962 and while it was inspired by Ruess's adventures, the main characters Clay and his older brother Mike journey across the southwest in a pickup truck in search of their long lost uncle.

Another of Hobbs's stories, *Far North* (HarperCollins, 1996), is set in Canada's Northwest Territories. The idea for the story came during a whitewater rafting trip on the Nahanni River that Hobbs, his wife Jean, and a friend decided to run. They hired a bush pilot to take them into the wilderness and during the trip, a ranger told the group about a floatplane that had stalled in the area of the 385-foot Virginia Falls; the plane barely avoided going over the falls. That gave Hobbs the story idea but in order to flesh out the details he made two more trips to the north, one to Canada and the other to Alaska. Hobbs read many books about the bush pilots, the adventures of others in the area, and the writing of anthropologists who had studied the native residents of the area.

As Hobbs researched and wrote, the images of his childhood days in Alaska came back to him and helped him create the vivid descriptions of the scenery. The place where the characters Gabe and Raymond attempt to escape down the river—and nearly lose Johnny Raven—is the same place that Hobbs and Jean had run the Figure-of-Eight Rapid on their whitewater rafting trip. As a boy from Texas, Gabe saw the Northwest Territories with a fresh perspective—the perspective of someone who had not before experienced the draw of the northern outdoors.

Inspiration for *Ghost Canoe* (HarperCollins, 1997) came when Hobbs hiked in Cape Flattery, on the Olympic Peninsula in Washington state, and visited a museum in a modern Makah town of Neah Bay. The museum included many artifacts from the island and its inhabitants in the 1400s. The old canoes and fishing gear in the museum made Hobbs think about the whaling hunts that continued well into the twentieth century. The most fascinating decade for this area, he thought, was the 1870s. So he researched the history of the region and used what he learned to write a fictional story. Later a visit to the Olympic Peninsula in Washington State and a lighthouse on the small island, Tatoosh Island, gave Hobbs the final inspiration and background that he would use to write the mystery tale, *Ghost Canoe*.

Hobbs wife, Jean, has played a significant role by bringing ideas or scenarios, which eventually become a book, to Hobbs. When she read an article about six young condors being released at Vermilion Cliffs, a place close to the starting point of their Grand Canyon River Trips, the incident seemed a natural prompt for a new book. *The Maze* (HarperCollins, 1998) grew out of this article and Hobbs's own fascination with flying.

As a teacher, Jean often worked with children that were sent to the Native American group home in Durango. One particular Ute boy was very homesick and that experience inspired the story of the character Cloyd in *Bearstone* (HarperCollins, 1989). A major element in this book is the Ute's bear dance. The old man, Walter, was based on an old rancher who often told Hobbs stories of a gold mine in the mountains. The story takes place in the upper Pine River country in the Weminuche Wilderness of southwestern Colorado. *Beardance* is the sequel to *Bearstone* and was spawned by an account of a sighting of four grizzlies in the mountains of southwest Colorado. This story included the Native American legend of the Lost Mine of the Window.

*Jason's Gold* (HarperCollins, 1999) came about after Hobbs visited Alaska and wandered into a museum in Dawson Creek. Hobbs was able to take photographs of the region and visit the cabin where Jack London spent a year during the days of the Klondike Gold Rush. He learned a lot about Jack London and incorporated that information into the book. A girl that Hobbs met in Alaska inspired Jamie, a character in the book.[7] Hobbs also included a few real-life people in this book. Many readers will recognize Jack Cervantes as the author of the well-known poem, "The Cremation of Sam McGee."

Another newspaper article and Hobbs's brother-in-law gave him the idea for *Jackie's Wild Seattle* (HarperCollins, 2003). The newspaper clipping that his brother-in-law sent to him was about a young rescue worker coaxing a wild coyote from an elevator in a Seattle office building. The setting was a familiar one for Hobbs, who has relatives in the area.

When Hobbs is not writing he is most likely found in the woods or on the water. He and Jean spend a lot time hiking in the San Juan Mountains and they often go whitewater rafting. Hobbs has rafted down the Colorado River in the Grand Canyon 10 times or so and each trip takes about three weeks. Usually others accompany Hobbs and his wife but once they ventured onto the river by themselves. Even though they had run the big rapids before, somehow it seemed much different when they were alone facing the foaming water.[8]

Similar to her husband, Jean has also changed careers. Once a classroom teacher, she now works as her husband's agent. The couple's 11 nieces and nephews figure into many of Hobbs's books and adventures. Their home overlooks a wildlife preserve and this allows Hobbs to look out his office window and see elk, bears, and a number of other wild animals. The canyons, mountains, and rivers are also close by. Directly out of the windows of his study, there are cliffs where Hobbs can see falcons nest and beyond that are mountains, which are capped with white snow much of the year.[9]

## Book Connections

Will Hobbs wrote his first fantasy novel about the magic flute player, Kokopelli. Kokopelli is a traditional Native American character that is often pictured in petroglyphs on cliff walls. *Kokopelli's Flute* (HarperCollins, 1995) was dedicated to Hobbs's sister. Later, Hobbs dedicated *Jason's Gold* to his three brothers. The character, Jason, has two older brothers just like Hobbs himself. Because the story is about brothers, Hobbs says, it seems just right for the dedication.

Hobbs and his mentor and friend, Richard Peck, share a love for the far north—the Northwest Territories and Alaska—so it seemed fitting that Hobbs's seventh book, *Far North* (HarperCollins, 1996), be dedicated to Peck.

## Books Written by Will Hobbs

*Beardance* (HarperCollins, 1993).

*Bearstone* (HarperCollins, 1989).

*The Big Wanderer* (HarperCollins, 1992).

*Changes in Latitude* (HarperCollins, 1988).

*Down the Yukon* (HarperCollins, 2001).

*Downriver* (HarperCollins, 1991).

*Far North* (HarperCollins, 1996).

*Ghost Canoe* (HarperCollins, 1997).

*Jackie's Wild Seattle* (HarperCollins, 2003).

*Jason's Gold* (HarperCollins, 1999).

*Kokopelli's Flute* (HarperCollins, 1995).

*The Maze* (HarperCollins, 1998).

*River Thunder* (HarperCollins,1997).

*Wild Man Island* (HarperCollins, 2002).

## For More Information

### Web Sites

Hobbs, Will. *Will Hobbs Official Website—Children's Book Author.* March 2004. <http://www.willhobbsauthor.com>.

## Notes

1. Will Hobbs, interview with the author, Indianapolis, Indiana, 18 Nov. 2001.

2. Ibid.

3. Ibid.

4. Ibid.

5. Will Hobbs, presentation at the American Association of School Librarians Conference, Indianapolis, Indiana, 18 Nov. 2001.

6. Will Hobbs, "The Story Behind the Stories," presentation at the Tri-Conference of the Kansas Library Association (KLA), Kansas Association of School Librarians (KASL), and the Kansas Association for Educational Communications and Technology (KAECT), Salina, Kansas, 11 Apr. 2003.

7. Hobbs, presentation.

8. Hobbs, interview.

9. Hobbs, presentation.

# Carol Otis Hurst

◆ Historical fiction ◆ Family stories

**Springfield, Massachusetts**
October 13, 1933

📖 *In Plain Sight*

📖 *Rocks in My Head*

📖 *Through the Lock*

## About the Author

Carol Otis Hurst's name is known to hundreds of readers of *Teaching K-8*, a professional journal for teachers, and to several hundred more that have heard her tell her wonderful stories at workshops and conferences across the country. Those who love her storytelling sessions now have some of her stories to enjoy in book form with more books to come in the future.

Carol Otis Hurst was the next to the youngest child in a family of five girls and two boys. She spent her childhood in her maternal grandmother's home. When Carol was just five years old the family moved to Westfield, Massachusetts. That same year, her mother broke both of her arms and Carol was sent to her grandmother Clark's home, also in Westfield, to stay until her mother's arms healed. Carol sums up the stay and the time spent at her grandmother's by saying, "stayed there from age 5 to age 21."[1] During those years with her grandmother, many of Carol's extended family members came for temporary visits—staying when they were temporarily out of work or in transit to find work. Carol says it was "normal for people to sit around the dinner table and tell stories."[2]

Carol attended the public schools in Westfield and after she graduated from high school she went on to attend and graduate from Westfield State College. Around the same time, in 1955, Carol, age 21, married John Hurst. Together they became parents of three children, Rebecca, Jill, and David (who died in infancy). During the six years of their marriage, the couple and their two daughters lived in Tennessee, Ohio, and Minnesota.

In 1961, Carol Hurst's marriage ended and she returned to Westfield with her daughters. Hurst turned her talents to teaching and became an elementary school teacher. Her knack for telling stories soon had other teachers requesting that she visit their classes. It wasn't long before she parlayed her storytelling and her love of books into a related career as an elementary school librarian. At first, because she was teaching in an elementary school that had no librarian, she organized the library. Then she decided to accept an offer to be the librarian, at least for one year, before she returned to classroom teaching.

Hurst continued to tell stories to the children and word of her stories spread. Before long she was visiting other schools and soon the editors of *Teaching K–8* discovered her talent. Hurst's career as a teacher and librarian spanned a period of 21 years. Her association with *Teaching K–8* continued for 25 years.

Hurst's emergence as a published writer seemed to be a natural extension of her other talents. She had been in and around the field of children's literature all her life and for a number of years had made her living as a storyteller but never thought she could write a children's book. She says, "when people would ask why I hadn't written a book for children, I would say that it was like asking an opera singer why she hadn't written any operas. I was on the performing and demonstrating end of things. But I grew up in a family that told stories: about themselves, about each other, about the past. Those family stories kept bubbling out in my presentations for teachers and librarians and, eventually, I sat down and played with bits of both my grandmother's and grandfather's stories and they began to mesh into a novel that became *Through the Lock* [Houghton Mifflin/Walter Lorraine Books, 2001]."[3] It wasn't long before she wrote *Rocks in His Head* (Greenwillow, 2001) because "my father was a really good guy with an incredible outlook on life and I wanted my kids and my grandkids to know a bit about him."[4]

Hurst's first novel, *Through the Lock,* is a fictionalized tale based on her grandmother and grandfather and the actual Farmington Canal, which was built in 1825. The story takes place in 1840 and three young people—Walter, Etta, and Jake—were for various reasons separated from their families—orphaned, alcoholic parent, and so forth. The three made a plan to operate a lock on the canal so that they could have a home in which to live. In the process they become embroiled in a feud between the canal operators and the local farmers, who look at the canal from adverse perspectives.

Hurst's first picture book, *Rocks in His Head,* tells a story about her father who had a love of rocks. He kept rocks in his filling station until the Depression forced him to close the station and he had to move the rocks home to the family's attic. One day while he was in the local science museum, he was offered a custodial job. Eventually the director learns of his love and knowledge of rocks and arranges that he be offered the curator position in charge of rocks. It is a gentle story based on actual events in Hurst's father's life.

Hurst turned to her family stories again to write *In Plain Sight* (Houghton Mifflin/Walter Lorraine Books, 2002). About this tale, Hurst says, "my great-great grandfather did go to California during the gold rush leaving his wife, son, and daughter behind as Miles Corbin did in *In Plain Sight*."[5] Her great-great grandfather did not return and neither did Miles Corbin. Hurst's family tradition always had it that he found gold and was returning home when he was robbed and killed but Hurst found evidence that he survived yet never came back to his family. Hurst says, "*In Plain Sight* has some of the reasons why I think he might have done that."[6]

Following her first three books, Hurst turned her attention to a ghost story, *The Wrong One* (Houghton Mifflin/Walter Lorraine Books, 2003). In the story, after their father dies, three youngsters and their mother move to an old farmhouse in western Massachusetts. The children, Kate, Jesse, and their adopted sister, Sookan, find a strange but perhaps valuable doll in the rafters of the barn. When an eerie and strange blue light appears, the three youngsters suspect a ghost may be the one causing the strange events

---

**Carol Otis Hurst**

Storyteller and Language Arts Consultant

*When I think about the things people need in order to survive, I list food, of course, and shelter. Then I add love, because the ability to give and to receive love is one of the chief ingredients of humanity. Next I list literacy. Even in today's world of telecommunication, with all its sound and images, literacy is what enriches the human experience.*

*I can't imagine a life in which books are not a part. Reading for information, reading for entertainment, reading for the sheer joy of diving into a book and emerging minutes, hours or even days later, richer for having experienced it is so vital to me that life without it seems totally impossible.*

*Carol Otis Hurst*

---

that are happening. They set out to solve the mystery and find a way to keep their home from foreclosure.

In *A Killing in Plymouth* (Houghton Mifflin/Walter Lorraine Books, 2003), Hurst and her daughter and coauthor, Rebecca Otis, take a journey further back in time to the 1600s. Here they tell the story of a murder and subsequent trial from the era of Governor William Bradford and his son John.

Carol Hurst, accomplished storyteller, educator, and journalist is now also a successful author of books for young readers. She still lives in Westchester, Massachusetts. Her two daughters are grown and she has two grandsons, Keith and Jesse Otis. When she is not telling or writing stories, Hurst enjoys cooking, giving dinner parties, or playing Canasta on the Internet.

## Book Connections

Real people and real events populate the pages of many of Hurst's books and although her first stories emerged from her vast collection of family stories, she also taps into stories that are set in her home state of Massachusetts. Yet to come is a picture book,

*The Terrible Storm* (Greenwillow), about the blizzard of 1988 and *And the Owl Called Back.* Hurst retells the family stories she heard around the dining table during her childhood in another book still to come, *One Thimble, Three Bicycles and a Bit of Ingenuity* (Houghton Mifflin/Walter Lorraine Books). This book will tell how a her grandmother's ingenuity and perseverance helps her and her siblings keep in contact and actually visit one another despite being separated and put into various foster situations.

## Books Written by Carol Otis Hurst

*In Plain Sight* (Houghton Mifflin/Walter Lorraine Books, 2002).

*A Killing in Plymouth.* Written with Rebecca Otis. (Houghton Mifflin/Walter Lorraine Books, 2003).

*Rocks in His Head* (Greenwillow, 2001).

*Through the Lock* (Houghton Mifflin/Walter Lorraine Books, 2001).

*The Wrong One* (Houghton Mifflin/Walter Lorraine Books, 2003).

## For More Information

### Articles

Romano, Katherine. "Carol Otis Hurst: The Stories in Her Head." *Teaching K-8* 31.8 (May 2001): 44–46.

### Web Sites

Hurst, Carol and Rebecca Otis. *Carol Hurst's Children's Literature Site—Reviews and Teaching Ideas for Kids' Books.* Nov. 2003. <http://www.carolhurst.com>.

## Notes

1. Carol Otis Hurst, letter to the author, 7 Sept. 2002.
2. Katherine Romano, "Carol Otis Hurst: The Stories in Her Head," *Teaching K-8* 31.8 (May 2001): 44.
3. Hurst, letter.
4. Ibid.
5. Ibid.
6. Ibid.

# Barbara Joosse

◆ Family stories ◆ Historical fiction

**Grafton, Wisconsin**
February 18, 1949

📖 *Stars in the Darkness*

📖 *A Houseful of Christmas*

📖 *Lewis & Papa: Adventure on the Santa Fe Trail*

## About the Author

Barbara Monnot Joosse was raised in Grafton, Wisconsin, in a family with three children, of which she is the oldest. The three siblings, according to Joosse, were raised in a family where each of the children and the parents loved one another. "This," says Joosse, "freed me to get on with the job of childhood: adventure, dreaming, fantasy, and down-and-dirty play." This resiliency and sense of courage, and boundless imagination and hope is a resource she says, "I draw on . . . in both my personal life and my work."[1]

Several factors influenced Joosse to become a writer. As a girl, her life's goals included several possibilities: a mom, nurse, nun, or teacher. After considering all the possibilities, Barbara decided to become a nurse. To find out more about being a nurse she read all of the Cherry Ames Student Nurse books. From those books she learned that nurses often had to clean up gross stuff so she decided that if she could clean up the horse droppings from her horse, she would be able to be a nurse. But one day Barbara went to shovel horse manure over a fence and the wet sloppy stuff slid back down the handle and landed in her hair and down her shirt. That ended her aspirations to be a nurse and, Joosse says, "is why I am a writer."[2] Besides, Joosse says she classifies herself as a bossy person and that writing books allows her to "make things happen exactly as I want."[3]

Barbara Joosse completed elementary and high school in Grafton and went off to Madison to attend the University of Wisconsin. She earned a bachelor's degree in journalism, married, and became the mother of two daughters. After submitting several manuscripts to publishers, she was successful in having her first book, *The Thinking Place,* published by Knopf in 1982. The story was one drawn directly from her experience as a mother. When her daughter, Elisabeth, was naughty she was sent to her thinking place.

Joosse has relied on the reservoir of her childhood and her experiences as a mother to write over 20 books for young readers. Some of her books, including *The Thinking Place,* are currently out of print but still available in libraries.

Joosse's first two children were just toddlers when she began to write. She became interested in writing books for children as she "watched [her] first child develop." Joosse said, "I saw the intricacies of her character—the fuss, frustration, jealousy, fears, and balkiness along with the sweetness, eagerness, passion and delight. It seemed a heroic struggle to tame down the first in order for the second to emerge. It did, most of the time. But watching the struggle made me want to write about it."[4]

In 1983, the year after her first book was published, her son Rob was born. As the three children—Maaike, Anneke, and Rob—grew, so did the ideas for more books. In fact, Joosse has commented that at one point her three children thought twice about whether they should tell her about the things that happened at school because they were afraid she would use that information in her books and their classmates would tease them. However, after awhile the children figured out that it would take long enough for the book to get published that their friends would no longer be interested in teasing them about it.

As Joosse's writing career progressed, the children became her best critics and often offered advice about what might or might not appeal to young readers. Incidents from their childhood behavior, memories from her own childhood, and even stories from her husband Pete's family made their way into her books.

Joosse's books vary in subject matter and in voice. She says, "if you like one voice, you might not find it again in another book . . . I think, however, that *Ghost Wings* [Chronicle, 2001] is my best story."[5] *Ghost Wings* is a story that involves relationships, family love, and tradition—all common elements in Joosse's books.

Today, Joosse lives alone in a hundred-year-old stone house on the banks of Cedar Creek, near Cedarburg, Wisconsin. During the winter, ice skaters populate the creek and in the summer geese and ducks swim in it. Joosse has a writing studio in an old woolen mill in downtown Cedarburg where she now lives. Her studio is on the second floor of the mill where she can look out and watch the people going about their daily business on the streets below. She walks to her studio each morning—stopping along the way to have coffee with her friends—and by late afternoon she is ready to go home to care for her garden and other things around the house.

Her two daughters and son are grown. Maaike is married, both she and her spouse are attorneys. Anneke will earn a Ph.D. in entomology, the study of bugs, and she and her husband have a crazy wiener dog named Edgar. Rob is studying anthropology at the University of Montana. When he comes home from college, Joosse says she puts her son's room back the way he left it and bakes him chocolate chip cookies.

Joosse loves to cook and eat and she celebrates the new Snickers candy bar, Cruncher. She says, "I like every single kind of food as long as it's not overly processed. I think maybe I'm most nuts about nuts." She has other favorites as well including sunny colors such as yellow and shades of orange. "Persimmon," she reflects, "is probably my favorite." She doesn't have any pets "except," she says, "for the dust bunny under my bed."[6]

When Joosse is not writing, one might find her reading *Anne of Green Gables* by Lucy Maud Montgomery, her favorite book *Peace like a River* by Leif Enger, or any book by her other favorite author, Elizabeth Berg.

## Book Connections

Barbara Joosse drew directly on her own childhood experiences along with those of her son, Rob, to write the Wild Willie series. In fact, Rob, "is really Wild Willie." Rob wrote many of the titles and provided many of the ideas so he actually gets a commission each time Joosse sells a new title. Rob also figures in another story. *Lewis & Papa: Adventure on the Santa Fe Trail* (Chronicle, 1998) is a story about a father and son traveling on the trade trail and the transformation of the son from a boy to a man. About the book's origin, Joosse says, "the house in the beginning of the story is my own. I was inspired to write the story as I watched my son, Rob, grow up, and discover what it was to be a man."[7]

When Joosse was growing up she remembers going to her grandmother's house in Chicago. There, she would see her cousins and the house was always filled with a lot of excitement and noise. Those memories were woven into a story, *A Houseful of Christmas* (Henry Holt, 2001), of a family get-together on Christmas Day with a snow that kept the whole family at Grandma's overnight. One of Joosse's favorite memories is of sleeping on the floor at her grandmother's house with grandmother's dog, Edgar, and her cousins all around and her grandfather's clock ticking the minutes away. Edgar, of course, is her daughter Anneke's dog and although the real dog is a wiener dog, the illustrator, Betsy Lewin, envisioned him as a hound dog.

*I Love You the Purplest* (Chronicle, 1996) came about one day when Joosse was signing books. A woman, the mother of twins, commented that her sons often asked her who she liked the best. The mother said that she always told them she loved them the same. Once Joosse began to think about the dialogue she knew she did not love her three children the same—not one more than another but just differently. She thought she "would not like the answer that she was loved just the same, she would want to be loved—not more!—but special."[8]

Joosse's relationship with her grandfather inspired the story *Ghost Wings.* Once when the two of them were at the family's cabin they went to pick strawberries. Joosse says she "worried that a bear was lurking in the dark forest shadows, and was waiting for a tasty girl to eat."[9] Her mom and dad tried to convince her that there was no bear but her grandfather stood right beside her until she got her strawberries picked. Joosse knew that her grandfather would not let any bear get past him.

Joosse's mother lives in Mexico for half of each year and Joosse visits her there every year. When Joosse sets her books in Mexico they are, she says, "based on the country of my heart, Mexico."[10]

*The Morning Chair* (Clarion, 1995) evolved from Pete Joosse's family story. Pete moved to the United States from the Netherlands when he was just five years old. On the trip across the ocean, the family ate in the dining hall of the ship and there were small dishes of olives on the table for each meal. The family thought that olives must be a real American food and that they would have to eat olives to be real Americans; but Pete did not like them. In the book, the character Bram and his parents sail to America. In Holland Bram enjoyed eating raw herring with his Papa but in America there were green olives served at meals. The story is about Bram's adjustment to his new life in America.

*Stars in the Darkness* (Clarion, 2002) is a picture book in which a young boy, Richard, lives in an inner-city home and attempts, with the assistance of his mother, to help his older brother get free of the gang he has joined. The story is based on a real story of courage and how Richard united his neighborhood residents to help his brother. When Joosse wrote the story, she interviewed the real Richard and used his street language as well as the details of his life for the book.

Subsequent books came from the success of previous ones. Joosse's Wild Willie Mystery series has at least four titles and one of her more recent books, *Papa, Do You Love Me?* (Chronicle, 2004), was spawned by the success of her 1991 title, *Mama, Do You Love Me?* (Chronicle, 1991), both illustrated by Barbara LaVallee.

## Books Written by Barbara Joosse

*Alien Brain Fryout: A Wild Willie Mystery* (Clarion, 2000).

*Bad Dog School.* Illustrated by Jennifer Plecas. (Clarion, 2003).

*Ghost Wings.* Illustrated by Giselle Potter. (Chronicle, 2001).

*Hot City.* Illustrated by Greg Christie. (Philomel, 2003).

*A Houseful of Christmas.* Illustrated by Betsy Lewin. (Henry Holt, 2001).

*Lewis & Papa: Adventures on the Santa Fe Trail.* Illustrated by Jon Van Zyle. (Chronicle Books, 1998).

*Mama, Do You Love Me?* Illustrated by Barbara LaVallee. (Chronicle, 1991).

*Papa, Do You Love Me?* Illustrated by Barbara LaVallee. (Chronicle, 2004).

*Stars in the Darkness.* Illustrated by R. Gregory Christie. (Clarion, 2002).

## For More Information

### Articles

Schroeder, Heather Lee. "Joosse Lets Children Imagine." *The Capital Times.* Nov. 2003. <http://www.madison.com/archives/read.php?ref = tct:2001:11:30:51438: EDITORIAL>, 30 Nov. 2001.

### Web Sites

Joosse, Barbara. *Barbara Joosse's Awesome Web Site!* March 2004. <http://www. barbarajoosse.com>.

## Notes

1. Barbara Joosse, letter to the author, 9 Sept. 2002.
2. Barbara Joosse, "The Story of Tex and How I Got to Be a Writer," *Barbara Joosse's Awesome Web Site!* June 2003, <http://www.barbarajoosse.com/tex.html>.
3. Barbara Joosse, "About Me—Barbara Joosse," *Barbara Joosse's Awesome Web Site!* June 2003, <http://www.barbarajoosse.com/me.html>.
4. Joosse, letter.
5. Ibid.

6. Ibid.
7. Ibid.
8. Ibid.
9. Ibid.
10. Ibid.

# Jackie French Koller

♦ Animals ♦ Family stories ♦ Fantasy

**Derby, Connecticut**
March 8, 1948

📖 *Bouncing on the Bed*

📖 *One Monkey Too Many*

📖 *Someday*

**Series**

📖 *Dragonling Series*

📖 *The Keepers Series*

📖 *Mole and Shrew Series*

## About the Author

Jackie French Koller was born and raised in New England. Much of her childhood was spent in Connecticut but she lived in Virginia and New York as well. She was the oldest of four children born to Margaret and Ernest French and with a younger sister, Laurie, and two younger brothers, Ernest James Jr. and Richard, she became the family story-teller.

When Jackie was in sixth grade, she told tales to her classmates chapter by chapter. She would write a chapter and pass it around the playground where her friends would read each episode and wait for the next. After graduating from Shelton High School, Jackie entered the University of Connecticut where she earned an undergraduate degree in 1970, the same year she married George Koller. It wasn't long before the Kollers were the parents of three children: Kerri (1973), Ryan (1975), and Devin (1980). Jackie French Koller's life was now filled with the two things she loved most: children and stories.

"When I had my first child, reading with her quickly became my favorite activity of the day. I soon started to get ideas of my own and wrote them down." In the beginning Koller wrote stories for her daughter Kerri "but then [Koller] got courage up to show them to others." By the time her third child was born and had grown out of diapers, Koller's husband had bought her a brand new electric typewriter. Receiving the typewriter marked the beginning of her serious efforts toward achieving her dream of being a children's book writer. Koller "got some positive feedback, so [she] decided to attend a conference and start a critique group. After that there was no turning back, even though it ended up taking ten years to get a first book published."[1]

Three years after the conference, in 1986, her first children's story was published in an anthology. However, it took another two years before her first book was accepted. *Impy for Always* (Little, Brown, 1989) deals with the efforts of eight-year-old Impy's attempts to keep her cousin, Christina, from growing up. Impy wants the two of them to continue to share dolls and funny nicknames but Christina wants to grow up.

Koller continued writing and submitting her work. Bits and pieces of her life and the lives of her children ended up in her books. "A character that is probably most like me as a child is Ana from *A Place to Call Home* [Atheneum, 1995]," she says. "The character who is most like the person I longed to be is Rebekah from *The Primrose Way* [Harcourt, 1992]."[2]

Koller's family moved often when she was a youngster, however, every year her parents rented a little summer cottage on the bay where the family would spend one or two weeks. Koller and her husband have now owned that cottage for more than a decade and it is a place they call home for three months a year. Koller's own search for a place to call home is explored in several of her books including *The Last Voyage of the Misty Day* (Atheneum, 1992), *A Place to Call Home* (Atheneum, 1995), *Nothing to Fear* (Harcourt, 1991), and *Someday* (Orchard, 2002).

When Koller's son, Ryan, was in second grade, his favorite animals were dogs but his second favorite were dragons. There were plenty of children's books about dogs but not enough about dragons so he asked his mother to write some books about dragons. The result was Koller's Dragonling series for middle-grade readers.

Jackie and her husband George Koller currently live on 10 acres on a quiet mountaintop in western Massachusetts with the family pets, two Labrador Retrievers. They spend the summer at their cottage on the bay. When she is not writing, Koller says she is most likely making plans for her annual gingerbread house. Each December she creates a themed house and in 2002 the house featured the theme Christmas with Mole and Shrew. In previous years she created a lighthouse, Thomas Kinkaid's cottage, a Christmas castle, and a New England farmhouse. Koller's children are now grown. Kerri is married and teaches middle school in eastern Massachusetts and after earning an engineering degree, Ryan designs aircraft engines. Devin, the youngest, is also an engineer who works in engineering sales.

## Book Connections

A couple years before Jackie French Koller wrote *Bouncing on the Bed* (Orchard, 1999), a story that follows a toddler from morning to night, her brother and his wife announced that they were expecting their first baby. The baby would be the first in the family for a long time. Everyone was very excited—especially Koller and she began to think about all the activity a baby would bring to the family. The baby turned out to be a boy named Noah and Koller said she was "quite astonished when I saw the illustrations that Anna Grossnickle Hines did for the book, because even though she's never seen Noah, she drew a little boy that looks enough like him to be his twin!"[3]

Koller has written books for all ages and each of her books differs from the others. Koller's Dragonling series and her Keepers series are, she says, "best read in order. While the Mole and Shrew series can be read in any order, but if readers start with *The Mole and Shrew Are Two* [Random House, 2000], they will get a good understanding of who Mole and Shrew are and how their friendship began."[4]

Dear friends,

There are so many things competing for your time these days - movies, video games, sports, computers, homework... How can you make time to read books? And why should you? Does it even matter? Well, for starters books can increase your vocabulary, reading speed and comprehension, and these things will help you all through your life, help you get into a good school, help you get a good job, help you become a valuable citizen of the world. But books can do a lot more than that. Take the word of the thousands of young people who have written to me over the years to tell me how much one or the other of my books has meant to them, has helped them better understand themselves and their world. You see, writers are the eyes and ears of society. While other people are busy with their jobs and daily lives, it's the writer's job to look and listen and think about things that most folks just don't have time to ponder. Then writers put their thoughts into stories and people read the stories and their eyes open wide. They have made a connection with the writer. They have understood something new, seen something in a different light. In this way, down through the centuries, books have changed the world in big + small ways. Each time you pick up a book you open the door to a new adventure, one that might change your life. Isn't that worth making time for?

Jackie French Koller

The sequence of the Dragonlings series is as follows:

*The Dragonling* (1990)
*A Dragon in the Family* (1993)
*Dragon Quest* (1997)
*Dragon of Krad* (1997)
*Dragon Trouble* (1997)
*Dragons and Kings* (1998)

Little, Brown Publishers and Pocket Books first published these books and in 2000 and 2001 the books became available in boxed sets. The first three titles were sold in a boxed set as Volume I of the Dragonling series and the last three titles were packaged together as Volume II.

The popularity of the Dragonling series has spawned a brand new series from Simon & Schuster called The Keepers. The Keepers series is fantasy similar to the Dragonling series but it features wizards, witches, dragons (of course), and many other fantastic folk. The most charming character, however, may be an enchanting miniature dragon named Minna. The first title in the series is *A Wizard Named Nell* (Simon & Schuster, 2003).

## Books Written by Jackie French Koller

*Baby for Sale.* Illustrated by Janet Pedersen. (Marshall Cavendish Books, 2002). Picture book.

*Bouncing on the Bed.* Illustrated by Anna Gossnickle Hines. (Orchard Books, 1999). Picture book.

The Dragonling Collector's Edition, Volume I—*Dragonling, A Dragon in the Family, Dragon Quest.* Illustrated by Jacqueline Mitchell. (Aladdin, 2000). Chapter books, Dragonling Series.

The Dragonling Collector's Edition, Volume II—*Dragons of Krad, Dragon Trouble, Dragons and Kings.* Illustrated by Jacqueline Mitchell. (Aladdin, 2001). Chapter books, Dragonling Series.

*Mole and Shrew Are Two.* Illustrated by Anne Reas. (Random House, 2000). Early reader, Mole and Shrew Series.

*One Monkey Too Many.* Illustrated by Lynn Munsinger. (Harcourt, 1999).

*Someday* (Orchard, 2002). Novel.

*A Wizard Named Nell.* Illustrated by Rebecca Guay. (Simon & Schuster, 2003). Novel, The Keepers Series.

## For More Information

### Articles

Koller, Jackie French. "Recommendation for Young People Who Want to Write." *Kid Authors.* March 2004. <http://www.kidauthors.com/Jackie_tips.asp>.

Smith, Cynthia Leitich. "Interview with Children's Book Author Jackie French Koller." *Children's Book Author Cynthia Leitich Smith's Official Web Site.* March 2004. <http://www.cynthialeitichsmith.com/auth-illJackieFrenchKoller.htm>.

"Women Who Rock the World Meet Jackie French Koller: Children's Book Author." *A Girls World.Com.* March 2004. <http://www.agirlsworld.com/amy/pajama/wmhistory/careers/jkollier/>.

### Web Sites

Koller, Jackie French. *Jackie French Koller's Author Page.* Nov. 2003. <http://www.Jackiefrenchkoller.com>.

## Notes

1. Jackie French Koller, letter to the author, 11 Sept. 2003.
2. Ibid.
3. Anna Grossnickle Hines, "The Story Behind Bouncing on the Bed," *Anna Grossnickle Hines: Children's Author & Illustrator,* March 2004, <http://www.aghines.com/bouncing.htm>.
4. Koller, letter.

# Jane Kurtz

◆ Family stories  ◆ Folk literature  ◆ Historical fiction  ◆ Poetry

**Portland, Oregon**
April 17, 1952

📖 *Bicycle Madness*

📖 *Jakarta Missing*

📖 *Rain Romp: Stomping Away a Grouchy Day*

📖 *Saba, Under the Hyena's Foot*

📖 *The Storyteller's Beads*

## About the Author

Jane Kurtz was born in Portland, Oregon but her family moved to Ethiopia when she was only two years old. Her parents spent 23 years in Ethiopia only making trips back to the United States once every five years. Jane spent most of her childhood in Ethiopia until she came back to the United States to attend college in Illinois. However, after she was back in the states, she says she "always struggled with the sense of not ever being at home with a culture."[1] She listed her grandmother's Iowa address in the student directory because she thought there was really no way to talk about Ethiopia with people in the United States. Twenty years later, Jane found a way to reconnect with Ethiopia through her writing a non-fiction book, *Ethiopia: Roof of Africa* (Silver Burdett/Dillon Press, 1991).

Jane says, "I always wanted to be a writer."[2] She says that she

> can't remember a time when my mom and dad didn't read to me—and when my dad didn't tell me stories. When I was two years old and on my way to Ethiopia for the first time, my mom says that my dad told the story 'This is the House that Jack Built' over and over in a London train station. The trip was long and my two sisters and I were bored. In Ethiopia, he learned new stories that he would tell us at night. I particularly remember lying in a tent with lions roaring in the distance and listening to stories. But I never thought about publishing a book for young readers until I had my own children. We would go to the library almost every week and come home with armloads of books. When I was reading them those hundreds of books, I fell in love with children's literature and set a goal of publishing my own book someday.[3]

Kurtz and her siblings, four sisters and one brother, were home schooled from kindergarten through third grade. By the time Kurtz reached the fourth grade, her parents

**143**

felt that they had reached the limits of their home-schooling ability. Kurtz was sent to a boarding school in Addis Ababa and the entire family moved there during her high school years. Soon, though, in the late 1970s, a revolution in the country disrupted their lives. The revolution brought gunshots and shouts telling all ferenjis (foreigners) to get out, ultimately forcing the family to return to the United States.

After the family left Ethiopia during the revolution, Kurtz's parents stayed in the United States for a period of time but they eventually returned to a missionary post in Kenya. Jane finished college and married Leonard Goering, a minister. The family lived in Illinois, Colorado, and by the time the family moved to North Dakota, Kurtz was the mother of three small children. Her husband was a busy minister so Kurtz's time for writing was at a premium. She helped to establish a mothers' morning out program at the church and after the program got going, Kurtz was able to have her own children in the program and capture time on Thursday mornings to write. Her first stories came from the lives of her children and spawned her first picture book, *I'm Calling Molly* (Whitman, 1990).

Her second book was the nonfiction book about Ethiopia. "I never studied Ethiopian history or geography or culture in school," she says, "because I had to be ready to fit back into American schools. It was a healing experience to go back and learn everything I could about the land of my childhood."[4] Kurtz began to research all the questions that she had about Ethiopia. She found information about the markets, peasant associations, legends, food, and festivals of Ethiopia. At the time, her younger brother, Christopher, was living in Ethiopia with his family. He had returned to Ethiopia from the United States as an adult and was spending time teaching in a school there. Because he was there, he was able to take pictures for *Ethiopia: Roof of Africa*.

Her next book, *Fire on the Mountain* (Simon & Schuster, 1994), came directly from her experience with the Ethiopian stories she heard during her childhood. Kurtz was able to send the illustrator, E. B. Lewis, photographs from Ethiopia and Lewis used the photographs to create the beautiful watercolors that show the Ethiopian countryside. A second folktale, *Pulling the Lion's Tail* (Simon & Schuster, 1995), was illustrated by Floyd Cooper.

Kurtz had always been fascinated by volcanoes and loved the obsidian that she and her sisters found on the Ethiopian mountain slopes where they often played. She realized that volcanoes were also found in a region of South America inhabited by the Incas. This piqued her interest in the Inca civilization and the tale she told next was *Miro in the Kingdom of the Sun* (Houghton Mifflin, 1996), an Inca tale.

*Trouble* (Harcourt, 1997), a traditional tale, is set in Eritrea, an area that prior to 1993, was part of Ethiopia. *Trouble* tells the story of a young boy, Tekeleh, who is kept out of trouble with a game of gebeta (sometimes called Mancala in other countries). Kurtz's own memories of the game include sitting on the dirt floor of her home in the village of Maji and scooping up pebbles and dropping them in the holes, one after another. Just as Tekeleh in the book, Kurtz also enjoyed poking at a line of ants with a stick.

When Kurtz's younger brother, Christopher, was teaching in a girl's school in Addis Ababa his students were middle-class Ethiopians who lived in houses much like those of his and Jane's childhood. Chris became acquainted with a young boy named Andualeum, who shined shoes outside of the school's complex. Through his friendship with Andualeum, Chris came to know the other side of Addis Ababa.

In Andualeum's world, many people were unemployed, families often had no home in which to sleep, and children who shined shoes might be the family's main source of income. Chris photographed Andualeum feeding and playing with a pigeon. When Andualeum fed the pigeon he chewed the food first and then fed it to the pigeon mouth-to-mouth (or mouth-to-beak). That photograph inspired Jane to suggest a book and together Jane and Chris crafted the manuscript for *Only a Pigeon* (Simon & Schuster, 1997). *Only a Pigeon* explored a part of Ethiopia that had not been part of Jane's childhood and she found it difficult to write about it. Jane's childhood had been one that emphasized the beauty of the country and she seldom saw the areas of Andualeum's world. Only as an adult did she realize how many Ethiopian children lived with the daily struggle to avoid starvation.

E. B. Lewis was asked to illustrate *Only a Pigeon*. This time, he and Chris (by now Christopher was back in the United States) returned to Addis Ababa to gather the images and Lewis photographed many images that would help him create the illustrations for the story.

That part of Ethiopia again surfaced when Kurtz set out to write her first novel, *The Storyteller's Beads* (Harcourt, 1998). After several revisions, she felt she was finally successful in telling about the Ethiopian children and their struggle to avoid starvation during the war. Through her revisions, the story took on its final form and as thoughts about two girls haunted her, Kurtz found the story's voice. From her readings, Kurtz found out more about the attitude of the Kemants (from northern Ethiopia), who considered the Jews in their country Buda—possessed by the devil. She thought about what would happen if a girl from each of these ethnic groups were put together in a specific situation. Kurtz also had another idea that she gleaned from a story that she came across during her research. That story told of a blind girl who walked all the way to the Sudan with her hand on the shoulder of her brother. The story of *The Storyteller's Beads* was the story of two girls, one Jewish and blind and the other Christian and from the Kemant group in northern Ethiopia. The two of them are among a group that in the 1980s fled the political situation in their homeland and became refugees.

*The Storyteller's Beads* describes the devastation that occurred in Jane's childhood home. However, while Kurtz was finishing the final rewrites for that story, she was, as an adult, experiencing another type of devastation, which began on her birthday in 1997. That is the day a great flood invaded the Kurtz's home on Lincoln Drive in Grand Forks, North Dakota. The family fled their home, each carrying only a bag of clothes except for Kurtz who took a few of her writing materials. They went to the home of friends in another part of the town but two days later, on April 19, her son David's birthday, the family had to evacuate again when the flood reached their friends' home.

The family was unable to return to their house for more than a month. During that month, Kurtz sat in the basement of a friend's house and worked on the revisions for *The Storyteller's Beads* while David and her other children, Jonathan and Rebekah, finished school in the town of Walhalla. In May that year, Kurtz kept her plans to attend the International Reading Association's annual conference in Atlanta, Georgia. There she shared a room with fellow writers: Deborah Hopkinson and Deborah Wiler. Kurtz was still very much affected by the events of the past month and her friends suggested that she follow the advice she often gave youngsters during her school visits. Write about it. So on Kurtz's return she did just that, she began to write poems about the flood and its effect on her family. Later, while the family attempted to clean their old home, they lived in a travel trailer provided by the Federal Emergency Management Agency (FEMA), which sat in their driveway. Many of their neighbors were also living in similar circumstances. The poems she wrote during that period became *River Friendly, River Wild* (Simon &

Schuster, 2000). Kurtz created the fictionalized girl who is telling the story in the book but Kurtz admits, "she is partly my daughter and partly me."[5]

Before that book was published another of Kurtz's manuscripts was published. *I'm Sorry, Almira Ann* (Henry Holt, 1999) was based on the story of her great-grandmother's trek west along the Oregon Trail. A scene in the book where Almira's mother's ring accidentally gets left behind when the covered wagons move on is based on an incident that really occurred.

Eventually the Kurtz family moved to another home in Grand Forks, where Kurtz continued to write and teach part time at the University of North Dakota. Another title, *Faraway Home* (Harcourt, 2000), brought together the themes of culture and identity by telling the story of a girl named Desta. Kurtz always felt a struggle with the sense of not ever being at home with any culture. That is a struggle Desta also feels but in a different way. When Desta's Ethiopian father is about to return to Ethiopia to visit his sick mother, Desta begins to worry that her father will not return—that he won't want to leave Ethiopia again. Kurtz says, "in many ways, it's my personal story as well as the story of so many immigrant families who have a cultural gap to bridge between parents and children."[6]

Kurtz says, "although it's not as obvious, *Rain Romp* [Greenwillow, 2000], also came from the flood."[7] Kurtz was driving her daughter to school one day during the aftermath of the flood and while the family was still living in the FEMA trailer. The day was very gloomy and rainy and her daughter's mood seemed to be just like the day. "That," says Kurtz, "is when the idea of a grouchy girl on a rainy day came into my head—along with the ending, that we would be a loving family even on grouchy days."[8]

Kurtz returned to her historical research to tell a story, *Bicycle Madness* (Henry Holt, 2003). The tale is about Frances Willard (1839–1898), a historical figure who was an advocate for women's rights and who learned how to ride a bicycle. In *Bicycle Madness,* Willard's story is told through a fictional relationship with a neighbor, a young girl Lillie, who Willard helps prepare for a spelling bee.

When Kurtz was asked to write a novel, *Saba: Under the Hyena's Foot* (Pleasant Company, 2003), for the Pleasant Company's Girls of Many Lands series, she again turned her attention to Ethiopia. More historical research was necessary for her to tell the story of Saba, a 12 year old who is kidnapped in the mid-1840s and taken to the palace in Gondar. Saba learns that she and her brother are part of the emperor's political plot to consolidate power. Kurtz's title is one in a series that has many notable authors including Kurtz's friend, Mary Casanova.

Jane's extensive travel commitments keep her on the road for several days each month. She has also been able to return to Ethiopia several times and her extended family made a pilgrimage back to Addis Ababa in 2002. Even though Kurtz herself did not grow up in Kenya, some of her siblings spent several years there. Now Kenya is often on Kurtz's itinerary when she travels to the continent of Africa with other members of her family.

The traditional Ethiopian foods Kurtz learned to eat as a youngster have influenced her favorites today. Other favorites include breads of all types, spicy food, and almost anything that is chocolate. Jane's enthusiasm for writing and children is never more evident than when she visits children in schools. She shares a realia kit, a kit with artifacts and objects from Ethiopia, so students can experience a little bit of Ethiopia and her research. She also brings pictures of those that have inspired her characters, her setting, and many anecdotes of how her stories came to be.

Dear Readers,

When I was in school, I never had a chance to meet an author or read a letter from one. If I had, I would have wanted to be an author because I loved books. Now, I always hope I can inspire young readers to spend as much time with books as I did because even though I've traveled all over the world, the greatest adventures of my life have happened while I was sitting in my own chair reading a book.

In one of my books, it says, "You are the hero of your own life." Life is tough, but books are a wonderful part of making people strong and hopeful and kind.

They did that for me. I hope they'll do that for you, too.

Best of times with reading —

Jane Kurtz

After living for a number of years in North Dakota, the Kurtz family home is now in Hesston, Kansas, where Jane and her husband, Leonard Goering, are closer to his parents. Kurtz's parents have lived for a number of years in Portland, Oregon and her fellow writer and brother Chris Kurtz lives near his parents. Kurtz's full-time attention is now given to her role as a children's author, which includes writing and school visits. Her daughter and both sons are grown, attending college, and establishing their own paths in life.

## Book Connections

Jane Kurtz's books are influenced directly by her childhood in Ethiopia. Sometimes her childhood allows her to tell a story that she heard during her youth—picture book stories such as *Pulling the Lion's Tail* and *Trouble*. Other stories draw on the emotions and cultural heritage that emerged from her years in Ethiopia, a country that wasn't really hers but kept her from being able to call the United States her own culture.

*Jakarta Missing* (Greenwillow, 2002) and *The Storyteller's Beads* made Jane face the impoverished parts of the country of her childhood that she had avoided for many years. *Only a Pigeon* helped her take a realistic look at the country she grew up in and to assess the conflicting emotions of belonging and not belonging. Recently, historical fiction became part of her repertoire. *I'm Sorry, Almira Ann* is historical fiction from the pioneer days. *Saba, Under the Hyena's Foot* takes place in Gondar, Ethiopia during the mid-1840s. *Bicycle Madness* is set in the middle and latter part of the 1800s.

Kurtz's experiences with her children and with contemporary events such as the Red River flood of 1997 continue to inspire her with new ideas and help her link the culture she grew up in and the culture she is part of today.

## Books Written by Jane Kurtz

*Bicycle Madness.* Illustrated by Beth Peck. (Henry Holt, 2003). Early chapter.

*I'm Sorry, Almira Ann.* Illustrated by Susan Havrice. (Henry Holt, 1999). Early chapter.

*Jakarta Missing* (Greenwillow, 2002). Novel.

*Rain Romp: Stomping Away a Grouchy Day.* Illustrated by Dyanne Wolcott. (Greenwillow, 2002). Picture book.

*River Friendly, River Wild.* Illustrated by Neil Brennan. (Simon & Schuster, 2000).

*Saba: Under the Hyena's Foot.* Girls of Many Lands Series. Illustrated by Jean-Paul Tibbles. (Pleasant Company, 2003). Novel.

*Waterhole Waiting.* Illustrated by Lee Christianson. (Greenwillow, 2001). Picture book.

## For More Information

### Article

"Author Interviews: September 2003: Jane Kurtz." *Downhomebooks.com: Jane Kurtz Interview.* March 2004. <http://www.downhomebooks.com/kurtz.htm>, Sept. 2003.

Kurtz, Jane. "Beyond Boundaries: Connecting Children with Modern Urban Ethiopia." *BookLinks* 7.4 (March 1998): 16–19.

Kurtz, Jane. "Writers & Readers: A Book Worm in High Places." *Booklist* 9.4 (1 March 2001): 1282–1283.

McElmeel, Sharron. "Author Profile: Jane Kurtz, Reflecting Homes Places." *Library Talk* 13.2 (March/April 2000): 24–26.

## Web Sites

Kurtz, Jane. *Jane Kurtz Children's Author.* March 2004. <http://www.janekurtz.com>.

## Notes

1. Jane Kurtz, interview with the author, Atlanta, Georgia, 4 May 1997.
2. Ibid.
3. Jane Kurtz, letter to the author, 12 Sept. 2002.
4. Jane Kurtz, letter to the author, 25 Oct. 1999.
5. Ibid.
6. Kurtz, letter, 1999.
7. Kurtz, letter, 2002.
8. Ibid.

# Loreen Leedy

◆  Mathematics  ◆  Family stories

| Wilmington, Delaware |
| June 15, 1959 |

📖 *Message in the Mailbox: How to Write a Letter*

📖 *Measuring Penny*

📖 *Mission: Addition*

📖 *Who's Who in My Family?*

## About the Author/Illustrator

Loreen Leedy's childhood began in Wilmington, Delaware where she grew up in a family with two older sisters, an older brother, and one younger brother. When Leedy was just two months old, the family moved to Chicago, Illinois and then when she was three, they moved to North Augusta, South Carolina. Leedy taught herself to read before she went to school and reading became her favorite pastime. By the time Loreen was nine, the family had moved back to Wilmington, where Loreen earned a scholarship to attend weekly art classes at the Delaware Art Museum. When she was just 13, her first published work appeared in *American Girl* magazine. During high school, Laureen was a member of the theater troupe and helped design the sets for the productions. After finishing high school in Wilmington, she entered the University of Delaware. She did not know what type of artist she wanted to be but she knew she wanted to work in the field of art so she studied that subject and earned her undergraduate degree cum laude in 1981.

After college Loreen Leedy established herself as a freelance craftsperson making and selling handmade polymer clay jewelry; mostly pins and earrings. She says, "many of my jewelry pieces were whimsical pigs, frogs, and other creatures." The animals were cats in pants, pig mermaids, mushrooms with tiny frogs on top and dozens of colorful critters. "In 1984, after a teacher friend introduced me to a children's author-illustrator, Olivier Dunrea," Leedy continues, "I thought they might make good characters for a children's book. I began to draw and paint critters and write stories for them."[1]

Dunrea became a mentor and a good friend to Loreen. Soon she was concentrating entirely on creating images and stories for children's books. Her first book was *A Number of Dragons* (Holiday House, 1985) and in less than three years, she produced another book, *The Bunny Play* (Holiday House, 1988), which was selected as a Junior Guild book.

**150**

Dear Readers,
    I hope you're discovering the wonderful world inside books. There are stories to entertain you and information that will enrich your life. Inside books, you can meet people, go places, and share experiences that you otherwise wouldn't be able to. So join me and . . .
    KEEP READING!

Loreen Leedy

Over time Leedy developed illustrative techniques with oils, watercolors, and gouache. With the publication of *Celebrate the 50 States!* (Holiday House, 1999), Leedy began to utilize a computer to create illustrations and many of the animals from her jewelry designs reappear in her books.

When asked about her favorite things, Leedy responds, "food is a top priority, preferably fresh and not full of chemicals." She feels her health has improved after educating herself about vitamins, minerals, and other supplements. In addition to food, Leedy says, "I love all animals, but prefer having a cat as a pet. Our cat's name is Photon, and he is very playful. As an artist, I love all colors (though not all together in one picture)."[2]

For many years Leedy lived in Winter Park, Florida where she worked in a large studio. From this location she traveled to many schools and conferences where she talked about her art and her writing. In 2002, Leedy married Andrew C. Schuerger, a scientist who works in the microbiology field. Much of his work is done for NASA and supports efforts to develop techniques for growing plants on Mars. After their marriage the couple moved to Titusville, Florida where Leedy became involved with her community. She is a voracious reader and one of her favorite activities involves reading and trying out all kinds of crafts. She also enjoys the flora and fauna of her Florida home. She loves to draw and paint.

## Book Connections

From the time Loreen Leedy's fourth grade teacher handed her a sheet of multiplication facts to memorize until the time she dropped out of a tenth grade geometry class, mathematics has not been one of her favorite subjects. However when an editor at Holiday House suggested that she write a book on some aspect of mathematics, she considered it and, realizing that mathematics is part of everyday life, she decided to write about it. She did a lot of research on the current curriculum standards for primary students and the first book she wrote on this topic was *Fraction Action* (Holiday House, 1994). Leedy included five short stories about a teacher, Miss Prime, and her students. The book served as a vehicle for teaching information about fractions. Miss Prime's students cut a tuna sandwich in half and folded a dollar bill in fourths. The stories involved dividing food fairly and selling lemonade at a fraction of its original price. The students even give their teacher a test on fractions. The success of that book spawned several additional titles including *2x2 = BOO! A Set of Spooky Multiplication Stories* (Holiday House, 1995), *Measuring Penny* (Holt, 1997), *Mission: Addition* (Holiday House, 1997), and *Subtraction Action* (Holiday House, 2000).

Because Leedy illustrated *Mission: Addition* before she began to use the computer to help create illustrations, she decided she would have to be extra diligent when she created the illustrations for its companion book, *Subtraction Action*. Even though she was now using a computer to help generate her art, she wanted both books to have a similar look.

In each of Leedy's books she manages to put in some images that are taken from her life and that of her friends. For example, a black cat that she once owned shows up in *The Edible Pyramid: Good Eating Every Day* (Holiday House, 1994). Her aunt's Boston Terrier is a featured character in *Measuring Penny* and *Mapping Penny's World* (Holt, 2000). Also, the photos used in the background of *Mapping Penny's World* are photographs from Leedy's former home town, Winter Park, Florida.

The art for *Celebrate the 50 States!* was created with scanned images of items Leedy had gathered. For example, the log on the Oregon Trail is really a small branch that fell from a tree in her backyard. She says, "the cereal on the Michigan page is from a box of corn flakes in my kitchen at the time. The fabrics in the title for South Carolina came from a box of scraps in my garage. The ring on the South Dakota page belongs to my mother. The map behind the title for Virginia came from my brother's used book store."[3] One of Leedy's nieces is featured in *Follow the Money!* (Holiday House, 2002). On page 17 of that book readers will see a candy store in the background. That store, Deborah's Candy, is named after her niece.

Generally Leedy writes and illustrates her own books but she has also illustrated a couple of books written by other writers and she recently coauthored a book, *There's a Frog in My Throat: 440 Animal Sayings a Little Bird Told Me* (Holiday House, 2003), with a teacher friend, Pat Street.

## Books Written and Illustrated by Loreen Leedy

*Celebrate the 50 States!* (Holiday House, 1999).

*Follow the Money!* (Holiday House, 2002).

*Look at My Book: How Kids Can Write & Illustrate Terrific Books* (Holiday House, 2003).

*Mapping Penny's World* (Holt, 2000).

*Messages in the Mailbox: How to Write a Letter* (Holiday House, 1991).

*Mission: Addition* (Holiday House, 1997).

*Subtraction Action* (Holiday House, 2000).

*There's a Frog in My Throat: 440 Animal Sayings a Little Bird Told Me.* Written with Pat Street. (Holiday House, 2003).

*Who's Who in My Family?* (Holiday House, 1994).


## For More Information

### Web Sites

Leedy, Loreen. *Loreen Leedy's Home Page.* Nov. 2003. <http://www.loreenleedy.com>.


## Notes

1. Loreen Leedy, letter to the author, 12 Sept. 2002.
2. Ibid.
3. Ibid.

# E. B. Lewis

◆ Historical fiction ◆ Family stories

**Philadelphia, Pennsylvania**
December 16, 1956

📖 *Dirt on Their Skirts: The Story of the Young Women Who Won the World Championship*

📖 *Sometimes My Mommy Gets Angry*

📖 *Talkin' About Bessie: The Story of Aviator Elizabeth Coleman*

## About the Author/Illustrator

Earl Bradley Lewis was born and raised in Philadelphia, the oldest in what became a family of five children. For the first four years of his life, he received a lot of attention as an only child and the only grandchild but when his sister came along, Earl was very jealous and he vied for attention in any way he could get it. Soon the family included another sister and two brothers. Earl became a problem child, the class clown, and the class artist. When he was in third grade he entered a citywide art contest where each entrant had to draw someone famous. Earl recalls, "I drew Ben Franklin, and I won."[1]

Despite his gift as an artist, Earl's behavior did not improve. He had two uncles who were artists, one of which ran a Saturday morning art workshop, the Temple University School Art League. After Earl finished sixth grade, his uncle began to take him to the school each Saturday morning and Earl's behavior began to change. He studied with a noted Philadelphia painter, Clarence Wood, and remained in the Saturday morning program until he entered the Temple University Tyler School of Art in 1975. He only applied to that one school because it was the only school he wanted to attend—the school associated with his uncle. Earl majored in graphic design and art education with a minor in drawing. At school, he honed his skills as a watercolorist.

When Earl graduated in 1979, he had a fine art portfolio but was ill prepared to enter the world of business as an artist. He says, "I had prepared as a fine artist and did not really know what to do with my portfolio."[2] He became disillusioned and decided to teach in order to make ends meet. For the next four years he taught second graders and then high school art, working on his own art during evenings and weekends. When teaching jobs began to be eliminated, Earl found himself without work. He went back to school to obtain certification to teach special needs learners and for 12 years he taught at

**154**

a psychiatric hospital school working with young adults who needed the controlled environment and a patient and gentle teacher. Art became an important part of their education, academically and emotionally.

By 1984, Earl Bradley Lewis had created many paintings and was offered a one-artist exhibit at the Downtown Philadelphia Gallery. All of his work sold and he gained wide recognition in the Philadelphia art community. Less than two years later he was exhibiting in the prestigious Rosenfeld Gallery in Philadelphia as well as in many other galleries throughout the United States. Many private collectors now have his work in their collections.

Lewis had not yet entered the children's book field and wasn't even interested in illustration—he only considered himself a fine artist. But one day an art editor saw his work on the cover of a fine art magazine. He called Lewis and asked if he would be interested in illustrating children's books. Lewis declined and explained that he was a fine artist, but the agent countered by sending him to a bookstore to look at some children's books and the art inside. Lewis went and browsed the children's section. He says he realized that "some of the best art in the country is inside the pages of children's books."[3] The agent then sent Lewis's slides and portfolio to seven or eight publishing house art editors. Within a week, the agent called Lewis back because four of those art editors had asked to have Lewis consider manuscripts for illustration. His first children's book project, *Fire on the Mountain* written by Jane Kurtz (Simon & Schuster), appeared in 1994 and since then Lewis has illustrated three to four children's books a year.

E. B. Lewis's recognition in the field of children's books began to grow and several of his books were recipients of the Coretta Scott King honor award for illustration. He often painted his images using photographs as source material. When he began to create the illustrations for *Fire on the Mountain,* he used photographs that Kurtz sent him along with photographs that he took of Ethiopian families who were now living in Philadelphia. Later he was contracted to illustrate another of Kurtz's books, *Only a Pigeon* (Simon & Schuster, 1997). After Lewis agreed to illustrate *Only a Pigeon,* he traveled to Ethiopia with Kurtz's coauthor, Chris Kurtz, so he could do the art research for the story.

When Lewis was working on the illustrations for *Dirt on Their Skirts* (Dial, 2000), a book about a 1950s women's softball team, he searched for authentic uniforms for the ball team. Eventually he found waitress uniforms from the era and adapted them for his models to wear. The models for the ball-team players were elementary school staff members who agreed to dress in the uniforms. Lewis photographed the models as they struck various player stances and these photographs helped him create his paintings for the book.

In *Talkin' About Bessie: The Story of Aviator Elizabeth Coleman* written by Nikki Grimes (Orchard, 2002) Lewis paid particular attention to the historic details of the era in which the story takes place. Lewis placed the character Bessie at the center of each oversized watercolor painting and each person who gives a testimonial at Bessie's funeral is included in a sepia-toned thumbnail portrait accompanying the appropriate illustration.

The models for Lewis's illustrations are sometimes friends or family but just as often they might be someone he identifies just for the specific purpose that is needed. Often he shows two of the people in his book in an embrace—a hug. Of his first 30 books or so, only 4 have lacked the hug.

Lewis's illustrative schedule typically is filled with children's book contracts that are five years in advance of the publication of the book. In addition to his illustrative work, he continues to exhibit his fine art and makes appearances in as many as 50 schools or conferences each year. Many of his paintings are in the collections of the Pew Charitable Trust and First Pennsylvania Bank.

Currently, E. B. Lewis teaches illustration at the University of the Arts in Philadelphia and is a member of The Society of Illustrators and the prestigious Salmagundi Club in New York City. He enjoys the time he spends with his two sons, Aaron (1986) and Joshua (1989), and his leisure time is often spent fishing. Says Lewis, "it's the thing I like to do best, it's my hobby."[4] He fishes both in the deep sea and in fresh water. Other favorites include the color purple and Thai food. Lewis currently lives in Folsom, New Jersey.

## Book Connections

E. B. Lewis has illustrated over 30 books since he entered the children's book field in 1984. He works for many publishers and has illustrated books by many authors including three titles set in Ethiopia and written by Jane Kurtz, three by Natasha Anastasia Tarpley, two historical fiction titles by Doreen Rappaport, a couple of literary folk stories by Tololwa M. Mollel, a series of books about Little Cliff by Clifton L. Taulbert, and other titles by Nikki Grimes, Elizabeth Fitzgerald Howard, Alice Schertle, John Steptoe, Fatima Shaik, and Jacqueline Woodson. He has received several awards for his illustrations including the 2003 Coretta Scott King Award for *Talkin' About Bessie: The Story of Aviator Elizabeth Coleman*. The award honors African American authors and illustrators of outstanding books for children and young adults.

## Books Illustrated by E. B. Lewis

*Bippity Bop Barbershop.* Written by Natasha Anastasia Tarpley. (Little, Brown, 2002).

*Circle Unbroken: The Story of the Sweetgrass Basket.* Written by Margot Theirs Raven. (Farrar Straus Giroux, 2004).

*Dirt on Their Skirts: The Story of the Young Women Who Won the World Championship.* Written by Doreen Rappaport and Lyndall Callan. (Dial, 2000).

*Faraway Home.* Written by Jane Kurtz. (Harcourt, 2000).

*Joe-Joe's First Flight.* Written by Natasha Anastasia Tarpley. (Knopf, 2003).

*Little Cliff and the Cold Place.* Written by Clifton L. Taulbert. (Dial, 2002).

*Sometimes My Mommy Gets Angry.* Written by BeBe Moore Campbell. (G.P. Putnam, 2003).

*Talkin' About Bessie: The Story of Aviator Elizabeth Coleman.* Written by Nikki Grimes. (Orchard, 2002).

## For More Information

### Articles

"E.B. Lewis Gallery." *R. Michelson Gallery.* March 2004. <http://www.rmichelson.com/Artist_Pages/Lewis/EB_Lewis.htm>.

## Web Sites

Lewis, E. B. *The Home of E.B. Lewis.* March 2004. <http://www.eblewis.com>.

# Notes

1. E. B. Lewis, interview with the author, 22 March 2003.
2. Ibid.
3. Ibid.
4. Ibid.

# Pat Mora

**El Paso, Texas**
January 19, 1942

📖 *Tomás and the Library Lady*

📖 *The Rainbow Tulip*

📖 *A Library for Juana: The World of Sor Juana Inés*

## About the Author

Pat Mora was born and raised in El Paso, Texas where she grew up with her brother, Roy, and her two sisters, Stella and Cissy. She has said that her father, who felt that others did not care if he was there or not, "was one of those disposal children. He dreaded the time when he was called upon to read." Their dual language household created an environment where Pat's development of both languages evolved very naturally. "I can't ever remember not speaking Spanish and English."[1]

Pat's family was a happy one. Always willing to take the four children to the library for a new batch of books, Pat's mother instilled in the children a love for reading. Pat's aunt often told them stories at night in both English and Spanish. Her elementary education was at St. Patrick's Elementary School in El Paso and she graduated from Loretto High School and then went on to Texas Western College, now known as the University of Texas at El Paso, where she majored in English. As a youngster, Pat loved words and writing but it wasn't until the mid 1980s, as the mother of three children and well into her adult life, that she began to set aside a regular time for writing. Pat Mora says she began to write for young readers simply because, "I became interested when I was reading books to my children when they were little. I love picture books and still give them to my three grown children."[2]

Mora is very aware of the image books give to children of Hispanic heritage. In 2002, she said that on one "notable reading list of 45 titles there was not one book by a Latino. Latinos are 13% of the population but less than 2% of the books published are about Latinos."[3] Her own ability to speak two languages has helped her to cross borders to build communities of readers. Mora often writes books in both Spanish and English or writes in English and inserts a few Spanish words to give the writing a little flavor. As a writer, she is "able to use árbol or tree in a poem."[4]

**158**

Yet, according to Mora, bilingual writers face stereotypic attitudes. For example, if a bilingual writer is from a segment of society that is typically undereducated, editors and others associated with book publishing and buying tend to assume that the writing is inferior to that of other writers. Conversely, if a middle or upper class author is bilingual and writes a story, that writing is viewed somewhat more favorably.

Mora has set out to present a much different image through her writing. Forty million adults have difficulty reading to children or helping them with homework. With her books, which are often bilingual, she hopes "to help families support a journey to family literacy." Her books are filled with playful words that focus on families and love. Mora has also created a collection of poems that use alliteration, *Confetti: Poems for Children* (Lee & Low, 1996). In another collection of poetry, *My Own True Name: New and Selected Poems for Young Adults* (Piñata Press, 2000), she includes a poem, "Alana," that deals with the situation when "Spanish is not enough."[5] But above all, her stories and poems speak to all of us about books and literacy.

*Tomás and the Library Lady* (Knopf, 1997) tells a story based on the true life experience of Tomás Rivera. Tomás was a young child who traveled each year from Texas to Iowa as a part of a migrant family that followed the agricultural jobs from state to state. Befriended by a librarian in Iowa, Tomás went on to earn a Ph.D. and to become the chancellor of the University of California at Riverside. The library at the university now bears his name.

Pat Mora has become known as the foremost Latino writer for children. She has taught at all levels, worked in a museum, in university administration at the University of Texas at El Paso, and as a consultant on U.S.–Mexico exchanges. For a time she was the Carruthers Chair, a Distinguished Visiting Professor at the University of New Mexico. She calls Santa Fe, New Mexico, her home although she spends part of the year in the northern Kentucky/Cincinnati area where her husband, Dr. Vern Scarborough, is a professor of archaeology.

Mora says New Mexico is a place of "continuing inspiration."[6] At times she has accompanied her husband on trips to Belize where he goes to study the Mayan culture. On one of those trips, Mora saw great large green lizards that reminded her of little dinosaurs. Lizards have always interested Mora and they sometimes show up in her books.

During her childhood, Mora's family always had a dog and lots of guppies. When her three children were young, they had fish, parakeets, and cats. But now because of her travel schedule, Mora does not have pets. But "because my daughters are such big cat lovers, I often tuck a cat into my books for them."[7]

Pat Mora connects each of her books to her life in some way. She says that "many are set in the desert because I love deserts and have spent much of my life in them. When I was spending a year in New Mexico, I was often on the hour-long shuttle ride between Santa Fe and the Albuquerque airport. I loved looking out at the wonderful vistas and began taking notes about what I saw. Those notes became the seeds for the poems in *This Big Sky* [Scholastic, 1998]."[8]

Mora's passions for reading and promoting literacy are evidenced in much of what she does. She actively promotes April 30 as "Children's Day/Book Day" or "El día de niños/El día de los libros," a day for families to read together and a day to share bilingual books.

Pat Mora now writes full time. Her youngest daughter, Cissy, is a veterinarian and works in an all-feline animal clinic. She loves cats and has two big cats and a little Chihuahua at home. Cissy also reads every night, just like Mora has done since her own

Pat Mora

Dear Girls and Boys,

Here's a poem for you about reading. Books are like wings. They take us to wonderful places.

Books and Me

We belong
together
books and me,
like toast and jelly
o queso y tortillas.
Delicious! !Delicioso!
Like flowers and bees,
books and me.

Your friend,
Pat Mora

childhood. Mora's older daughter, Libby, is an attorney and Mora's son, Bill, is a text-book editor.

When Mora was asked what some of her favorite things are she responded, "I like apples, tea, bread, cheese, and all sweets. I love so many colors! Green, yellow, orange, purple, gold, aqua, indigo blue and lots more."[9] And what does she like to do when she is not writing or playing with words? She likes to read, garden, visit with friends, cook, take walks, and travel. But perhaps most of all, she likes to laugh and hug.

## Book Connections

Many of Pat Mora's books deal with bilingual word play and are filled with positive relationships within the family and community. She has written books about three notable people—people who loved words and language and the visual images that inspire words. The first book in that category is *Tomás and the Library Lady,* which centers on young Tomás's friendship with the librarian and the inspiration he gleans from that friendship.

One of Mexico's most revered writers, Juana Inés, is profiled in Mora's *A Library for Juana* (Knopf, 2002). Juana loved words from the time she was three, always making up stories, songs, and poems. She could not wait to have her own library. When she became an adult, she became Sor Juana Inés de la Cruz, a nun who was able to devote her life to writing and learning.

The third book about a notable person is *Maria Paints the Hills* (Museum of New Mexico Press, 2002). Maria Hesch's paintings portray New Mexico through images of her life along the Santa Fe river and images of her grandfather's alfalfa field. Mora's words put story to the 17 paintings Hesch created to show the New Mexican way of life.

Another book, *The Rainbow Tulip* (Viking, 1999), is drawn directly from the experiences of Mora's own family. On Mother's Day a few years ago, Pat Mora presented her mother—Estela Mora, then well into her eighties—with a book about her own childhood. The story is set in El Paso, Texas and it describes Estela's first grade year. Mora tells a story about Estelita, also known as Stella, who is ashamed of her old-fashioned mother. But Estelita's mother values her Latino heritage and soon, during her participation in the May Day parade, Estelita comes to value her heritage as well.

Yet another of Mora's books deals with the joy of welcoming an adopted son into the family. *Pablo's Tree* (Simon & Schuster, 1994) was planted by Pablo's grandfather, Abuelito, on the day he found out that his daughter was going to adopt a baby. This adoption story features a Latino family and a single mother.

## Books Written by Pat Mora

*The Bakery Lady/La señora de la panadería.* Illustrated by Pablo Torrecilia. (Piñata Books/Arte Público Press, 2001).

*A Library for Juana: The World of Sor Juana Inés.* Illustrated by Beatriz Vidal. (Knopf, 2002).

*Maria Paints the Hills.* Illustrated by Maria Hesch. (Museum of New Mexico Press, 2002).

*Pablo's Tree.* Illustrated by Cecily Lang. (Simon & Schuster, 1994).

*The Rainbow Tulip.* Illustrated by Elizabeth Sales. (Viking, 1999).

*This Big Sky.* Illustrated by Steven Jenkins. (Scholastic, 1998).

*Tomás and the Library Lady.* Illustrated by Raúl Colón. (Knopf, 1997).

# For More Information

### Articles

Conlan, Maureen. "Writing from Two Worlds: Pat Mora Draws on Her Mexican Heritage." *The Cincinnati Post* 18 May 1996: 1B, 3B.

Versace, Candelore. "Pat Mora: Bringing the Latino Experience to Children's Literature." *The Santa Fe New Mexican* 6 Oct. 1996: D5.

York, Sherry. "Author Profile: Pat Mora." *Library Talk* 15.4 (September/October 2002): 26–27.

### Books

Ikas, Karin Rosa. "Pat Mora: Poet, Writer, and Educator." *Chicana Ways: Conversations with Ten Chicana Writers.* Reno: University of Nevada Press, 2002. 126–148.

### Web Sites

Mora, Pat. *Pat Mora—Author of Poetry, Nonfiction, and Children's Books.* March 2004. <http://www.patmora.com>.

# Notes

1. Pat Mora, "Bookjoy: The Magic of Words," presentation at the International Reading Association Conference, San Francisco, California, 28 Apr. 2002.
2. Pat Mora, letter to the author, 12 Sept. 2002.
3. Mora, "Bookjoy."
4. Ibid.
5. Ibid.
6. Ibid.
7. Mora, letter.
8. Ibid.
9. Ibid.

# Linda Sue Park

◆ Historical fiction

**Urbana, Illinois**
March 25, 1960

📖 *The Kite Fighters*

📖 *Seesaw Girl*

📖 *A Single Shard*

📖 *When My Name Was Keoko*

Photo by Klaus Pollmeier

## About the Author

Linda Sue Park was a relatively unknown writer when on January 21, 2002 the phone rang and she was catapulted into the limelight as the winner of the Newbery Award for *A Single Shard* (Clarion, 2001), her third novel about historic Korea.

Linda Sue's family story in the United States begins in the 1950s when each of her parents emigrated separately from Korea and settled in the American south. Her father, Ed, enrolled in Vanderbilt University in Nashville, Tennessee, and her mother, Sue, in Limestone College in rural South Carolina. They met through a Christian Youth group and soon married. Their first daughter was born in 1960 and they gave her two names, Linda Sue, in the tradition of many southerners.

Shortly after Linda Sue's birth, the family moved to the suburbs of Chicago and eventually two more children were born into the family. When Linda Sue was only four years old, her mother, in an effort to teach her the alphabet, "cut out every one of those cartoons (a series of phonic alphabet single-frame cartoons) and glued them onto the pages of one of her old college textbooks."[1] Because of her mother's efforts, Linda Sue entered kindergarten as the only child who knew how to read.

Linda Sue did not own many books but her family visited the library every two weeks. With each visit to the library, Linda Sue brought home an armload of books to read until their next visit. Because her father had not grown up in the United States, he had not read many American children's books, so the two of them selected books from the award lists. He kept files of newspaper articles and pamphlets that recommended books to read. Among the first books Linda Sue read were the Caldecott and Newbery award-winning books. One of the books that she was given was Frances Carpenter's *Tales of a Korean Grandmother*. In that book Linda Sue read that historically, Korean

**163**

girls from aristocratic families were kept in their homes. That bit of information intrigued Linda Sue and later it would become the seed that began her first novel, *Seesaw Girl* (Clarion, 1999).

Linda Sue's parents vowed to speak only English to their children because they wanted their children to be truly American. Linda Sue can speak a few phrases in Korean but she did not learn to speak Korean fluently. When she was a preteenager, she visited Korea and found that her relatives wanted to keep them comfortable in the Western style. One aunt, however, did have a more traditional Korean home with the courtyard in the center. Memories of that house later helped Linda Sue describe the setting for her first novel.

Even from her kindergarten year Linda Sue was interested in writing. She published her first piece of writing, a haiku, when she was just nine years old in the winter 1969 issue of *Trailblazer* magazine. She was paid one dollar for the poem and she gave the check to her father for Christmas. He framed it and hung it on his wall—and he still has it to this day.

Linda Sue's parents were very supportive of all of her endeavors and she published several more poems in magazines during her school years. She attended elementary school at Lincoln School in Forest Park, Illinois and along the way encountered several supportive teachers.

After graduating from high school, Linda Sue Park entered Stanford University where she participated on the gymnastics team and graduated with a degree in English. Her first job after college was back in Chicago with an oil company where she learned to present almost anything in an interesting manner. She also met and fell in love with a reporter, Ben Dobbin, who had come to Chicago from Ireland.

Dobbin was in the United States on a temporary visa and when his visa expired and he was scheduled to return to Dublin, Linda Sue decided to study in Dublin. She used her savings to enroll in graduate school at Trinity College. Later, when Dobbin's job took him to London, Linda Sue stayed in Ireland to complete her graduate studies and she earned a higher diploma in Anglo-Irish literature at Trinity. Most of the few Asians in Ireland were Japanese tourists so when Linda Sue traveled further west from Ireland she was often the first Asian person that people had met. Linda Sue then entered England on a fiancée visa, which stipulated that the young couple had just 90 days to marry. They married on the 88th day. Linda Sue then went back to school in London and earned a graduate degree in modern British literature from the University of London.

While in London their two children, Sean (1985) and Anna (1988), were born. The family lived abroad for seven years and then in 1990 they returned to the United States, settling in New York City and later, in 1993, moving upstate to Rochester. Park worked part time while the family lived in London and back in the United States she continued to teach non-native speakers of English. Shortly before winning the Newbery Award, she was teaching at the English Language Center in Rochester.

Park's first efforts at writing for children began with retelling some Korean folk tales. While she was submitting these stories without too much of a plan, she was also beginning to write *Seesaw Girl*. She sent off a query and three sample chapters to six publishers and all six asked for the complete manuscript. Several, after seeing the full manuscript, turned it down but Clarion's editor Dinah Stevenson asked to publish it and thereby established the relationship that eventually led to the publication of *A Single Shard*.

When Park first began to write she would write two or three days a week. Later, she found time to write every day. While she was still teaching, Park would go to school in the morning and then come home to write in her office until 4:00 P.M. When she emerged from her office, her children knew she was "home from work." Since winning the Newbery, however, Park has found that she is in greater demand as a speaker and she struggles to find the time to write. Shortly after publishing her fourth novel, *When My Name Was Keoko* (Clarion, 2003), she had five picture books in the works.

The town of Rochester, where the family makes their home, has feted Park as the town's artist of the year. The members of her writing group, in celebration of her Newbery Award, gave her two celadon pottery vases. These celadon vases are the type that play an important part in her Newbery Award book, *A Single Shard,* and one of the vases is small enough for her to take when she travels for author presentations.

As a thank you to everyone's hard work, on the January morning after it was announced that she won the Newbery Award, Park showed up at the Clarion offices with paper bags filled with gifts for everyone who had worked on her book.[2] The gifts were pieces of celadon pottery. On Father's Day, 2002, Linda Sue Park presented another gift. After accepting the Newbery Award, she gave the medal to her father, Eung "Ed" Won Park, for his support and encouragement.

Linda Sue Park, her husband Ben Dobbin, their son Sean, and daughter Anna, live in upstate New York. After winning the Newbery Award Park visited Korea once again and met Korea's First Lady, Lee Hee-ho, at the Blue House, Korea's presidential residence. This was in early November 2002 and since then she was also invited to the White House in October to attend the National Book Festival. Park actually met three first ladies within one month. At the White House, she met First Lady Laura Bush and also Lyudmila Putin, Russia's First Lady, who was a surprise guest at the Book Festival in Washington.

## Book Connections

Linda Sue Park's first book, *Seesaw Girl,* was born of Park's childhood memory of reading about girls in historic Korea who were not allowed out of their own homes. Park set the story in seventeenth-century Korea. The character Jade Blossom is a girl in a "good family," and as tradition dictates, she is not allowed to leave home. Nonetheless, twelve-year-old Jade devises a way to see what lies beyond the walls of her home. While researching *Seesaw Girl,* Park came across a reference stating that in the eleventh and twelfth centuries, Korea was world-renowned for pottery making. Park knew that China was credited with developing the art of porcelain pottery and that the country was known throughout the world for that pottery. She was curious about how a tiny country such as Korea could become known for its excellence in an area dominated by its huge neighbor, China. She set out to find the answer.

Park's research resulted in *A Single Shard,* the story of Tree-ear, an orphan who seeks to convince the master potter Min, that he deserves a chance to work with him. Throughout the novel Tree-ear strives to do his best and to convince Min of his sincerity. Tree-ear lives with Crane Man, another outcast living in Ch'ulp'o, a village known throughout Korea and beyond for the lovely celadon green glaze of the pottery created there. Tree-ear's relationship with Crane Man and with Min help form the story that has won a place on several honor lists and has garnered Park the Newbery Award.

Before writing *A Single Shard,* Linda Sue Park wrote and submitted a manuscript for *The Kite Fighters* (Clarion, 2000). She arranged for her father to make the decorations for *The Kite Fighters.* Eung Won Park had a special affiliation with kite making and this book was the story of two brothers, an eleven year old who tries to overcome his rivalry with his older brother who, as the first-born son, receives special treatment from their father. The two brothers combine their skills: one is skilled at kite flying while the other is a master in the field of kite making. Together the two hope to win the New Year kite-fighting competition. Park's fourth novel, *When My Name Was Keoko,* is set in 1940 and is based on her mother's story of living in Korea under the Japanese occupation.

Between novels, Park works on picture books as a break from writing the longer narratives. She also works on her first love, poetry, and some of that poetry enters into her author presentations when she incorporates some strategies for creating poems in the sijo form. Sijo is a traditional Korean syllabic form of verse similar to the more familiar haiku except that sijo is longer. Park has created a picture book poetry collection for elementary students, *Staying Green* (Clarion, forthcoming), that includes 30 sijo poems that focus on ordinary moments in a child's day. Rhyming texts also form the basis for two picture books, *In a Cottage Garden* (Clarion, 2004), a rhyming guessing game that follows a bunny through a garden and names colors and flowers, and *Bee-Bim-Bop!* (Clarion, 2004), a story about a mother and child who cook together and make a traditional Korean meal.

Other picture books by Park include *The Firekeeper's Son* (Clarion, 2003), which takes a page from Korean history, and *Mung-mung!* (Charlesbridge, 2004), a book of animal noises from around the world that is written as a guessing game.

## Books Written by Linda Sue Park

*Bee-Bim-Bop!* Illustrated by Ho Baek Lee. (Clarion, 2004).

*The Firekeeper's Son.* Illustrated by Julie Downing. (Clarion, 2003).

*The Kite Fighters* (Clarion, 2000).

*Mung-mung!* Illustrated by Diane Bigda. (Charlesbridge, 2004).

*The Seesaw Girl* (Clarion, 1999).

*A Single Shard* (Clarion, 2001).

*When My Name Was Keoko* (Clarion, 2002).

## For More Information

### Articles

Horning, Kathleen T. "Discovering Linda Sue Park." *School Library Journal* 48.7 (July 2002): 48–50.

Johnson, Nancy J., and Cyndi Giorgis. "Interview with the 2002 Newbery Medal Winner, Linda Sue Park." *Reading Teacher* 56.4 (December 2002): 394+.

Maughan, Shannon. "National Book Festival Draws Crowds." *Publishers Weekly* 249.42 (21 October 2002): 12.

Park, Linda Sue. "Newbery Medal Acceptance." *Horn Book Magazine* 78.4 (July/August 2002): 377–386.

Stevenson, Dinah. "Linda Sue Park." *Horn Book Magazine* 78.4 (July/August 2002): 387–392.

## Video

Podell, Tim, dir. *Good Conversations: A Talk with Linda Sue Park.* Videocasette. Tim Podell Productions, 2002. <http://www.goodconversations.com>.

## Web Sites

Park, Linda Sue. *Linda Sue Park: Official Website of Children's Author Linda Sue Park.* March 2004. <http://www.lindasuepark.com> or <http://www.lspark.com>.

# Notes

1.  Linda Sue Park, Newbery acceptance speech, American Library Association Conference, Atlanta, Georgia, 16 June 2002.
2.  Dinah Stevenson, "Linda Sue Park," *Horn Book Magazine* 78.4 (July/August 2002): 91.

# Nicole Rubel

◆ Family stories ◆ Humor

**Miami Beach, Florida**
April 29, 1953

📖 *A Cowboy Named Ernestine*

📖 *Grody's Not So Golden Rules*

📖 *No More Vegetables*

📖 *Rotten Ralph series*

## About the Author/Illustrator

Nicole Rubel began her career writing children's books when she was an art student in Boston. While the other students were creating impressionistic paintings, Rubel painted brightly colored scenes with giant goldfish and a big red cat. One instructor suggested children's book art and a representative from Hallmark Cards suggested she might have a future in their company as a greeting card designer. So, Rubel began to look at children's books and, she says, "the minute I saw *George and Martha* by James Marshall, I knew what I wanted to do for the rest of my life."[1]

After Rubel's art teacher told her that James Marshall lived in the Boston area, she picked up the phone and called him. Rubel and her friend Jack Gantos got encouragement from Marshall and more. "He invited Jack [Gantos] and myself to tea. I loved sitting in his parlor sipping tea and looking out his window at the Bunker Hill Monument. He saw my portfolio and said, 'I know you will do just fine. Call up Walter Lorraine at Houghton Mifflin but don't tell him I said so. He likes to discover his talent.' "[2]

So Gantos and Rubel made an appointment with Walter Lorraine and during that visit the two of them, according to Rubel, "showed Walter the many stories we created together. Walter liked a series of drawings about a little girl and her cat I was going to submit to Hallmark Card Company." Lorraine asked the pair to work on a story about the little girl with black hair and her large red cat with green eyes. "By the end of the summer Walter bought the story."[3] *Rotten Ralph* (Houghton Mifflin, 1976) was Jack and Nicole's first book and was such a great success that it spawned a series featuring Rotten Ralph.

Nicole's career goals had not always been clear or obvious. Leslie (later to be known as Nicole) Rubel and her identical twin sister, Bonnie, were born April 29, 1953 in Miami Beach, Florida. As babies, the two girls did not speak normal English but developed their own personal language that only the two of them could understand. Their parents worried that the two girls would never learn to speak normally but with several years of speech therapy, they did.

Their father owned a company that imported straw handbags and other accessories. Leslie (Nicole) loved one of the rooms at her father's company, the monkey room, so named because of the things that were kept there. Among other things the monkey room was filled with feathers, rhinestones, and felt flowers. Rubel says, "I played for hours in the monkey room gluing fabric and rhinestones into patterns."[4]

The Rubel family lived in Coral Gables, Florida where Leslie (Nicole) attended school along with her sister, Bonnie, and an older sister and a younger brother. They enjoyed picnics in the Florida Everglades National Parks while watching the alligators glide by in the water just a few feet from their blankets. In sixth grade, Leslie drew a Halloween drawing with a purple night sky and flying pumpkins but her teacher told her pumpkins did not fly and gave her a C. Every Sunday the family drove around Miami Beach and Leslie soaked up the images she saw. There were art deco buildings with colorful and unusual art. Huge sharks, large lobsters, and even alligators decorated places of business. Leslie fell in love with the bright colors and gargoyles and all the colors and images filled her head, even during her school days. She says her grades were B's and C's but her twin Bonnie's grades were considerably better.

During high school Leslie and her sister painted a large mural on their bedroom walls. Their inspirations were the artist Peter Max and the Beatle movie, *The Yellow Submarine*. In the mural, a large rainbow and sun looked down on a scene showing a classic struggle between good and evil. They also used papier-mâché to create a large butterfly on their door.

Throughout their childhood the two girls did everything together and when it came time for college, Bonnie was accepted to the University of Wisconsin in Madison. Leslie, however, did not qualify but she did manage to get accepted to college in nearby Beloit, Wisconsin. But after a year, Rubel realized that she did not want to be there. After some consideration, she decided that she wanted to attend the Boston Museum School of Art and because she had gotten good grades at Beloit, she was accepted and off she went. Her parents, Rubel says, "were furious. 'You, an artist? You'll starve!' I was determined and we compromised. I agreed to major in art education."[5]

That is how Rubel came to Boston and met James Marshall and Walter Lorraine. Rubel earned a joint degree from the Boston Museum School of Fine Arts and Tufts University in 1975. During her years at the Boston School, Rubel and other students were asked to think about who they were, what they liked, and what they disliked. They were to keep a diary of their ideas and thoughts. Rubel wrote one day that she didn't like her name, which was the beginning of her personal evolution. One of her first steps was to change her name and at the time she was reading *Tender Is the Night* by F. Scott Fitzgerald so she decided to call herself Nicole. She sent out birth notices to her parents and friends and has been Nicole ever since.

After the meeting with Walter Lorraine, Nicole Rubel and Jack Gantos worked on their books together. Lorraine encouraged them to work as a team on other books and although Gantos and Rubel's partnership on the books continued, their relationship did not; they had been a couple for six years. Rubel moved to New York City and began to create books and illustrations on her own. During the span of her career in children's books, Rubel has created numerous storybook characters. Rotten Ralph has been joined by dozens of other characters and Rubel has become a noted and popular writer and illustrator. Among the characters she has created are the twins Sam and Violet, Cyrano the Bear, the Ghost Family, Conga Crocodile, Ernestine the cowboy, and Grody.

In Rubel's books, readers will find alligators, palm trees, and many designs reminiscent of those busy and colorful patterns she created in the "monkey room" of her childhood. In fact, Rubel's childhood has had a great influence on not only the stories for her books but also the illustrations. Sometimes, even if twins are not in the storyline, readers will often spot twins in her illustrations. Rubel has an illustrative style that is wacky and wonderful. When she wrote and illustrated *The Ghost Family Meets Its Match* (Dial, 1992), she was able to use both text and pictures to attract readers to her silly, spooky yarn. There are palm trees on the wallpaper, an octopus chandelier, life-size monkey candleholders, a ceramic lion holding up the household toilet, and an excess of colors and patterns all of which create a visually interesting home. Several families attempt to live in the home but end up fleeing the haunted residence. When the Merry family shows up, Rubel cleverly uses a wolf motif in the new family's decorating scheme to provide a clue as to why they do not seem to mind the Ghost family's antics. Rubel has included 22 wolf clues in the book from the wolf-patterned wallpaper to the wolf hiding behind the tree.

Rubel's *Cyrano the Bear* (Dial, 1995) clearly is a fractured Old West version of the well-known, seventeenth-century French-verse drama, *Cyrano de Bergerac*. Cyrano, the bear with a large purple nose, is helplessly in love with the town librarian, Roxane. Fearing that he is not worthy, the shy bear helps his friend Wolfie aim for her heart. As in the *Cyrano de Bergerac* tale, Cyrano the Bear gets the poetry-loving Roxane.

Ernestine, a red-haired woman dressed as a rowdy cowhand, joins a cattle drive in *A Cowboy Named Ernestine* (Dial, 2001). Rubel also does illustrations for other authors and her wildly patterned images appear in several riddle books by Katy Hall and Lisa Eisenberg including *Dino Riddles* (Dial, 2002).

Rotten Ralph stories continue to be published as picture books and early chapter books. Ralph has even appeared as a television character. Rubel has illustrated more than a dozen Rotten Ralph titles and more than 30 other books, many of which she also authored. She has also created magazine illustrations and greeting cards. Her illustrations have been included in shows of children's book illustrations from Boston and New York to Key Biscayne and have spawned a plush Rotten Ralph doll and rubber stamps. Rubel also does some designing for an import company in Miami, Florida, owned by her family. Rubel's sister, Bonnie, is the president of the company and according to Rubel she is an "amazing person." Rubel sometimes accompanies her sister on buying trips in Asia.

Nicole Rubel regularly works in her home office. She says, "every day I'm at my drafting table from 8:00 A.M. to 4:30 P.M., Monday through Friday. When I'm writing, I do work on a computer."[6] Her art is created using ad markers and a technical pen.

After decades of living in New York City, Rubel and her husband Richard Langsen, a family therapist, left their loft apartment and migrated west to Aurora, Oregon, where they now live on the Red Cat Farm. The farm is an eight-and-one-half acre refuge for their Corgi, Siamese cat, two Saddlebreds, and two sheep. Touches of whimsy fill their home and one particularly spectacular feature is the hand-rolled and decorated clay tile surrounding the fireplace. The tiles are among Rubel's many artistic touches. Since December 1999, visitors to their home have been welcomed by a large wood image of Rotten Ralph, which was created by a local artisan who used a chain saw to carve the image from a tree trunk. It was a gift from Richard to Nicole.

# Book Connections

Twins are often a theme or are images that appear in Rubel's books and at times she has developed stories with twins as the main characters. Sam and Violet are twins that have been characters in some of her books and another book that she developed was about a set of twins named Skelly and Bones. The book was developed and offered to a publisher who was interested but wanted some rewrites. By the time the book was revised and rewritten, the twin characters became a funny talking dog and the star of *Grody's Not So Golden Rules* (Harcourt, 2003). Readers will want to look closely for unusual vases and teapots in the illustrations for these books. The illustrations were created as collages using fabric, photos, drawings, and fabric paint and many of the photographs in the artwork are photos of objects in Rubel's house. The craft store Jo-Ann Fabrics is going to reproduce some of the fabric designs from the book. The drawings of each double-paged spread contain many details that give evidence of Rubel's childhood interests and her love of colors. A purple alligator lamp with a "Florida" sign is in one room and images of palm trees and seashores fill the other pages. A pink flamingo hides in a closet and another stands in a goldfish aquarium. A frog reading a book sits under the bed in a cluttered room and pineapples and garish flowers are everywhere.

Farrar Straus Giroux spent several years preparing Rubel's book about twins and *Twice as Nice: What's It Like to Be a Twin* (Farrar Straus Giroux, 2004) is the result of many interviews with twins both identical and fraternal. These twins, young and old, shared their thoughts and ideas with Rubel about what it is like for them to be a twin. Of course, Rubel herself and her twin sister Bonnie have their own ideas about being a twin. The illustrations in *Twice as Nice* include photographs and many of Rubel's zany drawings.

# Books Written and Illustrated by Nicole Rubel

*A Cowboy Called Ernestine* (Dial, 2001).

*Conga Crocodile* (Houghton Mifflin, 1993).

*Cyrano the Bear* (Dial, 1995).

*Double Trouble: A Field Guide for Twins* (Farrar Straus Giroux, 2004).

*The Ghost Family Meets Its Match* (Dial, 1992).

*Grody's Not So Golden Rules* (Harcourt, 2003).

*No More Vegetables* (Farrar Straus Giroux, 2002).

*Twice as Nice: What's It Like to Be a Twin* (Farrar Straus Giroux, 2004).

# Books Illustrated by Nicole Rubel

*Back to School for Rotten Ralph.* Written by Jack Gantos. (HarperCollins, 1998).

*Bunny Riddles.* Written by Katy Hall and Lisa Eisenberg. (Dial, 1996).

*The Christmas Spirit Strikes Rotten Ralph.* Written by Jack Gantos. (HarperFestival, 1998).

*Dino Riddles.* Written by Katy Hall and Lisa Eisenberg. (Dial, 2002).

*Grizzly Riddles.* Written by Katy Hall and Lisa Eisenberg. (Dial, 1989).

Rotten Ralph series. Created with Jack Gantos. The first title, *Rotten Ralph,* was originally published by Houghton Mifflin in 1975 and was recently republished by HarperCollins.

## For More Information

### Articles

McElmeel, Sharron. "Author Profile: Nicole Rubel." *Library Talk* 13.5 (November/December 2000): 20–23.

### Web Sites

Rubel, Nicole. *The World of Nicole Rubel.* March 2004. <http://www.nicolerubel.com>.

## Notes

1. Nicole Rubel, interview with the author, 1 Apr. 2000.
2. Ibid.
3. Ibid.
4. Ibid.
5. Ibid.
6. Ibid.

# Margriet Ruurs

◆ Alphabet books ◆ Animals ◆ Humor

---
**Netherlands**
December 2, 1942

---

📖 *Emma's Eggs*

📖 *A Mountain Alphabet*

📖 *Spectacular Spiders*

## About the Author

Margriet Ruurs was born and raised in the Netherlands and she wrote her first stories and poems when she was just six years old. She is left-handed and in the beginning she wrote backwards so in order to read her writing, readers had to use a mirror. Margriet's childhood was filled with stories. She says, "I loved reading and listening to the stories my dad made up. It never occurred to me not to write [books]."[1]

Margriet had one sister who is ten years older than her. As a child Margriet wanted a dog but did not get one so the first thing she did when she considered herself grown-up was to get a dog.

At the age of 19, Margriet learned English and in 1972, when she was 20, she moved to Canada. That same year she translated from English to Dutch, Judith Viorst's *Alexander and the Terrible, Horrible, No Good Very Bad Day*. In 1983, Leopold Publishers, a publisher in the Netherlands, published Margriet's first book, *Apenkinderen* (*Baby Chimps*). Being bilingual allows Margriet to translate from English to Dutch and to translate from Dutch to English and she says, "being bilingual gives you twice as many ways to describe something."[2]

Margriet Ruurs married after she moved to Canada. In Canada, she attended Simon Fraser University in British Columbia to earn a graduate degree in education. Ruurs had already published several books when she decided to return to school. In an effort to help establish her fledgling writing career, she began to travel to promote her books. During one year she was in Newfoundland for Children's Book Week in November and in Iqaluit, Nunavut a short time later.[3] She says that in one two or three month period of time, she spoke to at least ten thousand children in British Columbia, Iowa, Nebraska,

Wisconsin, and Maryland. On these trips, Ruurs talks about her books and her writing career and she also helps her audience develop their writing skills.

Ruurs is known as a Canadian author and is popular in both Canada and the United States. She says, "I became a Canadian author not just by immigrating to Canada, but by doing alphabet books based on the scenery and wildlife characteristic of different Canadian locales—the Pacific coast, or the Rocky Mountains."[4]

Margriet Ruurs and her husband, a park ranger and park director, and their two sons have lived in many places including California, Oregon, northern Alberta, Kananaskis Provincial Park, and the Yukon, where Ruurs's husband was the park director. Ruurs spent some of her time writing news articles for a Yukon newspaper and for *The Whitehorse Star.* One year, in the late 1980s, the family traveled for a full year. Ruurs later wrote about the experience in an article for *Trailer Life,* "A Family Affair: Careful Planning and Precise Packing Help to Make Traveling with Children Enjoyable—Even for a Full Year."[5] Some of that information has also made its way into a more recent piece of writing, a book titled *When We Go Camping* (Tundra Books, 2001).

When Ruurs and her family lived in the Rocky Mountains of British Columbia, she contributed news articles to the local paper and continued to write books. She decided to create a book about mountain life. At the time her husband worked as a park ranger in the Kananaskis Provincial Park. The book, *A Mountain Alphabet* (Tundra Books, 1996), has become one of Ruurs's best-known titles. For this book she worked closely with the illustrator, renowned wildlife artist Andrew Kiss, who lived nearby in Armstrong, British Columbia, to tell and show a story of mountain life.

In *A Mountain Alphabet,* Ruurs's sons are represented in the drawings of the rock climbers and snowboarders. Kiss had only a few weeks to create 26 double-paged illustrations for the book—one for each letter of the alphabet. While Kiss was working on the pictures for the page representing the letter G, the branch of an old tree strangely seemed to form the letter. That gave him the idea to hide a letter on each page of the book. Readers seem to enjoy finding the hidden letters.

Among Ruurs's very favorite things is her dog Kaya, "my favorite dog in the world."[6] Other favorites include chocolate. If she is not writing or touring, one can find Ruurs curled up with a good book or sometimes in her garden. She and her husband had lived in Armstrong, British Columbia for several years when in 2003 he received an offer for a ranger job in Oregon. The couple moved to Cresswell, Oregon where Ruurs continues to write books and travel across the United States and Canada to talk to school children about books and writing.

## Book Connections

Nature and the wilderness influenced Margriet Ruurs's early writing. Later, she wrote about the chickens that she used to have—chickens that consistently followed her around. They became the stars of *Emma's Eggs* (Stoddart Kids, 1996), *Emma's Cold Days* (Stoddart Kids, 2001), and *Emma and the Coyote* (Stoddart Kids, 1999).

Several of her books are set in Canada. *Fireweed* (Burns and Morton, 1986) takes place in a northern Canadian city where a boy named Michael has trouble with his two dogs and his new cat, Fireweed. Another dog story is *No Dogs Allowed* (Chestnut, 2003), a story of a dog that followed his owner to the senior home. Wild animals are the subjects of other titles. *Wild Babies* (Tundra Books, 2003) provides tidbits about wild baby animals. *Big Little Dog* (Penumbra Press, 1992), besides being about dogs,

From the desk of
**Margriet Ruurs**

Dear fellow writer,

I'm so glad to know that you are interested in writing, too! When you write, you have to use your imagination and that makes writing fun and exciting!

I believe that you can become a better writer, by reading! Just read, read, read! Read every book you can get your hands on: fiction, non-fiction, poetry, everything! The more you read, the more you'll know to write about.

My other advise is, don't ever give up! Just keep writing and it'll get better and better. Writing is fun - just go for it!

Happy writing,

Margriet Ruurs.

www.margrietruurs.com

is set in the north as is *A Mountain Alphabet* and *A Pacific Alphabet* (Whitecap Books, 2001).

Ruurs's interest in the environment is evident in *Logan's Lake* (Hodgepog, 2001). The protagonist, Logan, tries to save a secluded lake from commercial development but eventually concludes that he is not going to be able to stop the growth around the lake. However, he does manage to interest the developer in building a resort lodge instead of a large hotel.

Two of Ruurs's books feature stories and libraries. *Ms May Bee's Magical Book Case* (Chestnut Books, 2003) is a funny story that tells how and where school librarians get their wonderful stories and *My Librarian Is a Camel* (Boyds Mills Press, 2003) is a nonfiction book about how children around the world get library books—sometimes by camel or elephant.

## Books Written by Margriet Ruurs

*Emma's Cold Days.* Illustrated by Barbara Spurll. (Stoddart Kids, 2001).

*Emma's Eggs.* Illustrated by Barbara Spurll. (Stoddart Kids, 1996).

*Emma and the Coyote.* Illustrated by Barbara Spurll. (Stoddart Kids, 1999).

*A Mountain Alphabet.* Illustrated by Andrew Kiss. (Tundra Books, 1996; 1999).

*My Librarian Is a Camel* (Boyds Mills Press, 2003).

*A Pacific Alphabet.* Illustrated by Dianna Bonder. (Whitecap Books, 2001).

*When We Go Camping.* Illustrated by Andrew Kiss. (Tundra Books, 2001).

*Wild Babies* (Tundra Books, 2003).

## For More Information

### Web Sites

Ruurs, Margriet. *Margriet Ruurs—Children's Author—School Visits, Writing Workshops, Professional Development, Conference Presentations.* March 2004. <http://www.margrietruurs.com>.

## Notes

1. Margriet Ruurs, letter to the author, 20 Sept. 2002.
2. Louise Donnelly, "Courage, Talent, Luck," *BC Bookworld* 15.13 (Autumn 2001): 36.
3. Iqaluit is the capital city of Canada's newest territory, Nunavut. This territory was created in 1999 after many years of negotiations between the government of Canada and the Inuit of the Nunavut area. Iqaluit is situated in the southeastern corner of the territory surrounding the northern and western perimeter of the Hudson Bay. Nunavut is comprised of a two million square parcel of land that was once the eastern part of Canada's Northern Territory.
4. Margriet Ruurs, session presented during the Canadian International Reading Association Regional Conference, Vancouver, British Columbia, Canada, 26 Oct. 2002.
5. Margriet Ruurs, "A Family Affair: Careful Planning and Precise Packing Help to Make Traveling with Children Enjoyable—Even for a Full Year," *Trailer Life* 51.5 (May 1991): 71–74.
6. Ruurs, letter.

# Pam Muñoz Ryan

◆ Historical fiction ◆ Family stories

## Bakersfield, California
December 25, 1951

📖 *Riding Freedom*

📖 *The Flag We Love*

📖 *Esperanza Rising*

## About the Author

Pam Muñoz Ryan grew up in California's San Joaquin Valley in a town surrounded by grape fields. In those fields grew "all the raisins of the United States." Pam was the eldest of three sisters and in her mother's extended family Pam was also the eldest of 23 cousins. Her childhood was filled with many aunts and uncles and her grandparents. Ryan says, "I think a lot of moral and values are reflected by the gossip and judgment heard from parents [and those other adults that are around a child in their childhood]."[1]

Pam's grandmother had a green thumb and her uncles "always said if she [grandmother] stuck a broom stick in a garden she'd have tiny brooms in her garden."[2] Pam spent many comfortable days in her grandparents yard watching her grandmother crochet blankets in zigzag rows and talking to her—in Spanish.

Ryan's maternal grandmother and grandfather came to the United States from Aguascalientes, Mexico in the 1930s. They wanted their own children, Ryan's mother and her mother's brothers and sisters, to learn and speak English so that they might succeed in their new country. However, to Pam her grandmother only spoke Spanish and learning Spanish at a young age gave Ryan an appreciation for the cadence of both languages. Her grandmother fed her enchiladas, rice, and beans but when Pam was with her other grandparents, the food was different—black-eyed peas, fried okra, and peach cobbler. Her paternal grandparents were Italian and brought another set of cultural traditions to her life. Ryan says, "my life [then and now] is culturally diverse by background and choice."[3]

Pam's father drove a delivery truck and her mother was a clerical worker. Pam spent a lot of time with her maternal grandmother where there were few books and few toys. "I did not know there were so many books or libraries until I was in fifth grade or so." Ryan

**177**

says her childhood benefited from a "strong oral language tradition in the family." She spent a lot of time imagining stories in the backyard where she would then act out her stories. In school, children were seldom asked to write so the idea of writing down her stories never occurred to her. When Pam was in the fifth grade her family moved across town. About the change, Ryan says, "I didn't fit in—my feet were too big."[4]

So with her friends blocks away, Pam discovered the public library. During the hot summer months, she often hopped on her bike and headed for the East Bakersfield branch library where she could spend the afternoon reading in the air conditioning. By the time she was in junior high school, Pam was reading and rereading books about Sue Barton, Student Nurse, and many similar series. She also read *Treasure Island* and *Gone with the Wind.*

After earning her underground degree at San Diego State University, Pam Ryan worked as a bilingual teacher and an early childhood administrator. She married James Robert Ryan and after their children were born, Ryan quit her job in education and stayed at home. While the four children were still young, Ryan decided to return to San Diego State University, take classes at night, and earn her graduate degree in education. Ryan says:

> I didn't know I wanted to be a writer until I was an adult. Although I'd loved books from the fifth grade, it never occurred to me that I could write them. I knew that I wanted to do something that had to do with books and I thought that would be teaching . . . After I turned in several papers one of my professors asked me. "Have you ever considered professional writing?" Until that point in my life, it had never occurred to me.[5]

Shortly after that, a colleague approached Ryan and asked if she would help write a book. As soon as Ryan began working on this book for adults, she knew she had to write a children's story.

Ryan spends a lot of time thinking about what she might want to write about. She says, "when I get an idea or a thought about something I want to write about, I write the notes on anything that is available. I write on the backs of envelopes, napkins, and sometimes, if necessary, on the back of my hand."[6] At some point in this process the assorted collection of notes are put into an idea file, which usually marks the beginning of an official project.

Her normal routine begins early in the morning when she begins to write. She writes on a computer and initially pays little attention to punctuation, grammar, spelling, or neatness. Her first task is to get the main idea entered on her computer. Once that is completed, she lets the entire manuscript rest a few days. Over a period of weeks and months, Ryan rewrites the manuscript no fewer than 12 or 13 times—sometimes as many as 30. When she gets the manuscript to a stage where she is somewhat comfortable with it, she submits it to a publisher. If it is accepted, there are always more revisions and rewriting to do. These days, Ryan is always in the process of writing more stories. She says some of the stories will never get published and others will. If a book is accepted for publication it takes a year or more for all the revisions to be made and for the illustrator to create illustrations for the title.

When she is not writing or reading Ryan might be found taking a walk, going to the beach, or swimming in the ocean. When her children were younger, she spent many days watching soccer games. She says, "I read more than I write."[7] Among her favorite books are *The Relatives Came* by Cynthia Rylant and *The Talking Eggs* by Robert San Souci. The classic tale *Anne of Green Gables* by L. M. Montgomery is a long time favorite.

Dear Students,

Don't be discouraged with failure or starting over. I can't begin to tell you how many times I have started over in my life – on friendships, my education, writing a book, or something new that I wanted to learn. Starting over should be my middle name! I suppose that's why one of my favorite sayings is, "If you've never failed at anything, you're aiming too low." Failure is nothing more than a challenge to try again.

Pam Muñoz Ryan

Netty

When asked what books of hers she would recommend young readers read first, Ryan had a multiple part answer. Because she writes for many age levels this was a difficult question for Ryan to answer. For the younger children she suggested *Mice and Beans* illustrated by Joe Cepeda (Scholastic, 2001). *Mice and Beans* is the story of quirky and preoccupied grandmother, Rosa Maria. In this picture book, Rosa Maria is based on Ryan's grandmother. Ryan says that, "ironically, Joe Cepeda, agreed to illustrate the book because he thought the grandmother in the story was so much like his mother, whose name is coincidence, Rosa Maria."[8] Surely not all Mexican grandmothers are like this character but Ryan thinks there is a certain Hispanic verity that is captured within the story's whimsy—an adoration of children, big family celebrations, proverbs to live by, and of course, rice and beans. "That," says Ryan, "was all indicative of my early years, I also love the repetitive nature of the story and I think children do too. Of all my books so far, it's my favorite read aloud."[9]

Pam Muñoz Ryan and her husband, Jim, live in Leucadia, 30 miles north of San Diego and six blocks from the Pacific Ocean. Their four children, Marcie, Annie, and identical twin sons Matt and Tyler, are now grown and attending college or beginning their own careers. Where Ryan once worked in the family room she is now able to have a writing space for herself.

Ryan's view on her success in writing (and in life) is summarized by a quote that she often uses and that, for a time, has been on her bulletin board next to her computer. The quote says, "The harder I work, the luckier I get." Ryan says she views the failures and rejections that she receives as "opportunities to persevere."[10]

## Book Connections

Pam Ryan says, "I get my ideas for my stories based on what really happens in my life."[11] When some of her husband's corn snakes got loose they became part of an episode in *Esperanza Rising* (Scholastic, 2000). One Memorial Day Ryan went to the grocery story and found a display of beer covered by an American Flag. She complained to the manager but later the experience inspired her to write *The Flag We Love* (Charlesbridge, 1996).

Sometimes ideas come to her in other ways. In the early 1990s, the publisher Charlesbridge had some success with a book about the state of Texas. They decided that a similar book about California would be a good idea and because they knew that Ryan lived in California they asked her to write it. *California Here We Come!* (Charlesbridge, 1997) was the product of the research she did.

While Ryan was doing the research for *California Here We Come!* she discovered information about and became intrigued with a famous California stagecoach driver, Charlotte Parkhurst. Charlotte was an orphan living in New Hampshire in 1812. She loved horses and spent a lot of time in the stables at the orphanage, however, when she was 12 she was banned from the stables. Not willing to be forbidden to do the only thing she loved, Charlotte ran away, cut her hair, and dressed as a boy. Disguised as a boy she was able to do everything she wanted to. She made her way from New Hampshire to Massachusetts to Rhode Island and finally to California where she became a land owner, a sought-after stagecoach driver, and even voted in a federal election—52 years before any other female. Only when "Charles" Parkhurst died did others find out that Charles was actually a female. Ryan wrote the story in her first novel, *Riding Freedom* (Scholastic, 1998). In order to write that story, she had to research information about stagecoaches and how to harness a team of horses. Because there is not a lot of information available about Parkhurst, Ryan used her research and imagination to flesh out the story.

In other research for *California Here We Come!* Ryan read a statement saying that all the raisins in the United States are produced in the San Joaquin Valley—the area where she had grown up. That bit of information led her to do even more research and to write the book *How Do You Raise a Raisin?* (Charlesbridge, 2003).

One of Ryan's most notable works is *Esperanza Rising*. The book is based on the life of Ryan's maternal grandmother. Similar to the character Esperanza, Ryan's grandmother was born into a wealthy family that had a large ranch with many servants. After her father's death, Ryan's grandmother immigrated to the United States and in 1930 took up residence in a segregated farm-labor camp in Arvin, California. Her jobs included washing clothing in a communal washtub, packing fruit, and caring for her children. Just as in *Esperanza Rising,* Ryan's grandmother experienced the worker strikes, persecutions and mass deportations, and the deadly Valley Fever. This is the book that won Ryan the Pura Belpez Award, which honors the work of a Latino writer who writes of the Latino cultural experience.

Many illustrators have created the illustrations for Ryan's books. Ryan wrote *The Crayon Counting Book* (Charlesbridge, 1997) with author Jerry Palotta and Frank Mazzola Jr. created the illustrations entirely with a computer. Brain Selznick illustrated *Amelia and Eleanor Go for a Ride* (Scholastic, 1999) and Craig Brown used stippling and pastels to create the illustrations for *How Do You Raise a Raisin?*

## Books Written by Pam Muñoz Ryan

*Amelia and Eleanor Go for a Ride: Based on a True Story.* Illustrated by Brian Selznick. (Scholastic, 1999). Picture book.

*California Here We Come!* Illustrated by Kay Salem. (Charlesbridge, 1997). Picture book.

*The Crayon Counting Book.* Written with Jerry Palotta, illustrated by Frank Mazzola Jr. (Charlesbridge, 1997). Picture book.

*Esperanza Rising* (Scholastic, 2000). Novel.

*The Flag We Love.* Illustrated by Ralph Masiello. (Charlesbridge, 1996). Picture book.

*Hello Ocean.* Illustrated by Mark Astrella. (Charlesbridge, 2001). Picture book.

*How Do You Raise a Raisin?* Illustrated by Craig Brown. (Charlesbridge, 2003). Picture book.

*Mice and Beans.* Illustrated by Joe Cepeda. (Scholastic, 2001). Picture book.

*Mud Is Cake.* Illustrated by David McPhail. (Hyperion, 2002). Picture book.

*One Hundred is a Family.* Illustrated by Benrei Huang. (Hyperion, 1994). Picture book.

*A Pinky Is a Baby Mouse* (Hyperion, 1997). Picture book.

*Riding Freedom* (Scholastic, 1998). Novel.

*When Marian Sang: The True Recital of Marian Anderson.* Illustrated by Brian Selznick. (Scholastic, 2002). Picture book.

## For More Information

### Articles

Trevenon, Stacy. "An Inspiration for Authors Rising." *Half Moon Bay Review and Pescadero Pebble* 5 Feb. 2003: C1.

## Video

Podell, Tim, dir. *Good Conversations! Pam Muñoz Ryan.* Videocasette. Tim Podell Productions, 2002. <http://www.goodconversations.com>.

## Web Sites

Ryan, Pam Muñoz. *Pam Muñoz Ryan: Children's Author.* March 2004. <http://www. pammunozryan.com>.

# Notes

1. Pam Muñoz Ryan, presentation at the International Reading Association Conference, 5 May 1998.
2. Ibid.
3. Ibid.
4. Ibid.
5. Pam Muñoz Ryan, letter to the author, 10 Sept. 2002.
6. Ryan, presentation.
7. Ibid.
8. Ibid.
9. Ibid.
10. Ibid.
11. Ibid.

# April Pulley Sayre

◆ Humor ◆ Animals ◆ Nature

---
**Bakersfield, California**
April 11, 1966

---

📖 *Army Ant Parade*

📖 *Noodle Man: The Pasta Superhero*

📖 *Shadows*

## About the Author

April Pulley Sayre was born on April 11, 1966 to Elizabeth R. Pulley, the owner of a science book company, and David C. Pulley, an education professor at Furman University. Because of her parent's occupations, most people are not surprised that April grew up with an interest and curiosity about things around her. It was that curiosity that led her to write informational books for young readers, to explore the world of narrative, and eventually to write some very humorous picture books.

April had two older sisters, Cathy and Lydia. She says that they "grew up in Greenville, South Carolina with lots of adventures in the North Carolina Mountains near Boone." April loved the outdoors even as a little girl when she "picked flowers, collected leaves, watched bugs, read books, and wrote little poems and stories." She attended elementary and secondary school in Greenville and graduated in 1983, a year early. Even though she had always read books and wrote, April says, "I didn't start out trying to write for young people. My curiosity and my sense of humor led me in that direction." Her curiosity about wild animals, bugs, strange facts, and wondrous natural events led her to Duke University where she earned a degree in biology. April interned at the National Wildlife Federation where she wrote about the environment. She also interned at the National Geographic Society for *World* magazine. "Then," she says, "I took a full time job at National Wildlife Federation, where I helped create teacher's guides such as *NatureScope* and *Wildlife Week*. One day I answered an ad in the *Washington Post* for people to write biographies of scientists for kids. That led to my first book, which was cancelled when the company was sold. But the new owners contracted with me to write six more books—so I forgave them for canceling my first!"[1] In 1994, that publisher,

Twenty-First Century Books, published the series Exploring Earth's Biomes. Soon April was actively pursuing getting her works published.

April joined the Society of Children's Book Writers and Illustrators (SCBWI) and even attended a writing conference sponsored by *Highlights* magazine at Chautauqua. She says that conference changed her life and she came home so excited about writing that she started writing immediately. The writing she did became her first published picture book, *If You Should Hear a Honey Guide* (Houghton, 1995).

April Sayre enjoys her job, researching, talking to people, visiting museums, and traveling to exciting places. As an author, Sayre visits a lot of schools and she has found that children love animals and enjoy making a bit of noise—especially animal sounds, which made their way into her books *Crocodile Listens* (Greenwillow, 2001) and *Army Ant Parade* (Henry Holt, 2002). "One of my hobbies is learning to identify birdcalls, frog calls, and other animal calls. So many of my books describe animal sounds." A book she wrote for older readers, *Secrets of Sound: Studying the Calls of Whales, Elephants, and Birds* (Houghton, 2002), "includes interviews with scientists that study animal sounds." She says that interviewing the scientists for the *Secrets of Sound* book "was exciting because they were so passionate about their work, so engaged in their lives."[2] She often uses the sights and sounds of her own garden as part of the setting for her various books.

Although Sayre's forté is information books, she also writes some very interesting fiction but even her fiction books include interesting information. For example, when she wrote *Noodle Man: The Pasta Superhero* (Orchard, 2002) she managed to write in a lot of information about the different types of pasta and the flours that are used to make the pasta. She mentions durum wheat and all types of pasta including tortellini, ravioli, spaghetti, lasagna, angel hair, and macaroni. *Noodle Man: The Pasta Superhero* came from Sayre's personal experience, in a way. She says, "I wrote it right after having pasta for dinner."[3]

Since 1989, April has been married to Jeff Sayre. He is an ecologist who studies birds and is an expert in native plants. Together they travel to diverse locations including rain forests, deserts, seashores, and other areas. They also lead ecotours on which they listen for animals such as sloths, lemurs, capybaras, toucans, and of course army ants. "We identify the location of animals by the sound—and it seems as if we have found them by magic. But we find them because we have trained ourselves to listen."[4]

The couple has traveled to Ecuador, Madagascar, Panama, Alaska, Arizona, and other locations that become the settings for some of Sayre's books. Sayre says her heart "squeezed"[5] when, during a hike through the rain forest, she first saw an ant bird with its blue-ringed eyes. For more than seven years she had been studying these birds and here she was actually seeing one. In her books she tries to convey her feeling of excitement to her readers.

Sayre enjoys writing information books but she also likes being silly and making puns. She also has a long list of other favorites. She likes "chocolate chip cookies, sweet potatoes, Indian food, English Breakfast tea or cardamom tea." Because she travels so much, having pets is impractical but she does have a lot of bird feeders—some of which attract hummingbirds. Among her other favorite things are "the color periwinkle blue, butterfly bush (plant), bird watching, bug watching, dancing, snorkeling, and listening to comedian Wayne Brady."[6]

April Pulley Sayre and her husband Jeff Sayre live in Indiana where she often listens for animals in their backyard. It is a good day if she sees a dragonfly, or plants a prairie, or makes frog noises with children during a school visit.

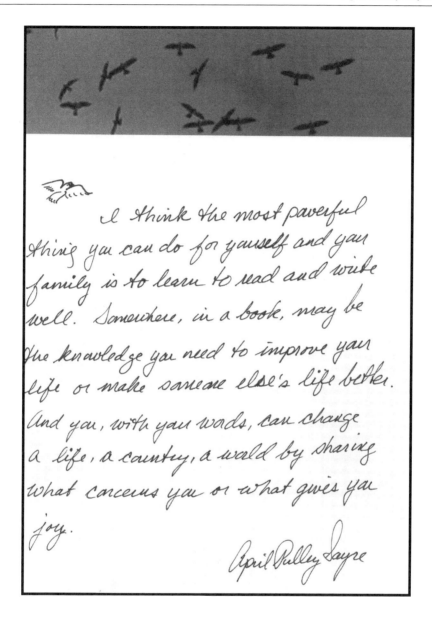

I think the most powerful thing you can do for yourself and your family is to learn to read and write well. Somewhere, in a book, may be the knowledge you need to improve your life or make someone else's life better. And you, with your words, can change a life, a country, a world by sharing what concerns you or what gives you joy.

April Pulley Sayre

## Book Connections

If young readers want to choose a book of Sayre's to read first she suggests *If You Should Hear a Honey Guide* or *Dig, Wait, Listen: A Desert Toad's Tale* (Greenwillow, 2001). "Both of these books draw the reader into natural stories that have underlying, amazing facts about animals. They reflect my joy in nature and the way I like to 'sink in' to the natural experience."[7] A trip to Tucson, Arizona and its nearby desert brought her the story of how toads who live on the desert throughout the year get water to survive. It was a question that she needed to research and tell and the result was *Dig, Wait, Listen: A Desert Toad's Tale*.

"Whenever possible," Sayre says, "I use my personal experiences to liven up my nonfiction. I let readers know what's its like to wade into a wetland, or wake up in a rain forest, or smell a swamp. My husband and I travel to rain forests in Madagascar, Ecuador, Panama, Costa Rica, and other countries, in order to see wildlife. For my book, *Army Ant Parade,* I traveled to see army ants in Costa Rica and Panama." [8]

## Books Written by April Pulley Sayre

*1 Is a Snail: A Counting by Feet Book.* Written with Jeff Sayre and illustrated by Randy Cecil. (Candlewick Press, 2003).

*Army Ant Parade.* Illustrated by Rick Chrustowski. (Henry Holt, 2002).

Continents of the World Series. (Millbrook Press, 2003).

*Crocodile Listens.* Illustrated by JoEllen McAllister Stammen. (Greenwillow, 2001).

*Noodle Man: The Pasta Superhero.* Illustrated by Stephen Costanza. (Orchard, 2002).

*Secrets of Sound: Studying the Calls of Whales, Elephants, and Birds* (Houghton, 2002).

*Shadows.* Illustrated by Harvey Stevenson. (Henry Holt, 2002).

*Turtle, Turtle, Watch Out!* Illustrated by Lee Christiansen. (Orchard, 2000).

## For More Information

### Articles

McDowell, Kate. "The Bulletin of the Center for Children's Books: Rising Star." *The Bulletin of the Center for Children's Books.* March 2004. <http://alexia.lis. uiuc.edu/puboff/bccb/0402rise.html>, April 2002.

### Web Sites

Sayre, April Pulley. *Author April Pulley Sayre.* March 2004. <http://www.aprilsayre. com>.

## Notes

1. April Pulley Sayre, letter to the author, 20 Sept. 2002.
2. Ibid.
3. Ibid.
4. Ibid.
5. Ibid.
6. Ibid.
7. Ibid.
8. Ibid.

# David Shannon

**Washington, D.C.**
October 5, 1959

📖 *No, David!*

📖 *The Rain Came Down*

📖 *Duck on a Bike*

## About the Author/Illustrator

David Shannon was born in Washington, D.C. but he grew up in the northwest in Spokane, Washington. As a youngster, he loved the book *Oliver Twist,* however, his favorite character was the Artful Dodger. He thought the villains in the Walt Disney movies he saw were always more interesting than the heroes. He had an older brother and a younger sister. David says his brother often got into trouble because David would "set him up."[1]

From the time he could hold a pencil or crayon, David was writing and drawing. His father was a radiologist and brought home the extra paper that was folded around the x-rays. When he was five years old David used some of that paper to write and illustrate a book, however, the only two words he could write were "No" and "David" so those were the only two words in the book and his illustrations showed him doing all the things he should not have been doing. Fortunately David's mother saved that book and years later, after David had begun to write and illustrate books, his mother sent that book to him. It became the basis for his award-winning title, *No, David!* (Scholastic, 1998).

When David was in junior high school he created illustrations for one of his favorite books, *The Hobbit.* After high school, he knew he wanted to be an artist but was a little leery of becoming a fine artist because of the uncertain aspect of the business. For a time he considered becoming a comic book artist. David attended and graduated from the art school at the Art Center College in Pasadena, California. It was while at the art center that he realized illustration was a way to make money in the art field.

After graduation David went to New York City to work as an artist in the publishing industry. His first jobs were creating serious political illustrations and he eventually ended up working at the *New York Times.* While at the *Times,* he created a piece for Toni Morrison's *Beloved,* which attracted the attention of an editor at Scholastic who asked

David if he was interested in illustrating Julius Lester's *How Many Spots Does a Leopard Have?* (Scholastic, 1989). That was David's first step into the world of books for young readers.

Over the next few years, David Shannon found that he liked working with children's books. He illustrated Jane Yolen's *Encounter* (Harcourt, 1992) and *The Ballad of the Pirate Queens* (Harcourt, 1995). Meanwhile, his editor was encouraging him to develop his own story to illustrate. In his editorial work, David was accustomed to creating dark paintings and didn't think he would feel comfortable portraying sunny days. When he came up with the idea of a time when there was no baseball and summer never came, he knew he had the right story for his gloomy day illustrations. *How Georgie Radbourn Saved Baseball* (Blue Sky Press/Scholastic, 1994) became David's first book with his own text and illustrations.

*A Bad Case of Stripes* (Blue Sky Press/Scholastic, 1998) came about a little differently. One day David wondered what would happen if, instead of chicken pox, one got stripes. The main character, Camilla Cream, came first. David says that, "the story started as a picture in my head, like the cover of the book. Usually I wait until the story is finished but this time it wasn't until I had some of the paintings completed that the story came."[2]

In 1996, David Shannon and author Audrey Wood began to work together with Bonnie Verburg, an editor at Scholastic. Verburg discovered that Shannon had an interest in the Paul Bunyan tales. She was actively seeking more titles for Shannon to illustrate and when she learned of his interest, she approached author Audrey Wood and asked if she was interested in retelling a Paul Bunyan tale. When first asked, Wood was not sure. As she thought about it, she began to be somewhat intrigued by the possibilities for the illustrations. She was also Shannon's friend so she decided to develop the manuscript. Wood read every version of the Paul Bunyan tales that she could locate and she found a lot of details, especially about Paul's family. She discovered that most references presented Paul's wife, Carrie McKinte, as crude. Carrie supposedly cursed a lot and was apparently very strong. They had two children, a son, Little Jean, and a daughter, Teeny. Neither child was very charming so Wood decided the make the family more respectable. She developed the manuscript for *The Bunyans* (Blue Sky Press/Scholastic, 1996) and the editor sent it to Shannon, who liked the manuscript and agreed to illustrate it. When he sketched the initial drawings for the story he decided to put a family pet, a cat, in the illustrations. When Wood saw the cat, she decided that it was a great addition and went back to her manuscript to add a role for the cat, which she named Slink.

Around this same time, Shannon's mother sent him his childhood book—the one he had made when he was just five years old—and when Shannon received the book, he thought it might make a good children's book. At first he drew the paintings for the story in a fairly realistic manner, as he normally does, but they did not seem to work with the text. They didn't seem to be as much fun as the original, Shannon says, "so I began to draw the characters like a 5-year-old."[3] The story seemed to work better with the more child-like illustrations but because the story is so simple, Shannon decided that there should also be a lot of detail in the background of the illustrations. The first David book was so successful that it earned Shannon a Caldecott Honor award for the illustrations. In each of the David books, the illustrations tell part of the story. In *No, David!*, the spunky character reacts to the authority of his mother and in the second book, *David Goes to School* (Blue Sky Press/Scholastic, 1999), he faces school authority. Shannon did not want to overdo the David books so after the second title he turned to other topics and characters. He created *The Rain Came Down* (Blue Sky Press/Scholastic, 2000) and *Duck on a Bike* (Blue Sky Press/Scholastic, 2002). Later he returned to telling another story about David in *David Gets in Trouble* (Blue Sky Press/Scholastic, 2002).

Shannon keeps notebooks filled with the doodles and ideas that pop into his head. Sometimes an idea becomes the beginning of a story, which is how *Duck on a Bike* began. At the time his daughter, Emma, was just learning to talk and liked imitating animal noises. Shannon was hiking one day and thinking about Emma and the animal noises. Someone rode by on a bike and the title popped into his head, duck on a bike. Shannon thought that was pretty funny so when he got home he wrote the phrase in his notebook. Later when he saw the phrase again, he thought of more ideas about a duck on a bike. Shannon kept collecting the ideas and soon had enough to form the beginning of a book.

Shannon creates his illustrations in the studio over his garage, which he sometimes calls his laboratory, in his home in Los Angeles. He jots down story ideas a little bit at a time, which come to him in little bits and pieces while he is painting. Once the story is almost done, he types it into his computer, which makes it easier to make little changes. Shannon often paints eight to fourteen hours a day but because his writing is done in a piecemeal fashion while he is working on other projects, Shannon says its difficult to determine exactly how long it takes him to write a book. Once he gets the manuscript completed, it takes anywhere from six months to one year to complete the illustrations. In his illustrations, he attempts to make every part of the picture tell part of the story and setting the tone or mood of the story is often done with the colors he chooses for the paintings.

Generally, Shannon likes to create the story first and then as the story begins to take shape, he starts thinking about the illustrations. Shannon's illustrations are created with acrylic paint and some prisma color pencil. Both the text and the illustrations must help to tell the story. Sometimes he has to write the text over and over again and when this happens he revises the pictures too. He usually begins the illustrative process by making a lot of thumbnail sketches. Some of the thumbnails are actually character studies where he tries to form an idea of what the character will look like, what the character will wear, and what the landscape or area will look like. Often Shannon will go to the library to check out books to give him accurate information about a particular geographic location or the clothing worn during a particular time period. If he is going to need the reference for a long time, he buys the book so that he has it while he is creating all the pictures for his book.

When David Shannon was a youngster, he knew he wanted to be an illustrator. He always liked to draw and his goal was to be a baseball player and an artist in the off-season. Now he is an artist who plays softball every Tuesday night. Besides softball he enjoys fishing and playing the guitar. In fact, at one time he even wrote songs but with his writing and painting taking up so much of his time, he hasn't had much time for song writing in recent years.

Shannon and his family live in a house on a quiet tree-lined street not far from the Walt Disney Studios. He works in his studio that is filled with keepsakes—a map of his home state of Washington, artwork from his nieces and nephews, and drawings and books made by his young daughter, Emma. His wife, Heidi, is an actress who sometimes does voice-over work. Emma began making her own books when she was two years old. One of her first books featured the only things she knew how to draw at the time—puppies, cats, people, and babies. Her favorite books at the time included some of Shannon's own childhood favorites: *Blueberries for Sal* and *Ferdinand the Bull* as well as books by

Eric Carle and Dr. Seuss. The family also includes the family dog, Fergus, a West Highland terrier who shows up in all of Shannon's books.

## Book Connections

When David Shannon illustrates a book, he tries to picture the characters by creating a visual character sketch of the people who will populate the book. When he writes, he does the same thing although he has said that "when I am writing I get to name the character and that's a big help in defining a character."[4]

Shannon feels that certain personality traits go with certain names but developing a character often requires research as well. When he was illustrating *How Georgie Radbourn Saved Baseball*, he had to make sure that his baseball scenes were accurate. When he created the illustrations for Jane Yolen's *The Ballad of the Pirate Queens,* he researched the clothing of eighteenth-century pirates. If the character is historical, he has to research but others can come from his own imagination.

After he completed the illustrations for *How Georgie Radbourn Saved Baseball*, Shannon realized that the villainous Boss Swaggert looked a lot like his sixth-grade math teacher. His real life neighbor—a retired fireman and folk artist who lived across the street and celebrated every holiday—inspired *The Amazing Christmas Extravaganza* (Blue Sky Press/Scholastic, 1995). Shannon's neighbor puts up elaborate decorations each holiday but unlike the neighbors in the book Shannon and his other neighbors enjoy the displays. When Shannon's neighbor saw the book, he liked it so much that he used some of the illustrations to design his display during his Easter extravaganza the following year.

Shannon's work often touches on deeper issues and several reviewers have commented that his first book, *How Georgie Radbourn Saved Baseball,* is a parable of totalitarianism. *The Amazing Christmas Extravaganza* deals with an excessive father. The character Camilla Cream in *A Bad Case of Stripes* suffers an extreme version of the chicken pox but story is really about the struggle Camilla has with herself to acknowledge her own individuality.

When Shannon decided to use his childhood book as the inspiration for *No, David!*, he experimented with the art technique. He also had to decide just what parts of the original he wanted to put into the manuscript for the published book. He omitted the scene from his five-year-old version that included guns and he consciously excluded any scenes, such as jumping off the top of a stairs with an umbrella, that might be potentially hazardous.

The palette for the illustrations in Shannon's first book was very dark, almost moody. Later, with the advent of the David books, his illustrations turned much lighter and colors emerged from the murky screen that sometimes covered his earlier work.

## Books Written and Illustrated by David Shannon

*The Amazing Christmas Extravaganza* (Blue Sky Press/Scholastic, 1995).

*A Bad Case of the Stripes* (Blue Sky Press/Scholastic, 1998).

*The Ballad of the Pirate Queens.* Written by Jane Yolen. (Harcourt, 1995).

*The Bunyans.* Written by Audrey Wood. (Blue Sky Press/Scholastic, 1996).

*David Gets in Trouble* (Blue Sky Press/Scholastic, 2002).

*David Goes to School* (Blue Sky Press/Scholastic, 1999).

*Duck on a Bike* (Blue Sky Press/Scholastic, 2002).

*Encounter.* Written by Jane Yolen. (Harcourt, 1992).

*Gawain and the Green Knight.* Written by Mark Shannon. (Putnam, 1994).

*How Georgie Radbourn Saved Baseball* (Blue Sky Press/Scholastic, 1994, 2000).

*No, David!* (Blue Sky Press/Scholastic, 1998).

*The Rain Came Down* (Blue Sky Press/Scholastic, 2000).

*The Rough Faced Girl.* Written by Rafe Martin. (Putnam, 1992).

# For More Information

### Articles

Bolle, Sonja. "David Shannon: A Merry Prankster." *Publishers Weekly* 246.29 (19 July 1999): 168.

*CBC Children's Book Council.* "David Shannon." March 2004. <http://www.cbcbooks. org/html/davidshannon.html>.

Cowee, Alessia. "Spotlight On: David Shannon (1999 Caldecott Honor Writer)." *Suite 101.* March 2004. <http://www.suite101.com/print_article.cfm/6025/32025>, 26 Jan. 2000.

Drennan, Miriam. "Back to School with David Shannon." *Bookpage Interview.* March 2003. <http://www.bookpage.com/9909bp/david_Shannon.html>, Sept. 1999.

# Notes

1. David Shannon, interview with the author, 27 June 1999.
2. Ibid.
3. Ibid.
4. Ibid.

# Judy Sierra

◆ Folk literature ◆ Humor ◆ Poetry

**Washington, D.C.**
June 8, 1945

📖 *Silly and Sillier: Read Aloud-Tales from Around the World*

📖 *The Gift of the Crocodile: A Cinderella Story*

📖 *There's a Zoo in Room 22*

## About the Author

When Judy Sierra was a child in Falls Church, Virginia, she walked the creeks on either side of her house and made up stories to tell the children she babysat. Her second-grade reports were written in rhyme. Judy also did word puzzles and she loved reading the dictionary. She wrote poetry, drew, made books, and wrote, costumed, and directed plays. She even created books that contained her stories but when she found that she did not have a way to copy the books to sell she turned to theater and charged admission to her backyard performances.

As the only child of Jean and Joseph Strup, Judy was encouraged for her entrepreneurship and her storytelling. At age two, she could recite poems by Robert Louis Stevenson and enjoyed the books of Dr. Seuss and the stories of Wanda Gág. Later, she shared her parents' love for the work of Ogden Nash, Cole Porter, and Gilbert and Sullivan. Her father, Joseph, a photographer for the U.S. Government, paid her a dollar for every poem she learned by heart. Judy memorized poems by many poets including Lewis Carroll and T.S. Eliot. Her mother, Jean, a librarian, also introduced her to many authors and books.

In high school, Judy edited a literary magazine and drew cartoons for the school newspaper. After graduating from high school, she attended college at the University of Lausanne, Switzerland and at the American University in Washington, D.C. She obtained an undergraduate degree in French literature with the idea of becoming a college professor. Along the way, however, she discovered that being a librarian—especially a children's librarian—might involve puppetry and storytelling so she decided to turn her studies in that direction.

After earning a graduate degree in library science from San Jose State University, Judy pursued another graduate degree in folklore. As a children's librarian, she honed her skills as a puppeteer and storyteller. Judy wrote plays and adapted stories for children's theater and then worked for a weekly children's television show in San Francisco as a puppeteer and a set designer.

From 1978 to 1985 Judy Sierra and her husband, Robert Kaminski, ran their own nationally touring puppet theater. They toured schools and museums across the country but after seven years they tired of setting up and taking down the puppet theater so they settled in Los Angeles.

Sierra began to think about writing down some of the stories she and her husband had been telling in their puppet shows. She joined the Society of Children's Book Writers and Illustrators, met other writers, and attended some of their workshops. About that experience she says, "being around published writers helped me develop a professional approach to my work."[1] Two of her books for adults, *Twice Upon a Time: Stories to Tell, Retell, Act Out, and Write About* (H.W. Wilson, 1989) and *Multi Cultural Folktales: Stories to Tell Young Children* (Oryx Press, 1991), were coauthored with her husband, Robert.

In 1993, Sierra enrolled in the Ph.D. program for folklore and mythology at UCLA but she continued to write while working on her Ph.D. Sierra's early books were written for teachers and librarians. However, after attending a workshop with children's author Uri Shulevitz, Sierra came away with the idea that a picture book is a small theater. That concept helped her focus her writing and she decided to write for children. She began retelling single tales as picture books and creating other books with poetry. After only four attempts, her first children's book, *The Elephant's Wrestling Match* (Dutton, 1992), was published. Sierra chose folktales from her puppet show repertoire, which she says, "had never before been published in [picture book] form."[2]

*The Elephant's Wrestling Match* was the first of these stories to be published and Brian Pinkney illustrated the book with scratchboard illustrations. Sierra says, "my picture books are meant to be performed." She also wrote *The House That Drac Built* (Harcourt, 1995) by using the rhythm of a traditional rhyme and while she was writing *Antarctic Antics: A Book of Penguin Poems* (Harcourt, 1998), she imagined them "to be Broadway show tunes sung by dancing penguins."[3] She even tracked down a well-known folktale about a clever little trickster who outwits a group of sea creatures and retold it in *Counting Crocodiles* (Harcourt/Guilliver, 1997). A classic Balinese story, which Sierra first encountered while studying and traveling in Bali, was retold in *The Dancing Pig* (Harcourt/Guilliver, 1999).

"Readers will find bits and pieces of the authors who influenced me in my work," Sierra explains. "For example, the rhythms of Lewis Carroll's poems ["The Lobster Quadrille"], which I memorized when I was six, can be found in *Counting Crocodiles,* though I did not realize this until the book was published."[4]

Some of Sierra's books turn out different than expected. One day Sierra was visiting a school library and as she was leaving the librarian commented that she wished there was a really good picture book about classroom pets. The same librarian also handed her a coloring sheet with an animal alphabet on it. Sierra recalls, "somehow those two ideas got mixed-up in my head and I began to think about a classroom with an animal for every letter of the alphabet."[5] In the library she found the information that helped her write the poems for *There's a Zoo in Room 22* (Harcourt, 2000). The troublesome letters were X, Q, and U but eventually Sierra found an umbrella bird. She knew about the quail and she could have used that for Q but she also found the quahog and liked that better. Only one good animal worked for X—the x-ray fish.

When Sierra collected some of her favorite Mother Goose verses in a volume titled *Monster Goose* (Harcourt/Gulliver, 2001), she transformed them into wacky versions of the traditional verses. Familiar nursery rhyme characters were replaced with their scary alter egos. Instead of a lamb "Mary has a Vampire Bat" and "Cannibal Horner" eats off his own thumb and declares, "a tasty morsel am I!" The book borders on dark humor but has just the right balance between hilarious and ghastly.

Sierra uses end-rhyme in her poems and searches for just the right words for every poem. She says she plays with the words and with their sounds within a line because the interplay between the words and the surprises each one brings are very important to her. She writes, then sets aside the writing for days or even weeks. When she picks the work up again, she says she can view it with a "fresh and critical eye."[6]

The actual writing of her verses or the retelling of other stories usually begins with traditional methods. Sierra says, "I always begin writing by hand on Embassy quadrille writing paper with a Uniball Micro Pen and revise with Le Pens of various colors. I switch to the computer as soon as I think that a computer printout will make revising easier. I wish I could say that I adhere to a schedule, but the truth is that I don't. I do my best creative work at the beginning of the day."[7]

The publication of a picture book from the beginning of the manuscript to actually having a published book in hand often takes three to five years so Sierra finds it necessary to work on more than one book at a time. Each might be at a different stage and because Sierra writes in a couple of genres and also continues to compile folklore collections for teachers and librarians to use with young readers she "may be doodling and brainstorming about one book while writing and rewriting another, and at the same time working with editors on revisions of accepted manuscripts. One project is usually on the front burner, receiving the greatest part of my attention."[8]

Sierra's single-tale picture books include a retelling of an Indonesian Cinderella story, *The Gift of the Crocodile: A Cinderella Story* (Simon & Schuster, 2000), which features a crocodile as the fairy godmother. Sierra also told a traditional Momotaro (Peach Boy) tale, *Tasty Baby Belly Buttons: A Japanese Folktale* (Knopf, 1999). Traditional Momotaro tales are among the best-known Japanese folk tales and the stories typically begin with a phrase such as "Mukashi mukashi aru tokoro ni" (Long, long ago, in a certain place). The characters in the stories often include *ojiisan* (an old man) and *obaasan* (an old woman), or a man or boy with a common name like Taro. Sierra's retelling of a Momotaro story has a female hero who is born from a melon rather than the peach that is part of most retellings.

Her fascination with folklore prompted Sierra to explore traditional oral tales. She collected several versions of many tales and has authored several collections of tales, many containing stories that have never before appeared in children's books. An anthology of 18 folktales from around the world, *Silly and Sillier: Read-Aloud Tales from Around the World* (Knopf, 2002), includes tales about small characters becoming successful or adults and large, frightening creatures making fools of themselves. Because these tales are intended to be shared with very young children (from ages three to eight), they use "a fair amount of repetition, amusing and onomatopoetic names and words, and participation [elements]."[9]

In *Nursery Tales Around the World* (Clarion, 1996), Sierra arranges 18 tales into 6 thematic groups: Runaway Cookies, Incredible Appetites, The Victory of the Smallest, Chain Tales, Slowpokes and Speedsters, and Fooling the Big Bad Wolf. The Runaway Cookies section includes runaway stories from Norway ("Pancake"), Russia ("The

Bun"), and America ("Gingerbread Man"). Sierra's sequel to the nursery tales volume, *Can You Guess My Name? Classic Tales Around the World* (Clarion, 2002), shares three little known variants of "The Three Pigs," "Rumplestiltskin," "The Frog Prince," "Hansel and Gretel," and "The Bremen Town Musicians."

Judy Sierra has many stories to tell and it delights her when others enjoy them. "The most satisfying single moment of my career occurred one Sunday morning in April, 1998. I awoke to the voices of Scott Simon and Daniel Pinkwater reading my penguin poems from *Antarctic Antics.* Such bliss!" Another exhilarating moment came when Sierra watched the animated video of that book. More books by Sierra are on the way. Stories are "always bothering me, whining 'Choose me! Choose me!' I find it difficult not to get carried away by new book ideas."[10]

Judy Sierra and her husband, Robert Kaminski, currently live across the San Francisco Bay in Oakland, California. They have a son and two granddaughters.

## Book Connections

Judy Sierra writes poetry and retells folktales, which she learns about by reading books and journals (usually old ones) and by asking people she meets about the stories they heard from storytellers when they were children. She often takes several versions of a tale from the same region or culture and uses the elements to create a version that she wishes to retell. She is especially interested in new versions of nursery tales such as "The Three Little Pigs" and "Hansel and Gretel."

Sierra creates a file folder for each story that she finds and thinks might have possibilities for retelling. Into that folder goes any other information she might come across that relates to the tale. She collects a slightly different way of telling the story, a different ending, a little rhyme, and so on. A story might stay in her file folder for several years until she gathers enough ideas for her to develop a book but as soon as she decides that she has enough background material and that she is ready to tell the story she is in a hurry to get the story told.

## Books Written by Judy Sierra

*The Beautiful Butterfly: A Folktale from Spain.* Illustrated by Victoria Chess. (Harcourt/Gulliver, 2000).

*Can You Guess My Name? Classic Tales Around the World.* Illustrated by Stefano Vitale. (Clarion, 2002).

*Counting Crocodiles.* Illustrated by Will Hillenbrand. (Harcourt/Gulliver, 1997).

*The Dancing Pig.* Illustrated by Jesse Sweetwater. (Harcourt/Gulliver, 1999).

*The Elephant's Wrestling Match.* Illustrated by Brian Pinkney. (Dutton, 1992).

*The Gift of the Crocodile: A Cinderella Story.* Illustrated by Reynold Ruffins. (Simon & Schuster, 2000).

*Monster Goose.* Illustrated by Jack E. Davis. (Harcourt/Gulliver, 2001).

*Nursery Tales Around the World.* Illustrated by Stefano Vitale. (Clarion, 1996).

*Silly and Sillier: Read Aloud Tales from Around the World.* Illustrated by Valeri Gorbachev. (Knopf, 2002).

*Tasty Baby Belly Buttons: A Japanese Folktale.* Illustrated by Meilo So. (Knopf, 1999).

*There's a Zoo in Room 22.* Illustrated by Barney Saltzberg. (Harcourt/Gulliver, 2000).

## For More Information

### Articles

McElmeel, Sharron. "Author Profile: Judy Sierra." *Library Talk* 15.3 (May/June 2002): 20–21.

### Web Sites

Sierra, Judy. *Judy Sierra's Official Web Site.* March 2004. <http://www.judysierra.net>.

## Notes

1. Judy Sierra, interview with the author, 11 Nov. 2001.
2. Ibid.
3. Ibid.
4. Ibid.
5. Ibid.
6. Ibid.
7. Ibid.
8. Ibid.
9. Ibid.
10. Ibid.

# Cynthia Leitich Smith

♦ Family stories ♦ Friends ♦ Native American

**Kansas City, Missouri**
December 31, 1967

📖 *Jingle Dancer*

📖 *Rain Is Not My Indian Name*

📖 *Indian Shoes*

## About the Author

As the only child of Harry E. and Caroline L. Smith, Cynthia Smith was cherished by her parents, her grandparents, and her extended family. Cynthia had "tea with Great-Grandma Bessie, fished with my Great-Grandpa Ernest, took long walks with my Grandma Melba, jostled with my cousin Stacy for rights to our Grandpa Clifford's chair, and lived with my Great Aunt Anne in Texas. They told stories about themselves, their parents and grandparents, our extended family and friends."[1]

The first 10 years of Cynthia's early childhood were spent mostly in Missouri, where she was born during a snow storm on December 31, 1967. Her early school years were spent at Highgrove Elementary in Grandview, Missouri. Later the family moved to Kansas where she attended school at Rosehill Elementary, Hillcrest Junior High, and Shawnee Mission High School in Overland Park. Summers were often spent at Lake Tenkiller in Oklahoma with her maternal grandparents, who played an important role in her life.

> I remember hearing stories about my Grandma Dorothy and her three sisters, about how my great-grandma had died young and so the girls had to all help raise one another. I always had a special fascination with stories about Grandpa Ray, who died the year I was born (maybe because it was the only way I could know him). I remember hearing again and again about how he was a man who cried at the movies, how he was deeply committed to his career in the U.S. Air Force, and how as a boy he'd grown up with his brothers and sisters at Seneca Indian School, a U.S. federal-run Indian boarding school in Oklahoma.[2]

While growing up in the Midwest, Cynthia did not go out of her way to tell people that she was a member of the Muscogee Creek Nation. "My grandfathers were Native, and

**197**

my grandmas were non-Indian. At first I thought of my identity as simply as extension of theirs. It took a while for the idea of biracial as a legitimate self-image to sink in." By the time Cynthia was in high school she says, "I found that there were boys who wouldn't date an Indian girl or wouldn't want their parents to know if they did." She tells of the time she was riding a bus to a football game in nearby Lawrence, Kansas. When the bus passed by the Haskell Indian Junior College (now Haskell Indian Nations University) some of the children she had grown up with began making "war whoops" and racist remarks. She says, "I was heartbroken."[3]

Cynthia's love of story sparked her interest in a journalism career. After graduating from high school in 1986, where many of her activities involved gathering news stories and writing as a reporter, Cynthia earned a degree in journalism from the University of Kansas in Lawrence. She worked for the next few years as a reporter and interviewed an African American civil rights lawyer, a city alderman who told about his decision to run for state representative, and a Tony Award–winning actress. During this time Cynthia also wrote poems and short stories but she did not really consider being any type of writer other than a journalist.

However, in the early 1990s, Cynthia decided to become a legal reporter and teach media law at a journalism school. In 1991 she entered the University of Michigan Law School at Ann Arbor and earned her Juris Doctor in 1994. Her studies took her to Paris, where she studied the French legal system and European Community Law and she also worked at the legal aid office in Hilo, Hawaii. Around this time, Cynthia also started to write fiction for adults. On September 4, 1994 she married Greg Leitich, a fellow attorney, who she often refers to as her "very cute husband."[4]

Cynthia and Greg moved to Chicago, to Austin, Texas, back to Chicago, and then in 1999, they settled again in Austin. During these moves Cynthia began to think about the stories she loved and to think more seriously about writing for adults. She tutored migrant students and reviewed books. For almost a year, Cynthia Smith worked in the law offices of the U.S. Department of Health and Human Services and of the Social Security Administration in Chicago.

During this time her mother encouraged her to write for children. Smith says, "at first I thought it was a terrible idea. I was just in my twenties and trying very hard to distance myself from being a kid. But, I'd already begun writing, scribbling stories on my lunch breaks and after work. As it turned out, all of my characters were young teens."[5] It took her a while but eventually Smith began to read children's books.

> What really cinched [my decision to write for children] was a visit I paid one autumn day to an independent bookstore located between my government law office and my skyscraper apartment in downtown Chicago. Walking past the children's section, I saw a display that included a face-out copy of *Dancing with the Indians* by Angela Shelf Medearis. I reached for it and began flipping pages. The book was about the long-term relationship between a runaway slave and the Florida Seminoles who'd taken him in. I'd been an avid reader all my life, especially as a young reader (even winning my local branch library's summer reading contest as a going-into-third-grader). But this was the very first time I ever saw a children's book that paired characters from two underrepresented ethnic communities in a positive and affirming way.[6]

Smith was entranced with *Dancing with the Indians* and she sat down in the bookstore and read the entire book. This type of story had not, to her knowledge, existed when she was a child. She says, "I had just missed the multicultural boom. Before that, every depiction of Native people I had ever seen in a children's or teen book was stereotyped, inaccurate, and offensive—so much so that I had stopped reading historical American fiction as a whole. The picture book in my hands was a revelation and an inspiration."[7]

Soon after this experience, Smith realized that she could not think of anything better to do than write children's books. Then, "after a few heartfelt conversations with my husband and [with] some ducks swimming in Lake Michigan, I did what everyone tells you not to do: I quit my day job."[8]

Cynthia and Greg moved back to Austin and she began to teach part-time at St. Edward's University and write for a couple of parenting magazines. She joined the Society of Children's Book Writers and Illustrators, read their publications, attended conferences and workshops, and met mentors and friends. She read all the children's books she could get her hands on. A year and a half later she and Greg moved back to Chicago where she sold her first children's picture book, *Jingle Dancer* (Morrow, 2000). After another year and a half they moved back to Austin where she sold her second book, a novel for young adults, *Rain Is Not My Indian Name* (HarperCollins, 2001).

Smith's love of story has brought her from a career as a journalist, through a career in law, to a career as a writer for young readers. Her writing career brings forth a voice for Native Americans in a contemporary setting. She says, "all children deserve to read at least some books that reflect the communities they portray in the deepest, most profound and accurate way possible. I'm trying to add one voice to that circle and gently draw them in."[9]

Smith's third title, *Indian Shoes* (HarperCollins, 2002), is a collection of related short stories for chapter book readers. Each short story in *Indian Shoes* revolves around a Cherokee-Seminole boy and his grandfather who live in the city of Chicago. The stories take place over the course of a year and Smith says, "they are (hopefully) humorous and touching."[10]

One of Smith's first manuscripts went to Rosemary Brosnan at Lodestar/Penguin who requested that the story be revised. Smith was happy to oblige and along with an acknowledgment of the editor's revision request, Smith sent Brosnan a draft of a picture book manuscript. Brosnan turned down the original manuscript but bought the manuscript for *Jingle Dancer.* After surviving a publisher buy-out, a released contract, the move of her editor, and a second publisher buy-out, *Jingle Dancer* was eventually published in 2000 by Morrow, under the HarperCollins umbrella.

As with most writers, there are bits and pieces of Cynthia Leitich Smith's life in her books. She says, "none of my manuscripts are retellings of [my family members] or their lives, but I'm honored if anyone can hear an echo of their voices in mine."[11] Smith devotes "every spare waking moment" to some type of writing activity. She spends about 20 hours a week working on her children's literature resource Web site. The site is an extensive multipaged resource for everything connected with books for young readers. One recent section includes 50 pages of information and extension activities intended to intensify the experience of reading *Rain Is Not My Indian Name.* Readers can learn more about the characters, how the story was put together, participate in many extension activities, and visit the dozens of related Web sites.

Another 10 hours or more of her time each week is spent on the business side of writing. This is the time when Smith responds to her editor's queries and requests for clarifications or revisions, answers fan letters, and other such activities. The rest of her time during the week is spent on the writing itself. In describing her writing schedule, Smith says, "if it weren't for my cats' management skills, I'd never actually produce a manuscript."[12]

When she refers to Native Americans within her books, Smith uses the term "Indian" and at other times she uses the term "Native American." When asked which she prefers, she explained, "like most Native people I know, I tend to alternate between terms. I was raised saying 'Indian,' and it's a habit for me, though I appreciate that many people prefer 'Native American.' I don't think that's too surprising really, the difference of opinion. After all, we're talking about folks from hundreds of distinct nations and cultures. . . . As an author, I tend to let my characters use the word that best reflects their own backgrounds and perspectives. The young attorney who says 'Native American' might well have a grandma who says 'Indian' . . . In writing, it's about story, characters, perspectives, not my own preferences or the political forces of the moment."[13]

When Cynthia Smith married Greg Leitich she says she "took his last name as my middle to distinguish Smith and still give people something they could pronounce."[14] Her husband, Greg, is a patent attorney who has also turned to writing. His first middle grade novel, *Ninjas, Piranhas, and Galileo* (Little Brown, 2003), was published under the pseudonym, Greg Leitich Smith. His adoption of his wife's surname is intended to help him keep his patent attorney persona separate from his author persona.

Together the two of them are involved with restoring their vintage home in Austin, Texas, which they share with at least two tabby cats, sometimes more. Among Smith's favorite things are sushi (especially hamache rolls), tater tots, caramels, blueberries, turtle soup, low mein, sunflower seeds, corn on the cob, pecan brownies, lobster, watermelon, barbequed burnt beef ends, and Cracker Jacks. Between 1:00 and 4:00 A.M. Smith and her cats might well be found in her office writing. Her first drafts are always written during that time of day. She says, "it's only then that I'm caught up on my email, that the phone stops ringing, that I've already gone to the gym and played in the city with my husband. In those quietest of the dark hours, I write to the whistle of the Union Pacific train and the flash of the neon signs on South Congress Avenue with one feline or another purring on my lap."[15]

## Book Connections

The idea for *Rain Is Not My Indian Name* had been growing in Cynthia Smith since she was 15 years old. During her beginning high school days, she says, "I attended a cross-country meet where a boy finished the race, fell to the ground, and died. It was my first brush with the death of a peer, and it happened right in front of me." The memory of holding the boy's mother as the paramedics worked to save him is a memory that long haunted Smith. *Rain Is Not My Indian Name,* according to her, is a book "about healing in a variety of contexts: cross culturally, in romance, between parent and child, between friends. I integrated a lot of humor, which for me is especially important in books with sensitive themes."[16]

Smith points out that she shares a background in law with the character Cousin Elizabeth in *Jingle Dancer* and similar to the character Flash in *Rain Is Not My Indian Name,* Smith was a journalism student at the University of Kansas and had a summer internship as a reporter in a small Midwestern town. Both Smith and the character Natalie from *Rain Is Not My Indian Name* were raised in Johnson County, Kansas. Smith's paternal grandparents enjoyed Las Vegas vacations just like the character Grandpa Berghoff. Smith says, "I share Marie's affection for Pez and Dmitri's affection for Superman [and] like Fynn, I spend way too much time playing on the Internet." In many ways Smith feels that

Dear Young Reader:

Books can help make you...

wiser...

more compassionate...

someone who smiles...

and inspires...

someone who steps forward...

when a HERO is...

needed.

The world needs heroes, needs you.

So Read Already!

Cynthia Leitich Smith

R
E
A
D
W
R
I
T
E
H
O
P
E

R·E·A·D·W·R·I·T·E·G·R·O·W·S·T·R·O·N·G

her favorite character, Aunt Georgia, is a "blending of her grandmothers and great aunties."[17] Smith also says that:

> Many of my characters are from Native families. I stick close to my own roots. Those in my direct line and people from places I've lived. Jenna of *Jingle Dancer* and I both share Muscogee (Creek) tribal membership, as does Rain from *Rain Is Not My Indian Name*. Likewise, the Berghoff family and Aunt Georgia from *Rain* share my Cherokee heritage, as does Grampa Halfmoon and Ray from *Indian Shoes*. Seminoles are first cousins to Creeks, and represented in both *Rain* and *Indian Shoes*.[18]

Many threads connect Smith to her stories. She is mixed-blood of Irish-, Scottish-, and German-American heritage. She says, "in many ways *Rain* is very much a German-American novel, set in a German-American town."[19]

There is also a connection to the geography through the settings in each book. "Every one of my stories is set in a place I've lived—Oklahoma, Kansas, Missouri, Illinois, Texas—or visited. My family went to Estes Park, Colorado for vacation every summer of my childhood. It was a retreat to return to in writing 'A Gentleman Cowboy.' "[20] "A Gentleman Cowboy" is a story contributed by Smith to a collection of stories, *Period Pieces* (HarperCollins, 2003), by various authors.

Character names often come from Smith's family members. In *Jingle Dancer,* she named characters after her cousin Elizabeth (*Rain* is dedicated to this same cousin) and others such as Mrs. Scott, Great Aunt Sis, and Aunt Georgia. "Aunt Georgia got a huge kick out of it. She's been known to introduce herself as 'Aunt Georgia from the book.' " In many small ways Smith resembles her main character, Rain, both of them like Cracker Jacks and Web design. Similar to Dmitri, Smith likes to read comic books and "Aunt Georgia's garden is based on my mother's." Smith says there are many connections from her own life that end up in her books, "who I am shows in my writing. It's very personal. Each story is a puzzle assembled with pieces of my soul."[21]

## Books Written by Cynthia Leitich Smith

"A Gentleman Cowboy." In *Period Pieces.* Ed. Erzsi Deàk and Kristin Litchman. (HarperCollins, 2003).

"The Naked Truth." In *In My Grandmother's House: Award Winning Authors Tell Stories About Their Grandmothers.* Ed. and illus. by Bonnie Christensen. (HarperCollins, 2003).

*Indian Shoes.* Illustrated Jim Madsen. (HarperCollins, 2002).

*Jingle Dancer.* Illustrated by Cornelius Van Wright and Ying-Hwa Hu. (Morrow, 2000).

*Rain Is Not My Indian Name* (HarperCollins, 2001).

## For More Information

### Articles

"Cynthia Leitich Smith, Author of *Jingle Dancer*—Interview." *ReadtheWest.com American Western Magazine.* March 2004. <http://www.readthewest.com/interviewCynthiaSmith.html>, April 2000.

Durango, Julia. "By the Book: Jingle Dancing with Cynthia Leitich Smith." *The Daily Times.* May 2004. <http://www.geocities.com/juliadurango/btbsmith.html>, 24 Oct. 2000.

Florence, Debbi Michiko. "An Interview with Children's Author Cynthia Leitich Smith." *Debbi Michiko Florence's Library—Children's Fiction.* May 2004. <http://debbimichikoflorence.com/index.2ts?page = cynthialeitichsmith>.

Hastings, Dr. Wally. "Cynthia Leitich Smith: *Rain Is Not My Indian Name*" *English 240—Literature for Younger Readers/Dr. Wally Hastings—Northern State University.* May 2004. <http://www.northern.edu/hastingw/smith-rain.html>.

McElmeel, Sharron. "Author Profile: Cynthia Leitich Smith." *Library Talk* 15.2 (March/April 2002): 30–31.

## Web Sites

Smith, Cynthia Leitich. *Children's Book Author Cynthia Leitich Smith Official Web Site.* March 2004. <http://www.cynthialeitichsmith.com>.

# Notes

1. Cynthia Leitich Smith, interview with the author, 18 Aug. 2001.
2. Ibid.
3. Ibid.
4. Ibid.
5. Cynthia Leitich Smith, letter to the author, 12 Sept. 2002.
6. Ibid.
7. Ibid.
8. Smith, interview.
9. Ibid.
10. Ibid.
11. Ibid.
12. Ibid.
13. Ibid.
14. Ibid.
15. Ibid.
16. Ibid.
17. Ibid.
18. Smith, letter.
19. Ibid.
20. Ibid.
21. Ibid.

# Chris Soentpiet

♦ Historical fiction

---

## Seoul, South Korea
January 3, 1970

---

📖 *Peacebound Train*

📖 *Molly Bannaky*

📖 *Coolies*

## About the Author/Illustrator

Chris Soentpiet's life took many turns before he became a renowned illustrator of children's books. Soentpiet is Korean by birth although his surname is Dutch. He spent his early childhood in Korea and when he was just six his mother died of a malignant brain tumor. Almost exactly a year later his father was killed in a car accident. Chris was the youngest of six siblings. The Soentpiet family was Mormon and his oldest Korean sister, who was 22, moved to Hawaii for a year. In Hawaii, she worked with a large Mormon adoption agency to find a home for Chris, her younger brother, and her youngest sister.

When Chris was eight years old and his sister was twelve, they traveled to the island of Kauii, Hawaii and were adopted into the Soentpiet family. Chris's brother and three sisters stayed in Korea including his oldest sister, who had since returned to Korea from Hawaii. Chris had a difficult time adjusting to life in the United States. At first he refused to speak English and finally, his English as Secondary Language (ESL) teacher asked him not to speak Korean. Eventually, Chris forgot the Korean language entirely. His sister had an even more difficult time adjusting but eventually she learned English and became bilingual.

In his new family, Chris's mother was German-English and his father was Dutch-Indonesian. The couple had three biological children—two daughters and one son who were older than Chris and his sister. At the same time that the Soentpiet family adopted Chris and his sister they also adopted a native Hawaiian infant son so there was a baby brother as well. Chris felt very comfortable in Hawaii because there were many other Koreans in his community as well as other cultures. Chris and his sister fit comfortably into the community, however, before Chris turned 10, the family moved to a suburb of Portland, Oregon. In Portland, their neighborhood had few minorities and most of the minority people were black.

**204**

Chris admired the way his American mom always just referred to him as her son—not as her adopted son. Others may have been left to figure out the situation but she treated him the same as she did any other member of the family. For a time, the Soentpiets lived in Alaska but then they returned to Oregon where Chris finished high school. During this time, Chris's American parents divorced and money was tight so it seemed that college was not in his future.

At Grant High School, Chris studied art and at age 16 he painted his first watercolor. Chris loved the way the paint could be layered to create brilliant colors and he knew he wanted to work more with the medium. His art teacher, Mr. Jannson, recognized his talent and encouraged him. Jannson actually challenged Chris to create 10 paintings and told him that if he did, he would get an A in the class. Once Chris completed the paintings Jannson took them home and made slides of them.

Unbeknownst to Chris, Jannson sent copies of the slides to several art schools and because of that, Chris was offered a full scholarship to the prestigious Pratt Institute in Brooklyn, New York. So once again, Chris Soentpiet packed his things and moved a long way from home.

At the age of 18, Chris was living in Brooklyn and doing construction work to meet his living expenses while he attended the Pratt Institute. At first, he studied commercial art but he was not too enthralled with it. He was nearing the end of his program when Ted Lewin, already a successful children's book illustrator, came to the school to speak. Chris used the opportunity to show Lewin some of his paintings and Lewin suggested Chris use them to enter the children's literature field. However, Chris's advisor tried to talk him out of making the change, telling him that there was little money in the children's book field. But Chris had already decided to change majors and he changed his final project to illustrative art. The paintings for that final project, paintings of scenes around the town, became the content for his first book, *Around Town* (HarperCollins, 1994).

Chris Soentpiet soon found out that his college advisor was right—there was not much money in the children's book field. In fact, for almost two years he had no income. "I lived on instant noodle soup for much of the time,"[1] he says. In 1992, after 10 different publishers had turned him down, Chris landed his first book contract. But it took more than two years before *Around Town* was actually published. Meanwhile, Chris got by with a job creating molds for belt buckles and doing some more construction work. He lived with his college roommate and continued to work on more books. Sometimes Chris had to decide whether to buy paints or food.

Chris often took as many as 60 rolls of film to have photos to use as references for his illustrations. He took pictures of locations and models in costumes and poses that would help him get the right details, angles, and perspectives. All of this took time, perseverance, and money, which he borrowed from his family, his roommate, and his sister.

Along the way, Chris met and married Rosanna Yin Lau, a Wall Street data analyst. After a few years, money started coming in from royalties for books on the market, advances for new contracts, and appearances. With these new opportunities, however, came more work on the business side of his work—contracts, appearance schedules, and other work usually done by agents. In 1997, his wife Rosanna gave up her career to become his agent, manager, and eventually collaborator.

Chris Soentpiet's first book used illustrations from his Pratt Art Institute project. He had created them using the neighborhood children and his old neighborhood in Brooklyn as models. Other models and a lot of research were necessary for every book he illustrated.

While researching and preparing to create the illustrations for his fourth book, *Peacebound Trains* written by Haemi Balgassi (Clarion, 1996), Soentpiet said, "I had to travel to Korea. While there, I took the opportunity to see my brother and sisters for the first time since I was adopted 16 years ago. It was a happy reunion. *Peacebound Trains* went on to win many awards, so it was a nice tribute to my Korean family."[2] The visit to Korea brought Soentpiet back in touch with his very early years. He says though, "the language barrier was a constant frustration."[3] His sister, who had been adopted along with Chris by the Soent-piets, went with him and because she was the only family member who was bilingual she translated for all of them. While Soentpiet was there he visited the war museum in Seoul and saw models of the peacebound trains with half-sized models of people in period costume. Care had to be taken that the family in *Peacebound Trains* was dressed in the proper Korean clothing. Chris took over 80 rolls of film for the book and many of the pictures were taken of the Korean countryside and housing; much of the area is still as it was in the 1950s.

Other books by Soentpiet also required research. For *Molly Bannaky* (Houghton, 1999), Soentpiet visited a recreation of an eighteenth-century village in Virginia and he contacted the Holstein Association to verify that Holstein cows were actually in America during the eighteenth century. For the cover illustration of *More Than Anything Else* (Orchard, 1995) he researched what type of hat a young man living in the 1880s would wear.

Even with his commitment to historical accuracy, Soentpiet does at times put a personal object in his books. For example, the number of the train in *Peacebound Trains* is 1370, numbers that represent his birth date, January 3, 1970, and Mrs. Chou in *Last Dragon* (Clarion, 1995) is modeled after his sister. Typically, it takes Soentpiet about six months to create the 20 or so illustrations for each book. However, that does not account for the research and arranging for models and photos that aid the illustrative process.

*Dear Santa, Please Come to the 19th Floor* (Philomel, 2002) was based on Soentpiet's wife, Rosanna's, childhood growing up on the nineteenth floor of a New York City apartment. Rosanna authored the story using her pseudonym, Yin. Soentpiet sketched the outdoor and stairway scenes from his wife's actual childhood apartment building in lower Manhattan. Rosanna (Yin) based the characters on neighborhood friends from her childhood—friends that shared common dreams and aspirations for a better life. Santa never did visit their nineteenth floor apartment.

After several frugal years as the traditional starving artist, Soentpiet has become one of the most lauded illustrators in the field of children's literature. Every year he creates the art for one to two books and visits thirty or more schools.

Following his school visits, Soentpiet often receives letters from children. One letter from a fourth grader in Columbus, Ohio said, "your books are very very good. I did not read any of them." Another letter also from a fourth grader said, "how did you get this job, friend, neighbor—who did you know?"[4] He and Rosanna (Yin) have collaborated on *Coolies* (Philomel, 2001), a historical novel that focuses on the contributions of the Chinese, *Dear Santa, Please Come to the 19th Floor,* and most recently on a sequel to *Coolies,* a story about the contribution of the Irish to the culture of America. Soentpiet has also been working on an autobiography tentatively titled, *Gift from Korea.* He has been working on it for five years and can't give a publication date for it yet.

For the first decade of Soentpiet's art career, he and his wife lived in a Brooklyn apartment. Now he has a spacious studio in Flushing, New York, can choose the manuscripts he wants to illustrate, and can take time off and still make a living. His wife, Rosanna, continues to be his business partner, agent, and sometimes collaborator.

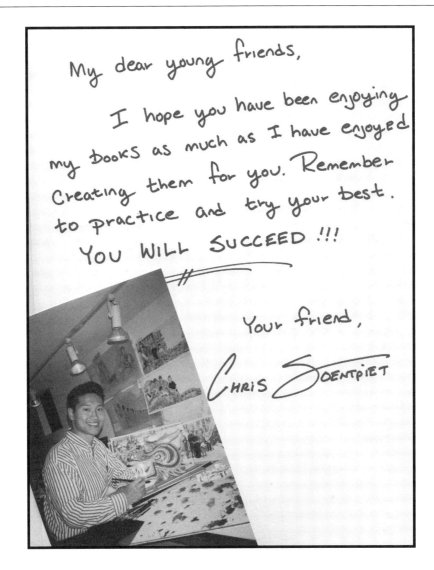

My dear young friends,

I hope you have been enjoying my books as much as I have enjoyed creating them for you. Remember to practice and try your best. YOU WILL SUCCEED !!!

Your friend,

Chris Soentpiet

## Book Connections

Chris Soentpiet says his work is marked by the fact that he is adopted and has been given a chance to travel to and live in many places from Korea to Hawaii to Oregon to Alaska, back again to Oregon, and finally to New York City and Flushing. His work is also influenced by the fact that his family is multicultural—a small United Nations. Soentpiet was born in Korea, has a German-Irish mother, a Dutch-Indonesian father, a Hawaiian brother, Korean (birth) brothers and sisters, and a Chinese wife. So he is drawn toward working on stories that are culturally diverse.

The popularity of *Peacebound Trains* gave Soentpiet a level of independence that has allowed him to pick and choose the manuscripts that he wants to illustrate. Among his choices are a book set in New York City (*Around Town*), a book honoring the work of the Chinese in building the transcontinental railroad (*Coolies*), two African American fictionalized biographical books (*Mary Bannaky* and *More Than Anything Else*), a story about wartime Korea (*Peacebound Trains*), a book set in Appalachia (*Silver Packages* [Orchard, 1997]), a book about Japanese American Internment (*So Far from the Sea* [Clarion, 1998]), and one about Lebanese immigration to the United States (*The Silence in the Mountains* [Orchard, 1999]).

Soentpiet selects the manuscripts that he wants to illustrate carefully. Each of those he chooses must "depict juveniles in a specific and well-defined ethnic and historical setting."[5] Another prerequisite is that the story must focus on the human struggle. Each of the main characters in the books he illustrates has a challenge to overcome. For example, Molly Bannaky overcame her status as an indentured servant and the ban on her marriage to a former slave and Booker T. Washington overcame his lack of a formal education. Other characters also face struggles of poverty and prejudice. Soentpiet's books seem to be as diverse as his own cultural heritage.

## Books Illustrated by Chris Soentpiet

*Around Town.* Written by Chris Soentpiet. (HarperCollins, 1994).

*Coolies.* Written by Yin. (Philomel, 2001).

*Dear Santa, Please Come to the 19th Floor.* Written by Yin. (Philomel, 2002).

*Jin Woo.* Written by Eve Bunting. (Clarion, 2001).

*Molly Bannaky.* Written by Alice McGill. (Houghton, 1999).

*More Than Anything Else.* Written by Marie Bradby. (Orchard, 1995).

*My Brother Martin: A Sister Remembers Growing Up with the Rev. Dr. Martin Luther King, Jr.* Written by Christine King Farris. (Simon & Schuster, 2003).

*Peacebound Trains.* Written by Haemi Balgassi. (Clarion, 1996).

*Saturday & Teacakes.* Written by Lester Laminek. (Peachtree, 2003).

*Silver Packages: An Appalachian Christmas Story.* Written by Cynthia Rylant. (Orchard, 1997).

*So Far From the Sea.* Written by Eve Bunting. (Clarion, 1998).

## For More Information

### Articles

Hong, Terry. "Picturing the Worlds of Chris Soentpiet." *AsianWeek.com: A&E.* March 2004. <http://www.asianweek.com/2002_09_20/arts_soentpiet.html>, 20 Sept. 2002.

Nowack-Kidd, Amy. "Picture the World." *KoreAm Journal: The Korean American Experience.* March 2004. <http://www.koreamjournal.com/search_detail.asp?id=450>, Dec. 2002.

Richardson, Clem. "For the Young at Heart Children's Book Artist Is a Medal Winner." *New York Daily News.* 10 April 2000: 3.

Romano, Katherine. "Chris Soentpiet." *Teaching K-8* 32.6 (March 2002): 48–50.

Shapiro, Sarah. "From Dark to Light: An Artist Paints a New Life Through His Books." *Newsday.* 1 June 2000: A33.

Vicker, Martha. "Evoking History with Art: The Multicultural Life and Work of Chris Soentpiet." *Korean Quarterly.* March 2004. <http://www.koreanquarterly.org/issues/ViewArticle.asp?ArticleID = 39&IssueID = >.

### Web Sites

Soentpiet, Chris. *Chris K. Soentpiet—Profile-author, illustrator of children's books.* March 2004. <http://www.soentpiet.com>.

## Notes

1. Chris Soentpiet, presentation at the Festival of Children's Books, University of Iowa, Iowa City, 3 Nov. 2001.
2. Chris Soentpiet, letter to the author, 19 Sept. 2002.
3. Soentpiet, presentation.
4. Ibid.
5. Ibid.

# Anastasia Suen

◆  Family stories   ◆   Science informational books

| Southern California |
| :---: |
| January 22, 1956 |

📖  *Air Show*

📖  *Raise the Roof*

📖  *Willie's Birthday*

## About the Author

Anastasia Suen grew up the oldest daughter in a family of four girls and three boys. Their father worked in the aerospace industry so they "lived on the Space Coast of Florida in the late 50's and early 60's in the early days of NASA, and on the California coast after that."[1] She says, "I was three when we moved to Space Coast in Florida. It was 1959, the year they selected the first astronauts. My father drove from California to Florida, but my mother flew with my brother and me. Eating pancakes on the plane is one of my first memories. I guess it should come as no surprise that the first book I sold (37 years later) was about a picture book poem about airplanes!"[2]

Because of her father's work, Anastasia and her siblings were very aware of the space industry and all of its activities. They watched space launches on their black and white television and then she says they would run "out into the back yard to see it in living color." The children watched the launches until the ball of fire rose into the sky and they couldn't see it any longer. They were very aware that someone's dad was inside the space shuttle. Anastasia says, "I also watched my Dad until I couldn't see him anymore. He sailed in a missile tracking ship, tracking spacecraft for NASA. When he sailed, we stood on the dock to see him off, and then watched until the ship reached the horizon, and disappeared. It looked as if the ship had sailed off the edge of the world!"[3]

Years later Anastasia Suen became a writer and used her childhood experiences as an inspiration for *Man on the Moon* (Viking, 1997), an account of the 1969 moon landing when Neil Armstrong became the first person to step onto the surface of the moon. Now, she also has written picture books and information books and has contributed books to series published by several publishers including the publishers of the Scott Foresman Reading 2000 series and the Wright Group.

Anastasia recalls, "they didn't have kindergarten when I was a kid, so in first grade, I finally learned how to read. I felt like I had been waiting forever to learn the magic. 'Oh! Oh! Look! Look!' said the pages of my Dick and Jane readers. I can still remember what the pages looked like."[4] Anastasia's mother read to her constantly and frequented the library on a regular basis. Anastasia's love of books inspired her to start writing at the age of 10, when she wrote her first picture book. She continued to write throughout her junior and senior high school days and even began to write poetry. During college Anastasia wrote and illustrated a nonfiction picture book as a project for one of her classes. After graduating from college Anastasia began to teach. Her first teaching assignment was with first grade and she wrote some little books for her students to read. Then she moved to a new area and taught in a fifth grade classroom where she wrote plays for her students to perform.

When her own son was young Anastasia Suen took time off from teaching. Later when she was expecting her daughter, she enrolled in a course with the Institute of Children's Literature. Because of health issues she dropped out of the course and never returned but her creative desires kept growing. Even though Suen wasn't writing for students anymore, she "didn't stop writing." Soon, she began to think about sending her work to publishers. When her son was just two, he decided that he wanted to read real books so she made him a picture book of trucks. "I shot photos of all the trucks we saw and put them into a book for him."[5] Her son's interest is partially responsible for Suen's interest in writing informational books and she has written books about many forms of transportation such as cars, trucks, trains, planes, and stories about travel into space.

As Suen was developing her writing career, she attended her first Society for Children's Book Writers and Illustrators (SCBWI) conference where she was given what she feels is the best writing advice she ever received. At the conference, Bonnie Verburg, then editor at Blue Sky Press, told Suen to "read every book in the library."[6]

Suen had already developed the habit of reading. During her junior high years she says, "I read my way through the library, from A to Z, from 000 to 999." Now she finds her own books on those shelves in both the fiction and nonfiction sections. Suen finds nonfiction particularly interesting as there is always something new to learn. She says, "I can never fit everything I learn about a topic into a single book. What ends up in a book is just the tip of the iceberg. I need to know more than I can ever include, so I can make choices. In nonfiction, I find that the simplest things are not as simple as they first appear. Facts and dates change as I dig deeper. The closer I am to the original source the more interesting the story becomes!"[7]

Suen's first experiences with submitting books to publishers, however, were not always successful. Her success began shortly after Suen and her family moved to Texas. Suen, who had grown up in Florida and southern California, was experiencing a day of being iced in but when she carefully made her way to her mailbox, she discovered some very good news; three publishers had accepted her stories for publication in magazines. A year later on January 23, 1996 she received a phone call offering her a contract for her first picture book. Two more offers came within the next three months and Suen's career was launched with three picture books.

Suen says her family inspires her picture books. Her maternal grandfather, a railroad man, was the inspiration for *Window Music* (Viking, 1998). "The scenes I wrote for *Window Music* are the same scenes that I saw along the rail line that passed by my house in California . . . hearing the train whistle blow at night as the train passed reminded me of

> Read and write
> like you breathe
>
> Words in
>         Read
> Words out
>         Write
> Words in
>         Read
> Words out
>         Write
>
> You need one
>         To do the other...
>
> *Happy reading and writing!*
>
> *Anastasia Suen*

[my grandfather]." Once the manuscript was submitted and the editors at Viking indicated they were considering it for publication, it took more than two years for them to make a final decision. Suen says, "the places in *Delivery* [Viking, 1999] are all places with a family connection. My brothers delivered papers as kids and later, one owned a grocery store. One of my brothers lived on a boat and I worked at the airport in college. In fact, the ideas for this book came to me as I drove to visit my brother. I passed by all the places in the book on a single trip."[8]

After her daughter was born, Suen kept a baby calendar, which she used as the basis for *Baby Born* (Lee & Low, 1999). "Month by month, I wrote about what she and her brother had done as babies."[9] When each of the children were two years old, Suen took them to a "Mommy and Me" class, which became the basis for her book *Toddler Two* (Lee & Low, 2000).

Suen says, "my mother played the radio all day when I was growing up, so I write poetry, music written into words. My father was an engineer, so I write about machinery. My husband is an architect; so after years of dust and noise I wrote a book about building a house called *Raise the Roof* [Viking, 2003]"[10]

Suen's favorite things include reading and writing, the color red, chocolate, and looking at flowers. She also enjoys going to the beach. Suen, her husband, and their son and daughter live in Plano, Texas. Every year her husband buys her a Dick and Jane calendar—a reminder of the readers she read as a child. Now she writes readers for the classroom and has published more than 40 readers for kindergarten through sixth grade.

## Book Connections

Viking publishes many of Anastasia Suen's trade books and an editor at Viking asked Suen to create some early chapter books based on the characters developed by the late Ezra Jack Keats. With Suen's words, Keats's characters Peter and his dog, Willie, his younger sister, Susie, and his friends Archie, Amy, and Louie, live on. Books in the series, Peter's Neighborhood, began to appear in 2001.

Suen has also written book for series for other publishers. She has written books about organizations such as *Habitat for Humanity* (PowerPress, 2002) and *Peace Corps* (PowerPress, 2002) for the Helpful Organizations series. She has also written about the earth's continents. Suen has produced controlled readers for the trade market as well as educational publishers such as Scott Foresman and the Wright Group.

When asked for a starting point for reading her books, Suen responds, "*Window Music* is a good place to start. It shows the scenes of my childhood and it also has the rhythm that I like to write in. The text is very spare. I only want to write just enough to give you a feeling of the experience. Let the pictures and your imagination fill in the void."[11]

Suen has also written a book for fellow writers, *Picture Writing: A New Approach to Writing for Kids and Teens* (Writer's Digest Books, 2003). This thorough guide can be described as a writing course in a book. In *Picture Writing,* Suen shares essential insider information to those who might want to write fiction, nonfiction, or poetry for young readers.

## Books Written by Anastasia Suen

*Air Show.* Illustrated by Cecco Mariniello. (Henry Holt, 2001).

*Baby Born.* Illustrated by Chih-Wei Chang. (Lee & Low, 1999).

*Delivery.* Illustrated by Wade Zahares. (Viking, 1999).

*Man on the Moon.* Illustrated by Benrei Huang. (Viking, 1997).

Peter's Neighborhood series: *The Clubhouse* (2002); *Hamster Chase* (2001); *Loose Tooth* (2002); and *Willie's Birthday* (2001). All illustrated by Allan Eitzen and published by Viking.

*Picture Writing: A New Approach to Writing for Kids and Teens.* (Writer's Digest Books, 2003).

*Raise the Roof.* Illustrated by Elwood Smith. (Viking, 2003).

*Toddler Two.* Illustrated by Winne Cheon. (Lee & Low, 2000).

*Window Music.* Illustrated by Wade Zahares. (Viking, 1998).

## For More Information

### Articles

Reichard, Sue. "Anastasia Suen: Prolific Non-fiction Writer for Children." *Suite101.* March 2004. <http://www.suite101.com/article.cfm/525/97061>, 1 Jan. 2003.

## Web Sites

Suen, Anastasia. *Anastasia Suen, Children's Author.* March 2004. <http://www. asuen.com>.

## Notes

1. Anastasia Suen, letter to the author, 1 Oct. 2002.
2. Anastasia Suen, letter to the author, 8 April 2003.
3. Ibid.
4. Ibid.
5. Ibid.
6. Sue Reichard, "Anastasia Suen: Prolific Non-fiction Writer for Children," *Suite101,* March 2004, <http://www.suite101.cm/article.cfm/525/97061>, 1 Jan. 2003.
7. Ibid.
8. Suen, letter, 2002.
9. Ibid.
10. Suen, letter, 2003.
11. Suen, letter, 2002.

# Simms Taback

◆ Folk literature

**New York, New York**
February 13, 1932

📖 *Joseph Had a Little Overcoat*

📖 *There Was an Old Lady Who Swallowed a Fly*

📖 *The House That Jack Built*

## About the Author/Illustrator

Simms Taback was born in the Bronx and grew up in a working class neighborhood. His father, Leon, was a painter and his mother, Thelma, was a seamstress. Simms says that he grew up in a terrific neighborhood—a neighborhood referred to as "The Coop." The neighborhood children frequented the community center where they participated in a camera club and a science club. The center also had its own library. Simms's teachers encouraged him to take the exam for the High School of Music and Art and he qualified for entrance and attended the high school. After graduation he thought about pursuing an engineering degree but instead enrolled in Cooper Union. Throughout the years, Simms worked as a graphic artist with CBS records, taught at the School of Visual Arts and at Syracruse University, and every year or two illustrated a children's book.

Simms Taback is one of those overnight successes that took nearly 40 years to achieve. Although Simms illustrated dozens of books, from the publication of his first book, *Jabberwocky and Other Frabjous Nonsense* (Harlan Quist, 1964) to his Caldecott Honor for *There Was an Old Lady Who Swallowed a Fly* (Viking, 1997) and the Caldecott Award for *Joseph Had a Little Overcoat* (Viking, 1999), he was relatively unknown until he received Caldecott recognition.

In fact, for more than 28 years, Simms Taback paid the bills as a freelance illustrator and designer for Ruffins/Taback Design Studio. Along the way, he illustrated dozens of children's books but few of them sold well enough to provide a stable income. His first book, *Jabberwocky and Other Frabjous Nonsense,* was published in several languages and seemed successful but according to Taback, the publisher "ran off to Europe with all the royalties." Later, Taback spent four months working on books for a new imprint to be

**215**

published as part of Mr. Roger's Library. However, on the day he delivered the completed artwork, "Mister Rogers had second thoughts and cancelled the whole project."[1]

The artwork for another book was lost before it was published so Taback had to recreate the art and other books were not successful at all. In the meantime, Taback achieved considerable success in other areas of the design business. One of his pieces of artwork, his design for the very first McDonald's Happy Meal, is actually in the Smithsonian Institute. But even that success was limited. Taback says he had accepted the job as a "low-budget assignment because it was only going to be a test print run. They produced over seven million boxes."[2]

For several years Taback and Reynold Ruffins, another artist who has also illustrated children's books, were partners in a design studio and later they shared a studio while doing their own freelance illustrative work.

Taback's father, Leon, was involved as a union organizer and his mother, a seamstress, was a member of the International Ladies Garment Workers Union (ILGWU). The benefits of workers joining together were not lost on Taback. In 1974 he began working to establish the Illustrators Guild. Eventually the organization affiliated with the Graphic Artists Guild and Taback served as the organization's president for several years.

As a designer, Taback created pieces for the *New York Times,* Columbia Records, Scholastic Press, various advertising agencies, and established his own studio and greeting card business. Although he has illustrated books by a dozen or more other writers, the illustrated books written by Harriet Ziefert are among Taback's best-known earlier works. He wrote and illustrated *Joseph Had a Little Overcoat* (Random House, 1978) but it was the second version of the story, released in 1999, by Viking, that eventually won him recognition. The first version was honored by the American Institute of Graphics but it wasn't a best seller. After illustrating more books by other writers, Taback came back to another traditional tale that did earn him recognition. In 1998 his illustrated version of *There Was an Old Lady Who Swallowed a Fly* earned him a Caldecott Honor Award, which was his first major recognition.

Taback's early illustrative style used pen and ink drawings and watercolor paintings. Eventually he mastered the art of collage, which is the technique he used for the illustrations for *There Was an Old Lady Who Swallowed a Fly.* In these illustrations Taback included many details and comments for the reader. Names of different types of birds are put in the illustrations along with a recipe for spider soup, and bogus newspaper headlines such as "Lady Wolfs Down Dog" add humor to the poem. A cutout allows the readers to see inside the gluttonous old lady. Even a small caricature of the artist, Taback himself, appears in one corner of the final page. The illustrations, which include various types of flies and birds and dogs, are clearly labeled and accompanied by a companion picture that accurately shows the animal.

After receiving the Caldecott Honor Award, Taback turned his attention back to the story of *Joseph Had a Little Overcoat,* which had become a novelty book sought by collectors. This story is based on a Yiddish folksong. For the second edition, Taback reillustrated the tale using colorful collages and die-cut cutouts. Taback reached into his cultural past for this second rendition of the story. He read books and viewed videos to learn all he could about Jewish life in Poland and Russia during World War II. He learned more about Sholom Aleikem—the author of many stories, including *The Fiddler on the Roof.*

Taback used a version of his mother's family name (Cohen) as Joseph's surname in the book—Joseph Kohn of Yehupetz, Poland. Taback visited a Jewish museum to research the clothing that was worn before World War II. He discovered that the clothing was usually drab and faded but sewn with much care. Taback decided to exercise artistic license and he mixed up the images with traditional Polish and Ukrainian designs. He used collage fragments from catalog images as fabrics of the ethnic clothing. So, in addition to the fact that the story is about making something from a soon-to-be discard item, Taback, by using the catalog scraps, was using discards to make the story illustrations.

The folk art quality of the collages made this edition of *Joseph Had a Little Overcoat* a favorite with readers. Taback filled the book's pages with references to Yiddish culture and tradition. In one illustration, Taback shows a man holding a book by Sholom Aleichem—a pseudonym for the most renowned author in the Yiddish world, Solomon Rabinowitz. In Yiddish Sholom Aleichem also means "peace be unto you."

Several Yiddish newspapers are shown in the illustrations. In one image, scraps from a Yiddish paper feature a village wedding. On a table Taback placed a menorah and matches and an opened letter, in Yiddish, addressed to "Joseph Kohn, Yehupetz, Poland." The photo on the table is of Molly Picon, a great Yiddish-American actress.[3] An open book on the table contains yet another reference to Sholom Aleichem and mentions a story, "If I Were a Rothschild," a possible reference to the song "If I Were a Rich Man" from the play, *Fiddler on the Roof.* Taback included photos in windows that most likely represent his family, friends, or people from history. A full page spread toward the end of the book has the character, Fiddler on the Roof, singing "Hob ich mir a shnips!"—"I had a little necktie."

In what seems to be a joke for the adults who will read the book, there is a page of a book by Sholom Aleichem called "A Tale of Chelm." The words translated from the Yiddish discuss how America is now involved in collecting money and reference former President Bill Clinton, Al Gore, and the 1996 democrats.[4]

Taback's clever and edgy illustrations can also be found in other titles. In 2002, Putnam released *This Is the House That Jack Built,* a retelling of a 1755 nursery rhyme. Taback illustrated this rhyme, which is based on a sixteenth-century Hebrew chant. The endpapers and back cover are covered with newspaper advertisements offering real estate and tools to fix a house. Taback illustrated the page that featured the phrase "This is the cheese that lay in the house," with many varieties of cheese and on the cat page he labeled mug shots of the Cat in the Hat, Felix the cat, and so forth. On the cow's image Taback has superimposed labels indicating the cow's parts—tail, hoof, and so forth. There are also labels on the cow for meatballs and the Big Mac. Each character moves across the page as the text becomes larger. As the tale ends Taback slips himself with many of his trademark artist tools into the story (wearing a beret that bears the words "Guess who?").

Simms Taback is married to Gail Baugher Kuenstler, who works as a business writer. Together, they raised a son and two daughters, Lisa, Jason, and Emily. Among Taback's favorite things are chocolate ice cream, making things with wood, swimming, and reading the newspaper. The Tabacks have four grandchildren. They live in Willow, in upstate New York.

## Book Connections

Simms Taback's illustrations of traditional folk rhymes or songs combine collage with pen, ink, and watercolor. His merry mix of media and images appeal on different levels to all ages. In each of his books Taback also includes a self portrait. In *There Was an Old Lady* an artist, a self-caricature of Taback, observes the woman meeting her gluttonous demise and says, "even the artist is crying." In *Joseph Had a Little Overcoat,*

Joseph bears an uncanny resemblance to Taback. Finally in *This Is the House That Jack Built,* readers can find the artist in a cameo appearance along with the many tools of his trade. Look for all the references to the Yiddish language and Jewish culture in *Joseph Had a Little Overcoat* and the humorous asides in *There Was an Old Lady* and *This Is the House That Jack Built.*

## Books Illustrated by Simms Taback

*Joseph Had a Little Overcoat.* Written and illustrated by Simms Taback. (Viking, 1999).

*Road Builders.* Written by B. G. Hennessy. (Viking, 1994).

*There Was an Old Lady Who Swallowed a Fly.* Written and illustrated by Simms Taback. (Viking, 1997).

*This Is the House that Jack Built.* Written and illustrated by Simms Taback. (Putnam, 2002).

*When I First Came to This Land.* Written by Harriet Ziefert. (Putnam, 1998).

## For More Information

### Articles

Debbon, Betty. "Meet Illustrator Simms Taback." Mini-Page supplement to *Cedar Rapids Gazette.* Cedar Rapids, Iowa. 10 Apr. 2001.

Ruffins, Reynold. "Across the Drawing Board from Simms Taback." *Horn Book* 76.4 (July 2000): 409–411.

"Simms Taback, an Interview with the Year 2000 Caldecott Gold Medal Winner." *Creative Parents.com.* Nov. 2003. <http://www.creativeparents.com/simmsinterv.html>.

"Simms Taback." *Children's Author at Embracing the Child.* Nov. 2003. <http://www.embracingthechild.com/booksspecialtaback.html>.

Taback, Simms. "Archives: Simms Taback." *CBC Children's Book Council.* Nov. 2003. <http://www.cbcbooks.org/html/simms_taback.html>.

Taback, Simms. "Caldecott Medal Acceptance." *Horn Book* 76.4 (July 2000): 402–408.

## Notes

1. Simms Taback, Caldecott Acceptance speech, American Library Association, Chicago, 9 July 2000.

2. Ibid.

3. Molly Picon (1898–1992) was known as an ethnic actress. She went to London to expand her reputation as an actress and to establish herself as an actress in the non-Yiddish theater. In London she successfully performed in the play, *Majority of One.* When she returned to the United States she was hired to portray an Italian mother opposite Frank Sinatra in Neil Simon's screen

adaptation of *Come Blow Your Horn* and in 1962 she received an Academy Award nomination for her performance. Later she starred in her first Broadway hit, *Milk and Honey.* when she was 64 years old, Picon also published an autobiographical tribute to her mother and grandmother, *So Laugh A Little!*

4. This book was created during the 2000 presidential elections when President Bill Clinton was finishing his last term and Vice President Al Gore was looking toward the presidential elections that eventually resulted with George W. Bush becoming the 43rd president of the United States of America.

# Deborah Wiles

◆ Contemporary fiction ◆ Historical fiction

**Mobile, Alabama**
May 7, 1953

📖 *Freedom Summer*

📖 *Love, Ruby Lavender*

📖 *One Wide Sky: A Bedtime Lullaby*

## About the Author

As a child, Deborah Wiles wanted to be a mother. She modeled her desires after her own mother's, and she says, "I didn't realize I could do other things—remember, this was the '50s, and I lived a very sheltered life."[1] Deborah was born in Mobile, Alabama to Thomas P. Edwards and Marie Kilgore Edwards, and she is the oldest of three children. Her father was an Air Force pilot so the family moved often and lived in many different parts of the world. Deborah was five when the family moved to Honolulu, Hawaii. In Hawaii, Deborah's younger sister, Cathy, was born and her Grandmother Eula came from Mississippi to help Deborah's mother with the new baby and the rest of the children.

After three years in Hawaii, the family moved to Camp Springs, Maryland, where Deborah attended Camp Springs Elementary School and Taney Junior High School. Because her family moved so often, she then attended high school for two years in Charleston, South Carolina and graduated from Wagner High School, in 1971 while living at Clark Air Force Base in the Philippines. Even though Deborah hating leaving one familiar place to make new friends and find her place in a new location, she says that she "liked the itinerant Air Force life. . . . I always settled in quickly. I read a lot as a child and was somewhat of a loner. I was never popular, but I always made a few very strong friendships. Friendship is important to me. I believe in the adage 'Family is a circle of friends who love you.' "[2]

As a young child Deborah says she also "loved Captain Kangaroo and her bicycle, cloud watching, puzzles, and Dr. Seuss." As she got older her favorites included "The Beatles, The Monkees, music of all kinds, school, and learning." Although Deborah loved learning of all types, she especially loved writing. At the time, however, she did not view writing as a career possibility. She says, "I wasn't even sure I realized that real peo-

**220**

ple wrote those books I loved reading. I love the natural world, and still do. There is something magical about the natural world. I had an insatiable curiosity and a sense of wonder about the world and the people in the world."[3]

Many of Deborah's summers were spent visiting her "wacky grandmother in a little Mississippi town."[4] Later those summers would contribute a great deal to her books. Deborah became a mother while she was still a teenager and she worked in a variety of jobs in order to make ends meet. "I was a school bus driver (not a good one), a burger queen (I flipped a mean burger at Hardee's), an underwear salesperson (don't ask), and more."[5]

Later she worked in a construction company as a timekeeper and eventually as an office manager but ultimately, the daily routine of a 9 to 5 job was not what Deborah wanted. For many years she wrote in the middle of the night after her children went to sleep and she also spent her time reading and writing essays. She says, "I loved words, and I realized, early on, that words were power, and that I had something I wanted to say."[6]

For a long time, Wiles says she did not know what she wanted to say through her writing. In the beginning she did freelance work, often writing for free, but at least getting a credit and later she was paid for her work. She wrote essays and for a time she wrote and edited the *Frederick Magazine.* She also hosted an AM radio show on WFMD, which featured longtime residents of Frederick County, Maryland. Both the magazine job and the radio show imposed deadlines and daily hours neither of which suited Deborah so she concentrated on her freelance work. She liked working at her own desk much better and in 1995, after attending a creative writing class at Frederick Community College, she became interested in writing children's books.

Now Deborah Wiles is a full-time writer and sometime teacher. She is paid for her freelance writing and often teaches writing in schools and at Lesley University in the Masters of Fine Arts (MFA) program. Her own MFA was obtained from Vermont College in 2003. She also, of course, writes books and her first titles, *Love, Ruby Lavender* (Harcourt, 2001) and *Freedom Summer* (Atheneum, 2001) received rave reviews.

Wiles says, "I love this job more than any job I have ever had. It suits my temperament." She doesn't like to do anything at a fast pace but after her first two titles were published, they did very well, very quickly. Wiles found herself on the road for two years just trying to keep up with her books. She talked at schools, signed books, and met many teachers at conferences and workshops. She says she loved her new experiences, they were "so gratifying" but she found herself "missing [her] slow rhythm."[7]

But Deborah Wiles's life has not always been so gratifying. "I feel grateful to be alive, and grateful for every experience I've ever had, even the tragic ones. I feel like I have lived several lives. There was a time I lived in my car, for instance, as a single parent, trying to take care of two children. I know what it is like to be very young and very hungry, to be very alone, to be scared . . . and I know what it is like to feel safe, to feel loved, and to be joyful. I learn so much from every person I meet, from every experience I have."[8]

Wiles has a deep appreciation of colors, which are laced and woven throughout her books. Ruby Garnet Lavender is the title character in her first novel, *Love, Ruby Lavender.* Wiles says she loves all shades of purples and shades of light orange and green. Her other favorites include good coffee, chocolate, and dinner. She actually likes dinner better than dessert and she loves good southern cooking, particularly the vegetables—broccoli, brussel sprouts, fried okra, eggplant, and tomatoes.

But her most important favorite is story itself. Wiles says, "I love story. Story can bring about laughter and tears and joy and pain. Story creates peace and understanding."[9]

Wiles believes that everyone has stories to tell—stories that can be told in words, song, art, or dance. That is how we tell our history. She believes that all history and everyone's history is important. Wiles's older daughter, Alisa (1972), is a Marine and the mother of Wiles's granddaughter, Olivia. Wiles's two sons, Zach (1982) and Jason (1974), live in Santa Fe, New Mexico. Wiles's younger daughter, Hannah (1985), graduated from high school in the spring of 2004 and is now starting on her own adventures. Wiles currently lives in Frederick, Maryland with her dog, Sandy, and her cat, Gus.

## Book Connections

In 1997, Deborah Wiles and two writer friends, Jane Kurtz and Deborah Hopkinson, were attending the International Reading Association's conference in Atlanta, Georgia. During a late night conversation, Wiles's friends asked her what topic she would write about if she could write about anything she wanted. Wiles says she knew just how to answer, "I said I would tell the story of the day the pool closed." Wiles had been writing for years but she had not yet written about the one day in 1964 that she said "stuck with me all my life. It was the meanest of the days that I remember."[10]

During her childhood, Wiles visited her grandmother every summer. In the summer of 1964, the summer the Civil Rights Act was passed, she was 11 years old. Rather than let African Americans use the swimming pools, the ice cream stand, or the roller rink, the people in charge closed down the pool, the roller rink, and many other businesses. The story of the day the pools closed is told in Wiles's first picture book *Freedom Summer.* It is the fictionalized story of two boys, one African American and one white. The two friends have eagerly awaited the day they will get to swim together in the town's swimming pool but when they arrive at the pool, the day after the Civil Rights Act of 1964 took effect, they find employees of the city pool filling the pool with cement.

Wiles's novel, *Love, Ruby Lavender,* is a tribute to Wiles's relationship with her grandmother. Her grandmother came from Mississippi and, in fact, had traveled to Wiles's home in Hawaii when her new baby sister was born. In the story, the images of Hawaii that the Grandmother character writes about are really Wiles's memories of the black sand beach and the volcano. The laughter in the book is the same kind of laughter that Wiles and her grandmother shared in Louin, Mississippi.

Wiles immortalized Louin as the town of Halleluiah in *Love, Ruby Lavender* the story of friendship between an irrepressible young girl and her fun-loving grandmother. Wiles says her three aunts actually became the three hens and "[the book] is filled with all the food that I loved as a child."[11]

Later, her family tradition of backyard camping turned into the beginning of *One Wide Sky: A Bedtime Lullaby* (Gulliver/Harcourt, 2003) a story in which counting verses form a bedtime lullaby that culminates a day filled with the activity of three little boys and two mischievous squirrels.

Books yet to come from Deborah Wiles include characters such as Comfort Snowberger (age 10) and her family, who own the local funeral home, from Snapfinger, Mississippi. The yet untitled novel about the Snowbergers begins "I come from a family with a lot of dead people."[12] Other novels that are in various stages of the writing and publication process include *Hang the Moon,* also know as "The Elvis Novel," and *End of the Rope,* a novel dubbed "The Cuban Missile Crisis Novel."

# Books Written by Deborah Wiles

*Freedom Summer.* Illustrated by Jerome Lagarrigue. (Atheneum, 2001).

*Hang the Moon* (Harcourt, 2004).

*Love, Ruby Lavender* (Harcourt, 2002).

*One Wide Sky: A Bedtime Lullaby* (Gulliver/Harcourt, 2003).

# For More Information

## Web Sites

Wiles, Deborah. *Deborah Wiles: Children's Book Author.* Nov. 2003. <http://www.deborahwiles.com>.

# Notes

1. Deborah Wiles, interview with the author, 16 June 2003.
2. Ibid.
3. Ibid.
4. Deborah Wiles, presentation, North-Linn Community Schools, Troy Mills, Iowa, 18 March 2002.
5. Wiles, interview.
6. Ibid.
7. Ibid.
8. Ibid.
9. Ibid.
10. Wiles, presentation.
11. Ibid.
12. Wiles, interview.

# Appendix

## Contact the Authors/ Illustrators

The primary job of a children's book author or illustrator is to write books for young readers. Although authors and illustrators welcome sincere letters to them, responding to letters and e-mails seriously cuts into the their time for writing or illustrating.

The volume of mail (both postal or e-mail) that many authors and illustrators receive often creates a time lag between the receipt of a letter and any answer. Some authors and illustrators simply do not have the time to answer mail and at the same time continue to write or illustrate. For that reason, many authors and illustrators have posted frequently asked questions (FAQs) on their Web site and have expressed the hope that those pages will aid readers in obtaining answers to their questions. Those personal author and illustrator Web site addresses are listed in this appendix.

If a reader decides to write to an author or illustrator it is suggested that the reader include a self-addressed stamped envelope if they think the author or illustrator will be able to answer their letter. Because answering letters and e-mail takes so much time, some writers hire someone to respond to their mail for them but hiring someone also costs money. Betsy Byars, profiled in *100 Most Popular Children's Authors,* clearly states that despite the fact that she has someone who maintains her Web site, she does not use e-mail. However, she does provide a postal mailing address on her Web site. Will Hobbs, who also has a Web site, tells his readers that he does not use e-mail and suggests that readers who want information about him consult his Web site or various resource books that have information about him.

I asked each of the authors and illustrators that I contacted in connection with this book to indicate what address they preferred fans use to contact them if the fan had a particular question or comment about their books. Those who provided a response suggested their preferred address (postal or e-mail). Some preferred their mail be sent through their publisher and others preferred it be sent directly to their office. I have honored those requests and have included contact information for each author and illustrator profiled in this volume.

Anderson, Laurie Halse
http://www.writerlady.com
Contact Anderson using the information on her Web site

Arnold, Tedd
http://www.teddarnold.com
Contact Arnold in care of
Scholastic, Inc., Author Mail
555 Broadway
New York, NY, 10012

Azarian, Mary
http://www.maryazarian.com
Contact Azarian using the information on her Web site

Balgassi, Haemi
http://www.haemibalgassi.com
Contact Balgassi in care of
Clarion Books, Author Mail
215 Park Avenue South
New York, NY, 10003

Bowen, Fred
http://www.fredbowen.com
Contact Bowen in care of
Peachtree Publishers, Author Mail
1700 Chattahoochee Avenue
Atlanta, GA, 30318–2122

Buzzeo, Toni
http://www.tonibuzzeo.com
Contact Buzzeo via e-mail using the link
    from her Web site

Bynum, Janie
http://www.janiebynum.com
Contact Bynum in care of
Harcourt, Inc., Author Mail
525 B. Street, Suite 1900
San Diego, CA, 92101

Carlson, Nancy
http://www.nancycarlson.com
Contact Carlson at
5900 Mt. Normandale Drive
Bloomington, MN, 55438

Casanova, Mary
http://www.marycasanova.com
Contact Casanova at
P.O. Box 141
Ranier, MN, 56668
or via e-mail at
    mary@marycasanova.com

Cobb, Vicki
http://www.vickicobb.com
Contact Cobb by using the e-mail link on
    her Web site

Creech, Sharon
http://www.sharoncreech.com
Contact Creech in care of
HarperCollins Children's Books, Author
    Mail
1350 Avenue of the Americas
New York, NY, 10019

Curtis, Christopher Paul
Contact Curtis in care of
Random House
Children's Books-Author Mail
1540 Broadway Ave.
New York, NY, 11036

Cushman, Karen
Contact Cushman in care of
Clarion Books, Author Mail
215 Park Avenue South
New York, NY, 10003

Davis, Katie
http://www.katiedavis.com
Contact Davis via e-mail at
    katiedavis@katiedavis.com or
by postal mail in care of
Harcourt, Inc. Author Mail
525 B Street, Suite 1900
San Diego, CA, 92101

Diaz, David
Contact Diaz in care of
Harcourt, Inc. Author Mail
525 B Street, Suite 1900
San Diego, CA, 92101

DiCamillo, Kate
Contact DiCamillo in care of
Candlewick Press, Author Mail
2067 Massachusetts Avenue
Cambridge, MA, 02140

Dyson, Marianne
http://www.mariannedyson.com
Contact Dyson at
15443 Runswick Drive
Houston, TX, 77062

Fleming, Denise
http://www.denisefleming.com
Contact Fleming via e-mail at
    denise@denisefleming.com

Florczak, Robert
http://www.robertflorczak.com
Contact Florczak via e-mail
at robert@robertflorczak.com

Frasier, Debra
http://www.frasierbooks.com
Contact Frasier via e-mail at
    DebFra@aol.com

Goldin, Barbara
http://www.barbaradiamondgoldin.com
Contact Goldin at
P.O. Box 981
Northampton, MA, 01061

Gollub, Matthew
http://www.matthewgollub.com
Contact Gollub at
PMB: 181 2777 Yulupa Avenue
Santa Rosa, CA, 95405

Gutman, Dan
http://www.dangutman.com
Contact Gutman by using the "contact
    Dan" link on his Web site

Hines, Anna Grossnickle
http://www.aghines.com
Contact Hines at
P.O. Box 1456
Gualala, CA, 95445

Halperin, Wendy
http://www.wendyhalperin.com
Contact Halperin by using the "Contact
    Wendy" link on her Web site

Hobbs, Will
http://www.willhobbsauthor.com
Contact Hobbs in care of
HarperCollins Books for Young
    Readers
Author Mail
1350 Avenue of the Americas
New York, NY, 10019

Hurst, Carol Otis
http://www.carolhurst.com
Contact Hurst at
41 Colony Drive
Westfield, MA, 01085

Joosse, Barbara
http://www.barbarajoosse.com
Contact Joosse at
W61 N764 Riveredge Dr.
Cedarburg, WI, 53012

Koller, Jackie French
http://www.jackiefrenchkoller.com
Contact Koller by using the
    "e-mail" link on her
    Web site

Kurtz, Jane
http://www.janekurtz.com
Contact Kurtz at
505 S. Weaver St.
Hesston, KS, 67062
or through the "contact" link on
    her Web site

Leedy, Loreen
http://www.loreenleedy.com
Contact Leedy via e-mail address listed
    on her Web site

Lewis, E. B.
http://www.eblewis.com
Contact Lewis by using the
    "Contact E. B. Lewis" link on
    his Web site

Mora, Pat
http://www.patmora.com
Contact Mora in care of
Clarion Books, Author Mail
215 Park Avenue South
New York, NY, 10003
or in care of Random House
Children's Books-Author Mail
1540 Broadway Ave.
New York, NY, 11036

Park, Linda Sue
http://www.lindasuepark.com
Contact Park in care of
Clarion Books, Author Mail
215 Park Avenue South
New York, NY, 10003

Rubel, Nicole
http://www.nicolerubel.com
Contact Rubel via e-mail at
    nicole@nicolerubel.com

Ruurs, Margriet
http://www.margrietruurs.com
Contact Ruurs at
145 C Street
Creswell, OR, 97426
or via e-mail at
    Margriet@margrietruurs.com

Ryan, Pam Muñoz
http://www.pammunozryan.com
Contact Ryan in care of
Scholastic, Inc., Author Mail
555 Broadway
New York, NY, 10012

Sayre, April Pulley
http://www.aprilsayre.com
Contact Sayre in care of
Henry Holt & Co., Author Mail
115 West 18th Street
New York, NY, 10011

Shannon, David
Contact Shannon in care of
Scholastic, Inc., Author Mail
555 Broadway
New York, NY, 10012

Sierra, Judy
http://www.judysierra.net
Contact Sierra in care of
Harcourt, Inc. Author Mail
525 B Street, Suite 1900
San Diego, CA, 92101

Smith, Cynthia Leitich
Contact Smith at
P.O. Box 3255
Austin, TX, 78764

Soentpiet, Chris
http://www.soentpiet.com
Contact Soentpiet at
P.O. Box 205
Flushing, NY, 11358-1428

Taback, Simms
Contact Taback in care of
Viking Children's Books
A division of Penguin Books, Author
    Mail
345 Hudson Street,
New York, NY, 10014

Wiles, Deborah
http://www.deborahwiles.com
Contact Wiles in care of
Harcourt, Inc. Author Mail
525 B Street, Suite 1900
San Diego, CA, 92101

# Photography Credits

Photograph of Laura Halse Anderson by Chris Whitney and provided courtesy of Pleasant Company. Reprinted wih permission.

Photograph of Tedd Arnold provided courtesy of Tedd Arnold.

Photograph of Mary Azarian by Sharron L. McElmeel

Photograph of Haemi Balgassi provided courtesy of Haemi Balgassi.

Photograph of Fred Bowen by Sharron L. McElmeel; photograph of Fred Bowen and his brother Rich from the Bowen family album and reprinted courtesy of Fred Bowen.

Photograph of Toni Buzzeo provided courtesy of Toni Buzzeo.

Photograph of Janie Bynum provided courtesy of Janie Bynum.

Photograph of Nancy Carlson provided courtesy of Lerner Publications.

Photograph of Mary Casanova by Sharron L. McElmeel.

Photograph of Vicki Cobb provided courtesy of Vicki Cobb.

Photograph of Sharon Creech provided courtesy of HarperCollins and Sharon Creech.

Photograph of Christopher Paul Curtis by Sharron L. McElmeel.

Photograph of Karen Cushman by Sharron L. McElmeel.

Photograph of Katie Davis by Jerry Davis and provided courtesy of Katie Davis.

Photograph of David Diaz by Sharron L. McElmeel

Photograph of Kate DiCamillo by Sharron L. McElmeel.

Photograph of Marianne Dyson courtesy of Marianne Dyson.

Photograph of Denise Fleming by Sharron L. McElmeel.

Photograph of Robert Florczak provided courtesy of Robert Florczak.

Photograph of Debra Frasier by Sharron L. McElmeel.

Photograph of Barbara Diamond Goldin by Sharron L. McElmeel

Photograph of Matthew Gollub by Sharron L. McElmeel

Photograph of Dan Gutman by Sharron L. McElmeel

Photograph of Wendy Halperin by Sharron L. McElmeel.

Photograph of Anna Grossnickle Hines courtesy of Anna Grossnickle Hines.

Photograph of Will Hobbs by Sharron L. McElmeel.

Photograph of Carol Otis Hurst courtesy of Carol Otis Hurst.

Photograph of Barbara Joosse courtesy of Barbara Joosse.

Photograph of Jackie French Koller courtesy of Jackie French Koller.

Photograph of Jane Kurtz by Sharron L. McElmeel.

Photograph of Loreen Leedy by Sharron L. McElmeel.

Photograph of E.B. Lewis by Sharron L. McElmeel.

Photograph of Pat Mora courtesy of Cynthia Farah Haines.

Photograph of Linda Sue Park by Klaus Pollmeier. Courtesy of Clarion Books, an imprint of Houghton Mifflin Company.

Photograph of Nicole Rubel by Sharron L. McElmeel

Photograph of Margriet Ruurs courtesy of Margriet Ruurs.

Photograph of Pam Muñoz Ryan by Sharron L. McElmeel.

Photograph of April Pulley Sayre by Harriet Hamblin. Courtesy of April Pulley Sayre.

Photograph of David Shannon by Sharron L. McElmeel.

Photograph of Judy Sierra by Sharron L. McElmeel.

Photograph of Cynthia Leitich Smith by Sharron L. McElmeel.

Photograph of Chris Soentpiet by Sharron L. McElmeel. Photograph of Chris Soentpiet working in his studio courtesy of Chris Soentpiet.

Photograph of Anastasia Suen courtesy of Anastasia Suen.

Photograph of Simms Tabeck by Sharron L. McElmeel.

Photograph of Deborah Wiles by Sharron L. McElmeel.

# Cumulative Author/ Illustrator Index

Those authors/illustrators profiled in my previous reference books, *100 Most Popular Children's Authors: Biographical Sketches and Bibliographies* and *100 Most Popular Picture Book Authors and Illustrators: Biographical Sketches and Bibliographies* are included in this index along with those authors and illustrators profiled in this volume *Children's Authors and Illustrators Too Good to Miss.*

**CA** = *100 Most Popular Children's Authors*
**PBAI** = *100 Most Popular Picture Book Authors and Illustrators*
**TGTM** = *Children's Authors and Illustrators Too Good to Miss*

# Genre/Theme Index

This index groups authors and illustrators, featured in this volume, according to the genres or themes with which their books are associated. The major genres/book categories that are part of each profile's header is included in this list, as well as, additional genres and major themes associated with the author's or illustrator's books. This reference volume is arranged in alphabetical order by each author's or illustrator's last name; thus page numbers are not included with this index.

# General Index

In this index, the page numbers that refer to the main entry for each author are included in the bold type. Titles that are within the narrative about each author are included with references to the appropriate page numbers. References to titles/resources in the selected bibliographies at the end of each chapter are not included in this index. References to specific genres written by authors included in this volume can be found in the genre index.

# About the Author

SHARRON L. MCELMEEL is an Adjunct Instructor at the University of Wisconsin–Stout, and at Mount Mercy College, Cedar Rapids, Iowa. She is also is a writer and educational consultant who has built a national reputation in the area of children's and young adult literature and is an often-requested conference speaker. She was named Iowa Reading Teacher of the Year in 1987, and in 2003 she received the Iowa Reading Association's State Literacy Award in recognition of her lifelong efforts to build literacy and literature appreciation in the community. In 2004, she was named one of the top ten online educators by Innovative Teaching Newsletter. She maintains a website at http://www.mcelmeel.com.